Public Defenders and the American Justice System

Paul B. Wice

PRAEGER

Westport, Connecticut
London

Library of Congress Cataloging-in-Publication Data

Wice, Paul B.
   Public defenders and the American justice system / Paul B. Wice.
       p.   cm.
   Includes bibliographical references and index.
   ISBN: 0–275–98576–8 (alk. paper)
   1. Public defenders—United States. 2. Legal assistance to the poor—United States.
3. Criminal justice, Administration of—United States.   I. Title.
   KF9646.W53   2005
   345.73'01—dc22   2005006491

British Library Cataloguing in Publication Data is available.

Library of Congress Catalog Card Number: 2005006491
ISBN: 0–275–98576–8

First published in 2005

Praeger Publishers, 88 Post Road West, Westport, CT 06881
An imprint of Greenwood Publishing Group, Inc.
www.praeger.com

Printed in the United States of America

The paper used in this book complies with the
Permanent Paper Standard issued by the National
Information Standards Organization (Z39.48–1984).

10   9   8   7   6   5   4   3   2   1

To Robert Donaldson,
a great friend and wonderful teacher
whose support and encouragement has
meant so much to me for so many years.

Contents

Preface

It is a typical Tuesday morning in courtroom 1104 in the Essex County, New Jersey, criminal courts building. The courthouse, a sixteen-story building, is located halfway up a hill from the heart of Newark's shopping district, sandwiched between the county jail and the county administrative building. All three are functional, depressing, gray structures built in the late 1960s. As ten o'clock draws near, the two public defenders assigned to this courtroom anxiously wait for the judge to commence proceedings. They sift through a two-foot pile of case folders preparing for the day's scheduled series of sentencing hearings, rulings on pretrial motions, determinations of the status of parole violations, and a miscellany of additional pretrial decisions. The majority of the day's clients jam into the six rows of seats behind the defenders. The remainder are being transported from the jail to the adjoining courthouse to be carried by elevator, four or five at a time, up to the courtroom.

By 12:30 P.M., the pair of defenders and prosecutors along with the judge and assisting court clerks have cleared nearly two-thirds of the day's scheduled cases. The public defenders now exit the courthouse and trudge a half mile down the hill to their offices located in a nondescript ten-story office building on a side street, squeezed between two of the city's major thoroughfares. Their compact offices are found on the sixth and seventh floors. After checking for any new messages from clients, the two defenders join a handful of other staff attorneys preparing to have lunch in the office's modest law library. With a large table dominating the room, it is more of a social gathering point than the locus of legal research. The camaraderie of the eight to ten public defenders seated around the table is palpable. Animated conversations range from humorous anecdotes and gossip to more serious discussion of defense tactics. Following the convivial lunchtime gathering, the attorneys either return to their solitary offices, meander back up the hill for an afternoon court appearance, or continue a conversation in an adjacent hallway.

The nearly fifty lawyers working as staff attorneys at the Essex County regional public defender office are responsible for representing all adult defendants arrested for an indictable (felony) offense who cannot afford an attorney. The Essex office is part of a statewide public defender program based in Trenton with regional offices in virtually every county (with the exception of a few of the state's less populous counties, which share an office). Although the overwhelming majority of clients served by the Essex County defender office come from the more populous, impoverished, and crime-ridden cities of Newark, East Orange, and Irvington, the office occasionally represents someone from the more suburban middle-class communities to the north and west such as Montclair, Nutley, or Livingston.

Nationally, public defender programs operating within an urban criminal justice system typically represent three-fourths of the defendants facing serious criminal charges (i.e., those facing the possibility of being sentenced to more than a year in prison if convicted). These beleaguered attorneys are often inexperienced, just commencing their legal careers. They are handicapped by staggering caseloads and inadequate resources such as the absence of investigative assistance. Beyond these institutional hardships are significant social and psychological difficulties that can undermine their effectiveness. Public defenders are keenly aware of the low esteem in which they are held by the general public as well as the rest of the legal profession. Contaminated by their association with their clients—impoverished defendants generally assumed to be guilty of at least some of the charges facing them—the defenders are further disillusioned to learn that their clients also share the public's low opinion of their professional abilities. The clients mirror the rest of society, which is very skeptical about the value of something received for free. Street-wise indigent defendants question the commitment of public defenders who are paid by the same treasury that also funds the judges and prosecutors. How viable an adversary can exist when both defense and prosecutors receive their salaries from the exact same source? How aggressive can assigned public defenders be in challenging the very institution—the criminal courts—that controls their economic livelihood? Furthermore, defendants realize that a public defender will be paid a salary regardless of whether he or she is victorious in the courtroom.

Although the American justice system is based on an adversarial process in which the prosecution and defense are assumed to be operating on level playing fields with fairly equal resources, the local prosecutors usually have several advantages. They are better paid, more experienced, backed by competent investigators (often former police officers), and assisted by an impressive support staff. Prosecutors also have the important discretionary power to select which cases they choose to pursue, thereby eliminating any cases that appear difficult to win.[1] By contrast, the public defenders *must* defend any indigent client the prosecution attempts to convict. Through control over caseloads as well as superior resources, it is not surprising that the prosecution is able to win over 90% of their cases, either through guilty pleas or after trial. By contrast, the public defenders are constant losers. Forced to settle so many cases by a negotiated plea bargain because of the strength of the prosecution's case, public defenders often devote their professional effort to minimizing a client's period of incarceration, or if they are even more successful, obtaining a probationary sentence instead of jail or prison time.[2] With less than 10% of their cases going to trial, dramatic courtroom acquittals are a statistical rarity. Thus, more public defenders are forced to redefine a successful outcome for their clients and their own self-esteem. Being able to convince a prosecutor to reduce the charges, have a sentence run concurrently instead of consecutively, or simply count the time spent in jail awaiting the outcome of a defendant's case are all significant factors in a public defender's evaluation of his or her performance.

In response to the numerous difficulties facing current public defender programs operating in the nation's urban justice systems, there has been an effort to implement numerous reforms designed to both improve the quality of professional life for the individual public defender as well as elevate the quality of legal defense for their clients. The Essex County regional defender program (as part of the New Jersey statewide defender agency) represents a public defender system that has embraced a reform model of indigent defense in an attempt to avoid the many problems found in the older, traditional defender programs that were described in the preceding paragraphs. Chapter Two will present a more detailed examination of two traditional public defender programs that have been in operation for over seventy-five years—New York's Legal Aid Society and Chicago's Cook County public defender agency.

The majority of this book will analyze the Essex County regional defender office located in Newark, New Jersey. It embodies a reform defender agency striving to improve the quality of legal defense for the county's indigent defendants. Additionally, the Essex regional office has tried to foster a professional work environment that will create a satisfied, energized, stable group of staff attorneys who are committed to the broader programmatic goals of improved indigent defense.

In order to complete a detailed yet comprehensive picture of the Essex regional defender office, approval first had to be obtained from the state defender agency in Trenton, followed by the consent of the Essex County deputy director. During the next eighteen months interviews were conducted with nearly the entire office legal staff (only three of the fifty attorneys declined to participate in the study). The interviews averaged two hours in length, with a combination of specific demographic and background questions asked of all the attorneys as well as a series of open-ended questions that allowed for more subtle and complex responses. The interviews were conducted primarily in the defenders' offices on Clinton Street but several were also completed at the courthouse during breaks in the proceedings. A number of attorneys who were especially interested in the research project spoke to me on numerous occasions. First Deputy Michael Marucci, who directs the Essex regional office, set a cooperative tone for my work with his enthusiastic support, which spread to the entire office and was a major factor in the project's success. Members of the support staff and team of investigators were also interviewed.

In addition to the personal interviews, extensive time was spent observing the public defenders carrying out their professional responsibilities both in the Essex County Criminal Courthouse as well as in their Clinton Street offices. By viewing the public defenders as they interacted with clients, prosecutors, judges, courtroom staff, and private criminal lawyers, information was obtained that enriched the interviews as well as validated some of the responses. Once members of the courtroom workgroup learned of my research project, they were frequently interested in speaking with me, offering their personal insights on public defenders and the Essex justice system. The majority of the interviews were conducted from October 2000 through the following summer, while courtroom observations continued for an additional six months.

What emerges from this detailed examination of the Essex regional public defender office is a reform program that appears to succeed against all odds. They appear to be a group of committed attorneys with an unexpected degree of experience and competence who are the adversarial equals of the county prosecutors who they battle on a daily basis. Additionally, the Essex defenders' salaries, support staff's investigative assistance, and office leadership actually surpass that of their prosecutorial opponents. How do the traditional public defender programs as well as the variety of reform defender agencies differ from the Essex County model? What are the critical variables that have allowed the Essex regional office to achieve an admirable level of success? Does the Essex program provide feasible features that can be incorporated into these other defender agencies? This volume will attempt to answer these difficult, important, and challenging questions. The fate of our nation's indigent defendants facing criminal charges by their local justice system depends on the answers to these perplexing issues that lie at the very foundation of our adversarial process and the basic constitutional guarantees that underlie our justice system.

Acknowledgments

This book could not have been written without the cooperation and candor of the Essex County regional defender office. This includes several staff support members as well as nearly ever attorney. I must also acknowledge the help of my research assistants at Drew University in the completion of the final edition–Katy Carnevale, Bill Pope, Anastasia Sheffler, and Cass Vreeland–as well as the tireless work of my two sons, Andy and Matt, in polishing up the final copy of the manuscript. Special thanks also goes to Senior Editor Suzanne I. Stasza-Silva at Praeger for her continuous and reliable assistance in preparing the manuscript. Finally I owe a deep debt of gratitude to Phyllis Schutze, Criminal Justice Librarian, Rutgers University, Newark, for her never-ending help, not just on this book but in all nine of my previous efforts.

Essex County Public Defenders (Fall 2000)

Regional Deputy Director:
  Michael Marucci

First Assistants:
  Al Kapin
  Joe Krakora
  John Mask
  John McMahon
  Yvonne Segars

Assistant Public Defenders:

Paul Arlt
Matt Astore
Janice Beer
Peter Berger
Ray Black
Bob Blumenfield
Shawn Burks
Denise Cobham
John Convery
Bill Cucco
Michellen Davis
Ollis Douglas
Whitney Fisher
Bill Fitzsimmons
Sue Freedman
Bill Friel
James Jukes
David Kervick
Sterling Kinsale
William Latimer
Peter Ligouri

Charles Mantone
Kevin McLaughlin
Wanda Moore
Ray Morasse
Regina Morrow
Ed Peranio
Joan Richardson
Chris Rojas
David Rosen
Robert Schaff
Donna Scocozzo
George Shire
O.C. Smith
Jerry Soffer
Ann Sorrel
Bill Strauss
Anita Treasurer
Ann Truncale
John Whalen
Elaine Wladyga

CHAPTER ONE

The Right to Counsel for Indigent Defendants: A National Perspective

The Essex County New Jersey criminal courts, like all other legal systems within the United States, operate under the adversary system of justice. Inherited from England, it has remained a fundamental principle of our justice system. Roscoe Pound termed it a "contentious procedure," and anyone observing legal proceedings in the Essex County criminal courthouse would certainly agree. In criminal cases the opposing adversaries are the prosecutor representing the state (the plaintiff or injured party) and the defense counsel representing the accused defendant whose guilt must be established "beyond a reasonable doubt." The basic assumption underlying the adversary system is that the legal struggle between these two protagonists—the prosecutor and the defense counsel—before a neutral judge will uncover the truth and permit the court to reach a just decision. Closely paralleling a boxing match, the two adversaries are required to battle vigorously yet fairly before a judge acting as a referee responsible for ensuring that it is a fair fight.

By utilizing the adversary system, it is imperative that the American justice system guarantee that both contesting parties be on reasonably equal footing. Thus in the criminal courts where the injured party is the state and is represented by the prosecutor, who is a trained attorney, it would seem necessary in order to guarantee fairness that the defendant also be granted legal representation.

Intensifying the importance of guaranteeing competent counsel for a defendant in a criminal case are the serious consequences of conviction, loss of freedom through imprisonment, financial penalties, and, in capital cases, death. Judge Walter Schaefer of the Illinois Supreme Court summarized the importance of a fair fight and the necessity for both sides to have legal defense by writing, "Of all the rights that an accused person has, the right to be represented by counsel is by far the most pervasive, for it affects his ability to assert any other rights he may have."[1]

Ensuring the right to counsel in a criminal case is also of critical importance because in contrast to a civil case where the adversaries are usually private individuals, the plaintiff or victim is represented by the powerful legal arm of the state—the prosecutor, who is publicly financed and assisted by the police, investigators, and a trained support staff including forensic experts and psychiatrists. State funds will also pay for the prosecutor's law library as well as any necessary expert witnesses.

Without the assistance of counsel in a criminal case, the defendant will most likely be ineffective in gathering critical pretrial research through investigation and interrogation of witnesses as well as the timely filing of crucial pretrial motions designed to prevent damaging evidence from being introduced into the trial or eliminate his or her identification during an improper line-up. Once the trial begins the layman's disadvantages are even more apparent, beginning with the selection of the jury, a procedure that many lawyers believe can significantly affect the ultimate outcome of the trial. Knowing who to use as a witness and how to directly examine him or her as well as the critical ability to cross-examine prosecution witnesses are also extremely important skills that lawyers develop over time. Additional stages in the trial such as opening and closing statements as well as when to make timely objections to the prosecution's accusations combine to indicate the monumental disadvantages of a layman facing a legally-trained adversary. Obviously, if the adversary system is to function as originally intended by our founding fathers and the constitutional guarantees they wrote into the Bill of Rights are to be assured, the defendant must be given the opportunity to be represented by competent counsel.

Right to Counsel: A Brief Constitutional History

The right to counsel in federal criminal cases is guaranteed in the Sixth Amendment to the Constitution. It was ratified as a key element of the Bill of Rights in 1789 with other provisions ensuring a fair trial for the defendant. These include the Fourth Amendment's protection against unreasonable searches and seizures, the Fifth Amendment's right to not be compelled to be a witness against oneself, the Sixth Amendment's right to a jury trial and opportunity to confront one's accusers, and the Eighth Amendment's prohibition against cruel and unusual punishments. The judge must ensure that all of these Bill of Rights guarantees are protected.

Despite the apparent plethora of defendant's rights protected by the federal constitution, there is a major problem for the vast majority of defendants without legal representation who find themselves charged in state rather than federal criminal proceedings. Constitutional law scholar Professor Mason Beaney explains this contradiction by stating that "Only a few states guaranteed in their constitutions the right to appointed counsel; more commonly, state and federal statutes provided for appointed counsel under particular circumstances, while judicial discretion to appoint counsel was sometimes exercised in special cases. In most jurisdictions counsel was appointed in none but the most serious cases, often only when the crime was punishable by death."[2]

The opportunity to extend the right to counsel to defendants in state criminal courts arose in 1868 with the passage of the Fourteenth Amendment. Although this amendment, along with the Thirteenth Amendment giving black Americans their freedom from slavery and the Fifteenth Amendment guaranteeing their right to vote, was thought by many to also ensure the rights of black Americans following the Civil War, there were two important sections that would affect the legal rights of all Americans. The first section was the Fourteenth Amendment's due process clause, which prohibited states from depriving citizens of their life, liberty, or property without due process of the law. The second section was the equal protection clause, which would also prove relevant in right-to-counsel cases.

The vagaries of the Fourteenth Amendment's due process clause in addition to the post–Civil War political climate contributed to the Supreme Court's reluctance to clarify the applicability of this ambiguous constitutional clause to problems of defendants in state courts unable to afford legal representation. It was not until the 1930s, nearly sixty years after the amendment's ratification, that this important issue was addressed by the U.S. Supreme Court in the landmark case of *Powell v. Alabama* (287 U.S. 45 [1932]), the first of the infamous Scottsboro cases. These cases thrust this sleepy Alabama town into the national spotlight when a handful of impoverished, young black farm boys were charged with raping two white women. The boys were riding a slow-moving freight train winding its way from Tennessee through the northeast corner of Alabama. The nine young black men jumped into one of the boxcars and were surprised to find two white women and their two male companions. The tense situation erupted into a fight. The white men were thrown off the train. They ran to local authorities reporting that the black men had raped their women. The train was halted at the next stop, where the young men were dragged off the train by the police and thrown in jail as an angry crowd surrounded the building and demanded lynching.

The nine black defendants, aged thirteen to twenty-one, were charged with rape and faced the death penalty. None of the illiterate, penniless young defendants could afford an attorney. The trial judge, rather than appoint a specific individual attorney for each defendant, called upon the entire local bar to volunteer their services. After a week, when no lawyer came forward, the judge selected "all members of the bar," but this also failed to elicit any legal representation. In frustration, the judge finally selected a solitary young Chattanooga attorney with almost no trial experience, shortly before the trials were about to commence.

The trials progressed rapidly, completed in one day per defendant, resulting in eight defendants receiving the death penalty. Only the thirteen-year-old (the youngest defendant) was spared, being sentenced a life term. The highly publicized case made the nine young men *cause celebres,* gaining their case a national notoriety that allowed the defendants the opportunity to receive the legal assistance of a famous New York City civil rights lawyer, who appealed their conviction and was ultimately able to have the U.S. Supreme Court hear their case. The attorney argued that the young men had been denied effective assistance of counsel because of the lateness of the appointment of their attorney as well as the attorney's questionable competence and palpable reluctance to represent them.

The Supreme Court agreed with the defendants, reversing their conviction. Justice Sutherland's majority opinion declared that they had been unconstitutionally denied counsel. Because they were young and barely literate, facing the death penalty, and on trial in an intensely hostile environment, they required the assistance of effective counsel. The Fourteenth Amendment's guarantee of due process against state deprivation of liberty had been violated by the Alabama justice system. The majority opinion clarified the importance of a defendant's right to counsel by explaining, "Left without the aid of counsel he may be put on trial without a proper charge, and convicted upon incompetent evidence, or evidence irrelevant to the issue or otherwise inadmissible. He lacks both the skill and knowledge to adequately prepare his defense, even though he may have a perfect one. He requires the guiding hand of counsel at every step in the proceedings against him. Without it, though he may not be guilty, he faces the danger of conviction because he does not know how to establish his innocence. If that be true of men of intelligence, how much more true it is of the ignorant and illiterate, or of those of feeble intellect."[3]

Unfortunately, the *Powell* decision was construed rather narrowly. It soon became clear that only the defendant whose case contained similar circumstances as well as the unusual characteristics found in the *Powell* case would establish an unconstitutional denial of a right to counsel in violation of the Fourteenth Amendment's due process requirements.

Ten years later in *Betts v. Brody* (316 U.S. 455 [1942]), the Supreme Court had an opportunity to reexamine and possibly expand the *Powell* ruling. Betts was a middle-aged Maryland farmer charged with robbery. He was indigent and requested a court-appointed lawyer, but he was denied. The appellate courts, both state and federal, concluded that Betts had defended himself adequately in the uncomplicated case. In a 6-3 decision, the U.S. Supreme Court agreed with the appellate courts. The majority opinion explained that the Sixth Amendment's right-to-counsel provisions applied only to federal criminal cases, while the Fourteenth Amendment did not require the state to appoint an attorney in every criminal case where the defendant was impoverished and could not afford an attorney. The court acknowledged that several states, on their own volition, did provide legal defense to indigents through either public defender programs or appointed counsel; such actions, however, were not constitutionally mandated for all states.

The *Betts* decision left the Court sharply divided on the right-to-counsel issue. Justices Douglas and Murphy joined with Justice Hugo Black in his strongly worded dissent that would in another two decades become the majority opinion. Black's dissent was founded upon his firm belief that the right to counsel in a criminal case was a "fundamental" due process right that was intended by the Fourteenth Amendment. Despite Black's eloquent words, the *Betts* majority opinion clearly rejected the declaration of right to counsel as an important fundamental procedural guarantee and therefore did not necessitate the nationalization of the Sixth Amendment. The nationalization process means that the Supreme Court has decided that certain specific elements or provisions of the Bill of Rights are so critical to the American system of justice that they must be applied to the states as well as the federal government based upon the due-process clause of the Fourteenth Amendment. The majority opinion clarified that states need to provide attorneys only in "special circumstances" where the defendant was clearly unable to defend him or herself.

During the next twenty-one years, the U.S. Supreme Court danced around the "special circumstances" rule. More significantly in terms of foreshadowing a shift in the Court's attitude toward indigent state defendants and their right to counsel was a change in the Court's membership. The most important new addition was Chief Justice Earl Warren, who arrived in 1953 and immediately showed a favorable disposition toward poor defendants and their constitutional rights in state proceedings. Additional changes occurred in April of 1962 when Justice Whittaker, the most ardent supported of the *Betts* decision, retired and Justice Frankfurter, who also voted with the majority, suffered a stroke and would not participate in the upcoming *Gideon v. Wainwright* case that would radically alter the state's obligations in providing counsel for indigent defendants. Thus in late April 1962 when the *Gideon* case reached the Supreme Court, a new liberal, activist Chief Justice and three associate members from the minority *Betts* opinion were poised to reconsider the right-to-counsel issue.

Clarence Earl Gideon, an unemployed fifty-one year old drifter who had been in and out of jails most of his life, would lend his name to a 1963 Supreme Court case that would be synonymous with a defendant's right to counsel. Gideon was tried and convicted of breaking and entering a Panama City, Florida poolroom. Gideon declared his indigence and requested that the State of Florida appoint an attorney for him. The trial judge refused. Gideon unsuccessfully served as his own counsel. He was convicted and sentenced to five years in the Florida State prison in Raiford. While serving his term, Gideon, who had a reputation as a "jailhouse lawyer" because of his previous experience with the criminal courts, petitioned the U.S. Supreme Court requesting that his conviction be overturned on the basis of the state's failure to provide him with the assistance of counsel.

The Supreme Court soon notified Gideon that not only would they hear his appeal, but they would also provide an attorney for his case. The justices chose Abe Fortas, a highly respected Washington lawyer who in three years would be named to the U.S. Supreme Court himself. Fortas had recently gained national recognition for his successful argument before the Supreme Court in the important *U.S. v. Durham* decision that expanded the legal definition of insanity. Gideon's good fortune was not entirely serendipitous. Chief Justice Warren had told his new clerks to be on the lookout for a case that would allow the Court to overrule the *Betts* decision. He thought the special circumstances rule was unworkable and the Sixth Amendment's right-to-counsel protection should be extended to indigent state defendants.

On March 18, 1963, Justice Hugo Black delivered the Court's unanimous opinion overturning *Betts*. Black declared that the assistance of counsel is a fundamental right protected by the Fourteenth Amendment's due process clause. Thus, the Sixth Amendment's right-to-counsel guarantee was extended to state defendants such as Gideon. The essence of Black's decision is contained in the following excerpt from the opinion.

> Reason and reflection require us to recognize that in our adversary system of criminal justice, any person hauled into court, who is too poor to hire a lawyer, cannot be assured a fair trial unless counsel is provided for him. This seems to us to be an obvious right. . . . That government hires lawyers to prosecute and defendants who have money hire lawyers to defend are the strongest indications of the widespread belief that lawyers in criminal courts are necessities, not luxuries.[4]

The impact of this case would be felt both personally and nationally. On the personal level, Gideon would return to Panama City for a retrial. This time he would have the assistance of counsel, Fred Turner, an experienced local criminal lawyer appointed by the judge. The jury at the retrial would take only an hour to return a not guilty verdict. Clarence Gideon was now a free man after two years in prison.

The broader significance of the *Gideon* decision would be for all of the states to be prepared to now provide legal counsel for their indigent defendants facing felony charges. (It would be another ten years before the *Gideon* mandate would be extended to misdemeanors as well.) Interestingly, the large majority of states had already been providing assistance of counsel to indigent defendants prior to the *Gideon* decision. In fact, the decision had its greatest impact on the five southern states (including Florida) that had previously failed to appoint lawyers for indigent defendants in any cases except one involving a capital offense or other special circumstances. Most states, according to a study by Lee Silverstein, made immediate plans to redesign their right-to-counsel provisions. He estimated that by 1964 at least twenty-six states had made major changes in their appointment-of-counsel process for indigent defendants, while a number of counties also implemented reforms.[5]

In the years following the *Gideon* decision, the Supreme Court has ruled on a defendant's right to an attorney at all critical stages of a criminal proceeding and on the right to legal assistance for nearly all categories of crimes. A more complex, related issue that the Court also had to resolve was defining what was meant by "effective assistance of counsel." In other words, what should be the constitutionally acceptable level of performance for a defendant's lawyer. Establishing a clear, workable standard of professional competence for defense attorneys has been elusive and challenging but the Supreme Court had little choice in attempting to resolve this dilemma. Complicating the problem have been the practical difficulties of implementing the *Gideon* mandate. With at least three-fourths of all defendants dependent on the state for competent counsel, local governments have been overwhelmed by the expense of providing this legal defense, either through public defenders or assigned-counsel systems.

The Supreme Court confronted the competence question in the 1973 case of *Tollet v. Henderson* (411 U.S. 258 [1973]). The Court held that defendants had to assume a certain degree of risk that their attorneys would make some common or minor errors in attempting to obtain their freedom. If these errors did not combine to create a "mockery of justice," then there would not be a sufficient basis for reversing a decision. Both the Berger and Rhenquist courts have continued to take a more critical view of the defendant's claim to have received less-than-competent counsel. The trend reached its high-water mark in 1984 with two important cases defining this ambiguous standard. The first case, *Strickland v. Washington,* held that even if a lawyer's errors were so serious that counsel was not functioning as guaranteed by the Sixth Amendment, a conviction should not be reversed unless the defendant shows "there is a reasonable probability that but for counsel's unprofessional errors, the result of the proceeding would have been different."[6] The Court's decision in *Strickland* sent a clear message to the nation's courts that it maintained a strong presumption that the lawyer's conduct was constitutionally adequate. Justice O'Connor, who wrote the majority opinion, explained, "It is all too tempting for a defendant to second-guess counsel's assistance after conviction or adverse sentence, and it is all too easy for a court, examining counsel's defense after it has proved unsuccessful, to conclude that a particular act or omission of counsel was unreasonable."[7]

The second case was *U.S. v. Cronic* (466 U.S. 648 [1984]), decided on the same day. A unanimous court held that an appeals court had erred in concluding that a defendant had been denied the right to counsel because the appointed counsel lacked criminal law experience and did not have much time to prepare for trial. These inadequacies must be supported by evidence of serious errors by the lawyer to the degree that they were so prejudicial as to deny the defendant a fair trial. These cases do not negate the Supreme Court's overall commitment to the *Gideon* decision, but they are a clear warning that challenges to a lawyer's competence must be of a grievous nature and so prejudicial as to deny the defendant a fair trial.

In 1975 the Court decided a related problem by clarifying how a defendant may constitutionally decide to waive his or her right to counsel. This universal problem was clarified in *Faretta v. California* (422 U.S. 806 [1975]), which explained that defendants do have the right to conduct their own defense and the right to reject counsel appointed to represent them. Justice Stewart, who authored the majority opinion, was quick to add that "It is one thing to hold that every person, rich or poor, has the right to assistance of counsel, and quite another to say that a state may compel a person to accept a lawyer he does not want."[8] The Court recognized that even more important than granting a defendant the right to refuse counsel was the formulation of procedures to ensure that this decision was neither coerced nor irrational.

The *Faretta* case and several other federal decisions have combined to require the court to follow carefully this procedure before a waiver can be accepted.

1. Advise the defendant that he has the right to retain counsel and that time will be allowed for him to do so if need be, and if he is indigent, counsel will be appointed him at no cost.
2. Ascertain that the defendant knowingly, intelligently, and unambiguously waives his right.
3. Make a record that each of the above precautions has been taken.

Because so many defendants plead guilty without the assistance of counsel, it is especially important that trial court judges ensure that the waiver is being made intelligently and in compliance with these noted procedures. It is very rare for a defendant to waive his right to counsel and then choose to defend himself in a trial. The waiver is most typically done by defendants who, shortly after their arrest, believe that it is in their best interests to accept the prosecution's offer of a lighter sentence in return for a plea of guilty. The general rule understood by most defendants and prosecutors is that the earlier the plea arrangement is finalized, the more advantageous the settlement for the defendant; simply stated, the sooner the plea, the lesser the sentence.

A final issue in defining a defendant's right to counsel is the determination of how early in the proceedings his or her legal defense is initiated. The issue was first addressed in *Escobedo v. Illinois,* and it was then stated more definitively two years later in the historic *Miranda v. Arizona* decision that held that a defendant had a right to counsel once he or she was a suspect placed in custody and subject to interrogation. One year later in *Gilbert v. California* and *U.S. v. Wade,* the Supreme Court declared that police lineups conducted without a defendant's attorney present were unconstitutional. Thus, any in-court identification of a defendant based on pretrial lineups conducted without an attorney present would be inadmissible. Five years later, however, the Supreme Court retreated from the *Wade* and *Gilbert* standard. In 1971 in *Kirby v. Illinois,* the Court held that the assistance of counsel was not constitutionally required until formal prosecutorial proceedings were underway. Justice Potter Stewart, writing the majority opinion, explained why the Court selected the prosecution's decision to charge the defendant as the initial critical stage requiring legal representation in the following statement: "It is then that a defendant finds himself faced with the prosecutorial forces of organized society, and immersed in the intricacies of substantive and procedural criminal law. It is the point, therefore, that marks the commencement of the 'criminal prosecutions' to which alone the explicit guarantee of the Sixth Amendment are applicable."[9]

Presently, as we enter the twenty-first century, nearly forty years since the *Gideon v. Wainwright* decision, our state courts are cognizant of the defendant's right to counsel in any case where he or she can face imprisonment (all felonies and misdemeanors). This protection should begin as soon as the prosecution has charged the defendant with a crime and placed him or her into custody. The defendant's attorney is held to a reasonable level of competence, although the Supreme Court maintains a strong presumption that the quality of the representation is constitutionally adequate, satisfying the Sixth Amendment's protection.

At the conclusion of this brief constitutional history of the right to counsel, the most puzzling aspect of its evolution is why it took so long for the Supreme Court to recognize its critical importance. Particularly because this nation operates within an adversary system where the legal representation is so important to the outcome of each case, why did it take the Supreme Court nearly one hundred years to guarantee this right to indigent defendants in all fifty states? Was it a fear that with adequate legal representation too many defendants would be able to gain their freedom? Given the incredibly high percentage of cases that are resolved through negotiated plea bargains—a long-standing procedure in which defendants plead guilty in exchange for a reduced sentence—this fear is probably not justified. A second troubling possibility resulting from the guaranteeing of legal representation to indigent defendants, however, is a more legitimate concern. This is the inevitable costly expense to state or county governments operating a viable system of public defense. With the typical urban public defender system required to represent approximately three-fourths of all defendants being prosecuted, it is going to be a costly public expenditure. The next section of this chapter will examine the variety of programs that have been devised to satisfy the *Gideon* decision.

Varieties of Public Defense: A National Response

Following the *Gideon* decision in March of 1963, most state and local governments began either developing new systems or modifying existing programs in order to accommodate the increasing number of indigent defendants they were required to serve. Lee Silverstein, in his national survey for the American Bar Foundation, estimated that by 1964 at least twenty-six states had made significant changes in their appointment of counsel practices, while several others were implementing reforms in particular counties.[10] Within ten years, as a result of the decision in *Argensinger v. Hamlin* that expanded the required coverage from felony to misdemeanor (or any case involving the possibility of the defendant spending time in jail if convicted), even more pressure was placed upon state and local governments to comply with their new constitutional responsibilities.

Presently, there are four general categories of indigent defense operating in the United States: public defender, assigned counsel, contract, or mixed, which has elements of the first three programs. The most recent survey by the U.S. Justice Department's Bureau of Justice Statistics in 2000 found that in the nation's one hundred most populous counties $1.2 billion dollars was spent by indigent criminal defense programs that primarily handled felony cases at the trial level. These programs received approximately 4.2 million cases. Public defender programs received 73% ($880 million) of the total expenditures. They employed over 12,700 individuals, approximately half being attorneys, with the average programs utilizing thirty-three lawyers. Assigned-counsel programs accounted for 21% of the funding, leaving the remaining 6% for awarded contracts. In absolute numbers, this meant that over 30,700 attorneys received appointments through assigned counsel in 1999, while over one thousand contracts were administered in the one hundred counties surveyed during the same period. County governments provided 60% of the funding, with states contributing 25% and city, federal, and private agencies paying the remaining 15%. All three systems combined to provide representation for eight out of every ten defendants in the counties surveyed.[11]

Public Defender Programs

Public defender programs can be distinguished from assigned-counsel systems because they are comprised of salaried lawyers who represent nearly all of the indigent defendants within their jurisdictions. (They are unable to represent more than one defendant in a multiple defendant case because of possible conflict-of-interest complications.) Public defender programs are most commonly found in populous jurisdictions because they are a fairly effective bureaucratic approach to defending large numbers of indigent defendants. By contrast, assigned-counsel systems would be cumbersome and overburdened in an attempt to keep up with the thousands of indigent defendants passing through our urban criminal courts. The recent Justice Department survey confirmed these trends by finding that although assigned-counsel programs operate in 2900 out of the 3100 counties in the United States, public defenders are found in 90 of the nation's 100 largest counties.[12]

Public defender programs usually receive their funding from state or local sources, although private philanthropic organizations occasionally contribute. The primary characteristic of a public defender program is its use of salaried attorneys serving on a continuing basis. They are criminal law specialists since all of their cases involve defendants being prosecuted by the local justice system. A few jurisdictions, including Pittsburgh, Pennsylvania, have experimented with allowing public defenders to work part-time while continuing with a civil practice during their off hours. These efforts have proven unfeasible despite their savings in salary costs to the local jurisdiction. They do little to reduce the additional expenses of support staff as well as rental of office space.

The typical public defender office is housed in a building in close proximity to the criminal courthouse. Even though it might be more convenient for their clientele, defender programs wish to preserve their independence from the prosecution and judiciary by not being housed within the same structure, the criminal courthouse. The defendants are already skeptical about the commitment of their publicly paid attorney so it is imperative to at least preserve a physical distance from their adversaries.

Public defender programs are usually organized in a hierarchical fashion with a director aided by a handful of top assistants. Beneath this modest supervisory level are the assistant public defenders who are responsible for the thousands of indigent defendants requiring their services. The staff attorneys are assigned cases either on the basis of being placed in a particular courtroom or being handed a case and then following it through the system. By being stationed in a courtroom, the staff attorneys offer a horizontal or zone coverage to their burdensome caseload. Beginning public defenders will be relegated to a courtroom where less important pre-indictment proceedings are being conducted, such as initial arraignments or preliminary hearings. Vertical coverage (also referred to as man-to-man coverage because a defender remains with his or her client throughout the proceedings) is most common during the post indictment period, especially after arraignment when the court often pressures the defendant to either plead guilty or go to trial.

Because defendants are likely to be represented by different public defenders at the pre- and post-indictment proceedings, they are often critical of their public defender representation because of its fragmented and somewhat impersonal nature. The bureaucratic style of defense frustrates many defendants, resembling other impersonal social service agencies such as the welfare department or public housing office where they have probably had unpleasant experiences. On the positive side, public defenders, as a result of their total immersion in the local criminal justice system, can use their familiarity with prosecutors and judges to their client's advantage. Given the plethora of plea bargain negotiations involving public defenders and prosecutors, public defenders can accumulate favors as well as develop a mutual respect with prosecutors that can all be used to benefit the client. At the very least, indigent defendants can be reassured that their attorney is not only knowledgeable in terms of the law but knows his or her way around the local criminal justice system.

Public defender programs experienced rapid expansion in terms of caseload and staff size following the 1963 *Gideon* decision, although many programs in the Northeast and West Coast had been in operation for nearly fifty years. Los Angeles, for example, has had a public defender program since 1914, although its staff and budget grew by 600% in the decade following *Gideon*.

Lee Silverstein, in his definitive national report for the American Bar Foundation entitled "Defense of the Poor in Criminal Cases in State Courts," concluded that public defender programs offered the following advantages.

1. Provide experienced, competent counsel
2. Assure continuity and consistency in quality of defense, especially in comparison to assigned counsel
3. Are better able to screen defendants for eligibility
4. Are more economical to operate in populous areas
5. Offer better cooperation between the defense and prosecutor, which can result in better (more advantageous) pleas[13]

Silverstein provided minimal empirical evidence to support these conclusions, but in the thirty-five years since his national study was published, his assertions have rarely been challenged.

Overall, public defender programs can be divided into two general categories, either traditional or reform. Traditional agencies are operationally defined as a bureaucratic organization resistant to change. Many traditional agencies are long-established and are located in the older, larger cities of the East and Midwest. They typically suffer from oppressive caseloads, inadequate budgets, inexperienced staff attorneys, and a lack of political independence. The reform public defender agencies, on the other hand, are distinguished by a more experienced staff, adequate funding, verticalized case management, and a merit-based system of hiring and promoting, independent of political influence. This volume will examine two traditional programs in Chicago and New York City and a pair of reform programs in Essex County (Newark), New Jersey, and Washington, D.C.

Assigned Counsel

While public defender programs may be the best form of indigent defense in large cities, assigned-counsel systems are the most effective in smaller jurisdictions that do not have heavy criminal court caseloads. As noted previously, 2800 out of 3100 counties in the United States utilize assigned counsel exclusively. Even in the populous urban and metropolitan areas that rely mainly on public defenders, assigned counsel must also be used because of the conflict-of-interest problems resulting from multiple-defendant cases. It has been estimated that approximately 10% of the cases fall within this category. Therefore, given the large caseloads of our cities, this necessitates the use of assigned counsel in hundreds of cases. Many cases involving the sale and distribution of drugs, as well as organized crime racketeering (RICO) cases, create the need for assigned counsel beyond the regular public defender system.

The typical assigned-counsel system is administered by a judge who appoints lawyers to indigent defendants on a case-by-case basis. The judge selects lawyers from a list of available attorneys, who may either volunteer for the work or who are appointed simply because they are a member of the local bar. Jurisdictions also vary in how carefully they monitor the qualifications of the bar, particularly their experience in criminal law. Generally care is taken with the more serious felonies, certainly any capital offense case where the defendant faces the possibility of the death penalty. It is common for some judges to favor certain attorneys in terms of either granting them appointments to pick up some extra money or to purposefully exclude others who do not wish to be involved with defending indigent defendants. Younger attorneys trying to establish themselves fall into the first category whereas more experienced, financially solvent attorneys hope to avoid selection.

Assigned counsel are expected to perform on the same level of competence as privately retained counsel. The assigned counsel are paid on a fixed, per-hour basis, usually receiving slightly more money for time spent in court or during trial. The small amount paid creates a constant source of friction between the local bar and the judicial system. There is often no money available for hiring investigators or expert witnesses. Any expenses incurred by the attorney as he or she prepares a case will have to be absorbed by counsel. This paltry form of payment does little to motivate the assigned counsel to work long and hard on the defendant's case. Instead, assigned counsel are thought to offer a barely adequate defense sufficient to satisfy the Sixth Amendment's requirements. Their goal is to get through this professional obligation as quickly as possible without incurring the wrath of the client and being challenged in an appellate proceeding having to justify a meager performance. Also undermining the efforts of assigned counsel is the basic fact that time is money to attorneys since nearly all of their services are priced on a per-hour basis. Therefore time spent on an indigent defendant takes the assigned-counsel attorney away from the extremely more lucrative job of servicing his or her regular clients who will pay five to six times as much per hour.

The American Bar Association (ABA) in its Standards for Criminal Justice states clearly that "assigned counsel shall be compensated for all hours necessary to provide quality legal representation." State governments have not appropriated sufficient funds for assigned counsel to satisfy this ABA standard. In a study by Richard Klein and Robert Spangenberg for the ABA's Ad Hoc Committee on the Indigent Defense Crisis, they discovered that states vary widely in compensation. An example of the abysmal level of funding in certain states is South Carolina's hourly rate of payment of $5 out of court, $10 in court. Most state jurisdictions paid expenses in the range of

$20 to $30 an hour out of court and $30 to $40 per hour in court. Their study found that "[in] many states, low fee schedules are further discounted because fee caps are imposed for each case regardless of the number of hours worked. These maximum fees vary widely. Virginia has one of the lowest caps; the maximum fee for most felonies in the state is $350."[14] Even more troubling than the meager wages are the consequences of ineffective lawyering. Klein and Spangenberg write

> Some attorneys, whose practices are largely dependent on court appointments, find that they must make up for the low compensation per case by taking on more clients than they can properly represent. For others who take on indigent assignments, a temptation to devote their energies to paying clients and neglect their indigent clients exists.
>
> Even the most diligent and dedicated attorney, when adequately compensated, might have to forego necessary case preparation and consultation with expert witnesses and critical witnesses may be overlooked without proper investigative resources.[15]

Another ABA report by Professor Norman Lefstein to the Committee on Legal Aid and Indigent Defendants presented an equally depressing picture. In West Virginia, private lawyers are owed fees totaling $170,000 for work performed in 1978–1979. In one Louisiana parish, the private bar fees of more than $240,000 have not been paid and there is no apparent carryover to the next year. In Greenville, South Carolina, the county commissioners voted to discontinue the $240,000 spent by the county for a mixed-defender system and replace it with a $90,000 contract for five part-time lawyers. Similar proposals are presently pending in Oregon, Oklahoma, and Pennsylvania. Cases in Florida, California, Georgia, Massachusetts, Montana, Oklahoma, Missouri, Oregon, Nebraska, Iowa, Alabama, and Tennessee are raising questions of adequate compensation, improper reduction of fees, involuntary servitude, and the denial of due process for their clients.[16]

From personal observations gathered from thirty years of visiting criminal courts around the country, I found a disturbing number of assigned counsel to be inexperienced and weak adversaries for the prosecutor. They were commonly appointed late in the proceedings, further handicapping their efforts that were already less than enthusiastic, due primarily to insultingly low fees balanced against the professional demands of servicing their regular paying clients. Except for a limited number of multiple defendant cases, the assigned-counsel system appears inappropriate for most cities with a population exceeding 200,000.

Why has the assigned-counsel system continued in the five decades since *Gideon* despite its failure to appropriate the necessary funding, as documented in the ABA studies cited? I believe the reason is that the public officials responsible for the funding of these programs realize that the general public does not wish to see the quality of indigent defense improve. In other words, the electorate does not want to have its tax dollars spent on the defense of indigent defendants suspected of committing crimes in their community. Crime has long been a major concern in towns and cities across America. Public money spent on criminal justice is primarily directed to the police, prosecutors, and prisons. As an interest group lobbying for better indigent defense systems, the defendants and their families lack the numbers and the political clout to make much of a difference. This political reality does not portend well for future improvements in the quality of counsel serving indigent defendants.

Contract System

Large cities and counties have become increasingly dissatisfied with the delivery and effectiveness of numerous public agencies. Their response has been to turn to private contractors who offer to perform traditional governmental services at a savings while not compromising the quality of the product. The privatizing trend first appeared within the criminal justice system when private companies moved into the corrections field, taking over the operation of state and local prisons. (Massachusetts and Texas are two states that have invested heavily in this trend.) Within the past ten years, the criminal courts have also been attracted to the concept, specifically as a less expensive, more effective means of dealing with the rising costs of providing legal defense to indigent defendants.

Jurisdictions willing to experiment with a contract system for legal services will entertain bids from a group of lawyers working together in a modest-sized law firm who propose defending all or a percentage of indigent defendants at a set price for a designated length of time. In New York City, Mayor Rudolph Giuliani awarded a series of contracts to several groups of lawyers who will defend approximately 10% of the thousands of indigent defendants. The mayor's decision was prompted by his frustration with the city's primary defender of indigents, the Legal Aid Society, which had threatened to go on strike over work conditions and impossible caseloads.

(The public defender systems in New York City and Philadelphia appear on the surface to fall within the definition of a contract system. They can be distinguished, however, because they are both not-for-profit organizations, whereas law firms and associations of private lawyers designated as contract systems are clearly in the business of making a profit.)

Proponents of the contract system argue that it is a viable cost/savings measure. Alissa Worden, who has studied contract systems more thoroughly that any other legal scholar, explains that its recent growth is due to a belief in the following statements.

1. It is more efficient than public defender programs because competition motivates groups to bid at the lowest possible amount.
2. It induces more flexibility since it is outside the rule-bound public agencies.
3. The private producers are exempt from public regulations that therefore bypass costly procedures affecting public agencies.[17]

Professor Worden concludes that these claims of cost reduction have not been validated and remain inconclusive. She explains the difficulty in evaluating the quality of defense counsel is due in part to the lack of agreement over exactly what kinds of services participating lawyers should provide. There are also complications related to the questionable degree of accountability demanded by state and county governments. In attempting to compare acquittal rates across jurisdictions, researchers are dealing with miniscule variation because of the extremely high rate of plea bargaining, which is itself impossible to clearly unravel.[18]

In the last few years there does appear to be growing skepticism over the extent to which contract systems actually save money. Several cities have been frustrated by contract firms submitting increasingly higher budgets after their initial low bid. The rationale given is often unanticipated higher costs as well as rising numbers of indigent defendants. Thus after two to three years under the contract system, their revised budget requests have soared very close to the original public defender or assigned-counsel costs. Complicating matters is the difficulty in switching back to the original system. The most troubling critique of the contract system is its potential for encouraging lawyers to cut corners in their defense in order to make a profit for their contract firm. Given the previously noted difficulty in proving that an attorney's performance failed to satisfy the Sixth Amendment's competence standards, contract systems have little to fear in defendant challenges.

Mixed Systems

A few cities operated a mixed system of indigent defense, combining elements of the public defender with the assigned counsel. Washington, D.C., offers the best example of the blended alternative program. The district's public defenders handle only the more serious felony cases—approximately 25% of the total number of felonies—while they also administer an assigned-counsel system for the remainder. The D.C. program is blessed with excellent funding from the federal government, allowing them to utilize a large and experienced support staff, which explains their willingness to take on the more difficult cases. Detroit and Cleveland also operate on a modified "mixed system," although the public defenders' offices are not directly responsible for selecting assigned counsel. It should be noted that technically all cities with public defender programs operate a mixed system since they must rely upon assigned counsel in multiple defendant cases.

A Comparison Between Public and Private Defense in Criminal Cases

In addition to comparing different types of indigent defense systems, an equally significant issue is comparing public defender performance with that provided by privately retained counsel. This issue was examined in my 1978 book, *Criminal Lawyers: An Endangered Species,* based upon nearly two hundred interviews with privately retained attorneys, as well as subsequent research on public defenders that utilized over one hundred interviews and extensive mailed questionnaires.[19] Even though research has not uncovered perceptible differences in the case dispositions achieved by either group, the perceptions of the general public, legal profession, and especially indigent defendants distinguish clearly between the two groups.

From the perspective of the client, there is a strong belief that the performance of private attorneys is far superior to public defenders. This may, however, have more to do with *how* they are treated by privately retained counsel than differences in the outcome of their cases. The initial, and possibly most important, difference is that the defendants can *choose* their privately retained attorney whereas the indigent defendant has no choice, and must therefore be content with the attorney assigned to him or her. The only way a defendant can obtain a new attorney is on those rare occasions when he or she can convince a judge and/or the public defender program that there are irreconcilable differences between client and attorney that are likely to jeopardize the case. Even in those rare instances when a defendant's request for a new defender is granted, the client still has no say in the selection of his or her new lawyer.

Even public defenders acknowledge that private attorneys devote more time to the care and nurturing of their clients. The most common manifestation of this concern is their hand-holding for clients who are likely to be incarcerated for lengthy periods of time. The private lawyer can help prepare the client for an unpleasant outcome by trying to keep the defendant optimistic. The private attorney walks a fine line between hope and reality, as he or she tries to collect the bulk of the fees due before the defendant heads off to prison.

Given the overwhelming number of defendants who are forced to rely on public defense, anyone who has the economic capability of paying for private counsel stands out in the neighborhood as a unique individual. The defendant may still be going to prison, with the added financial penalty of having lost a great deal of money paying for his or her attorney, yet the defendant will impress his or her peers. Before sentencing, the defendant can travel downtown to visit the attorney in his posh office within a swank downtown high-rise. Lawyers often enjoy cultivating this image of a successful practice, allowing the client to vicariously experience the trappings of success.

Most defendants believe that private attorneys fight harder for their clients than public defenders and have significantly greater success. The perception of a more aggressive private attorney is a by-product of the defendant's jaundiced view of a public defender's adversarial efforts. Defendants believe that since public defenders are usually paid by the same public institution that is also responsible for the salaries of judges and prosecutors, it is reasonable to expect a collusive relationship between all three groups.

The state has a vested interest in protecting society and is viewed as encouraging the prosecution's efforts while undermining those of the defense. The end result is a blunted adversarial struggle between public prosecutor and public defender controlled or orchestrated by the judge. In such a hostile environment, the indigent defendant's fate lies in the supposedly compromised hands of his or her public defender, and it is easy to understand why blame is so readily placed on the ineffective efforts of his or her public defender.

Defendants have a difficult time accepting the fact that public defenders can be as effective as private attorneys because it runs counter to the commonly held belief that "you get what you pay for." Therefore, a public defender who does not cost an indigent defender anything cannot be as good as a private attorney who costs thousands of dollars. The empirical evidence presented at the end of this section refutes this assumption, yet most defendants refuse to accept the evidence, clinging stubbornly to their erroneous beliefs. Defendants' negative perceptions of public defenders are formulated in large part due to the impersonal style in which their defense is presented. As already noted, indigent defendants are given no choice in the selection of their defense counsel. Instead, during their first appearance in court they meet their public defender, who is also assisting another thirty defendants during this initial stage of the proceedings. A week or so later at the preliminary hearing, the defendant will be assisted by another public defender who he or she will meet seconds before the case is processed. Finally, by the arraignment, a permanent public defender will be assigned. This public defender will negotiate a plea or, in a handful of instances, take the case to trial, remaining with the client through sentencing. Contact between a lawyer and client is limited to a handful of conversations in the courthouse hallway with isolated meetings in the defender's office a few blocks away. The defendant's errant and peripatetic lifestyle makes even phone conversations difficult. Because most public defenders are hired directly out of law school and remain with the office only a few years, defendants frequently complain that their public defenders do not even look like lawyers. They are thought to be too young to know anything. The fact that many defenders are women, black, or Hispanic does not help to alleviate the defendant's concerns or prejudices. Frustrated by their legal difficulties and panicky over their probable future incarceration, it is not unexpected for those indigent defendants to lash out at their attorneys, blaming them in part for their seemingly intractable legal problems.

Despite a defendant's sharply contrasting opinion of private and public criminal lawyers, the two groups appear to coexist with no apparent animosity. The one area of possible tension that occasionally surfaces is when the private defense bar believes the local public defenders failed to adequately screen defendants regarding their financial capability. Public defender programs may be tempted to add as many clients as possible in order to justify their requests for budget increases, but very few defendants will actually opt for a public defender if they can afford private counsel. Bargain hunting when your personal freedom is at stake does not make any sense. On a one-to-one basis the two types of attorneys appear to have a mutual respect, each joining against their common protagonist, the prosecutor. Several private lawyers interviewed for my 1978 book on private criminal lawyers were appreciative of the public defenders taking most of the "lousier" cases off their hands. Public defender office libraries were frequently made available to private attorneys. On cases involving multiple defendants, the public defenders shared investigators and other support staff with the private bar. A few private attorneys went so far as to credit the local public defender with providing an excellent apprentice program for the private bar.[20]

It is interesting to learn from a recent Justice Department study of defense attorneys in the nation's seventy-five largest cities that the success rate of private attorneys and public defenders is almost identical. Their study shows that public counsel were able to gain acquittals in only 1.3% of their cases, while 23% of their clients had their cases dismissed and 71% pled guilty. The study did find, however, that privately retained attorneys see their clients earlier in the proceedings and more often before the trail and sentencing. The inescapable conclusion derived from this study shows that despite public perception, private and public criminal lawyers perform at nearly the same rate of effectiveness, as measured by dispositional outcomes.[21]

The Justice Department's aforementioned study is consistent with the following group of studies previously completed.

1. A study by Jean Taylor and others of the San Diego Superior Court for the *Denver Law Journal* found that 76% of the defendants with retained counsel were convicted while 77% of the public defender clients were similarly convicted. They also found that if one controls for offense, any difference between the categories of counsel disappears even further. The only hint of differential treatment was in the area of sentencing, where a larger proportion of convicted defendants with retained counsel were receiving suspended sentences. This probably is more closely related to the background characteristics and socioeconomic status of the wealthier clients who could afford private counsel than in the lawyering abilities of either category.

2. Also appearing in the *Denver Law Journal* a year later was a thorough analysis of the significance of counsel in Denver, and the report concluded that only slight variations in performance were found between the city's retained counsel and public defenders. Sixty-five percent of the retained counsel clients were convicted while 67.7% of the public defenders experienced a similar outcome. Again, the sentencing variation favored the retained counsel but, as noted earlier, he or she is blessed with clients who are more likely to appear to be better prospects for probation.

3. In April of 1975 the Joint Committee of the Judicial Conference of the D.C. Circuit Court and the D.C. Bar (Unified) issued a report on criminal

defense services in Washington. In their chapter on quality of representation, the following comparative statistics were presented which clearly indicate the similarity of performance between public and private attorneys.[22]

Disposition	Public Defender	Private Attorney
Dismissed at preliminary hearing	5%	5%
Dismissed after preliminary hearing	36%	38%
Pleaded guilty	29%	29%
Trial–acquitted	6%	5%
Trial–convicted	6%	8%

Even though these scholarly reports were completed nearly thirty years ago, there have been no recent studies in the past decade to refute their basic findings. Research has apparently waned on the issue, and the nearly equal competence between the majority of private and public criminal lawyers has evolved into an accepted fact within the legal community.

CHAPTER TWO

Public Defender Agencies: The Traditional Approach

Although several large cities operated public defender agencies prior to the 1963 landmark case *Gideon v. Wainwright,* the overwhelming majority of public defender agencies were created after the decision. Before 1963, cities such as New York, Chicago, Philadelphia, and Los Angeles provided representation for indigent defendants in only the most serious cases or unusual circumstances, such as the defendant being mentally incompetent or underage. This handful of programs, some of which had been in operation since the 1920s, developed a rough guideline for the multitude of public defender agencies that were being established during the 1960s.

By 1970, public defender programs existed in one form or another in nearly every large city in the United States, operating with a wide variety of institutional resources as well as diverse operational procedures, organizational structures, and working environments. (Depending on their rigidity or willingness to experiment with progressive procedures as well as their political independence, these public defender programs have been characterized as either traditional or reform. See Chapter One for a more detailed definition.) One critical factor that did not vary significantly, however, was the disposition rate for their clients. This was primarily due to the extremely high percentage of defendants pleading guilty and the resulting rarity of jury trials. These statistics and trends were recently validated in the United States Justice Department's Bureau of Justice Statistics survey report "Defense Counsel in Criminal Cases."[1]

National Overview: Critical Variables Affecting Public Defender Performance

The first section of this chapter will present an overview of the nation's public defender programs, describing the critical characteristics that affect

their performance and define their operation. The formulation and development of these institutional, structural, and procedural variables are usually of
great importance in determining the relative effectiveness of public defenders in providing a competent defense for indigent defendants.

Institutional resources are clearly a critical factor in public defender success. Such variables as the number of staff attorneys and their caseloads, the
number of investigators and their caseloads, the competence and number of
support staff, as well as the overall adequacy of the office's budget are of
obvious significance. Without the availability of adequate staff, even the
best-intentioned, intelligently organized defender office cannot offer effective legal representation for their clients. Wice and Pilgrim discovered in
their national survey that the average legal staff had twenty-one full-time
lawyers and seven who were part-time. The largest program was in Los
Angeles with 392 full-time lawyers. Nearly half of the cities in the sample
employed between five and fifteen attorneys. Trenton, New Jersey, part of a
well-financed statewide public defender system, had the best ratio of
defender to population with one lawyer for 1,600 inhabitants.[2] The more
recent (2000) Justice Department survey of the nation's one hundred largest
counties found an average of thirty-three lawyers for these more populous
jurisdictions. Of equal importance to the size of the legal staff is the amount
of their experience. In two national surveys, the average tenure of a public
defender was four years. Approximately half of the lawyers came directly to
a public defender program after graduating from law school.

The number of available investigators is also an important measure of the
capability of a public defender program. Investigators provide staff attorneys with information from interviews with critical witnesses and photos of
the crime scene, as well as verifying police reports. As with the legal staff,
the number of investigators varies greatly from city to city with the national
average at five, nearly one investigator for every four attorneys.[3] The Justice
Department survey of large counties found the average to be nearly ten
investigators, one for every three lawyers.[4] No information was uncovered
on the availability and number of expert witnesses, as well as secretarial,
clerical, and other support staff whose performance can directly impact the
quality of public defender services.

A third factor affecting the quality of performance of a public defender
program is the size of its caseload. Even with a large number of attorneys the
program can be overwhelmed by the number of cases it is forced to handle
at a particular time. An extreme example of this dilemma was reported by
Klein and Spangenberg in their ABA study entitled "The Indigent Defense
Crisis." The authors found that in New Orleans a public defender "who represented 418 clients in the first seven months of 1991, and had seventy cases
pending trial sought and obtained a court ruling that his excessive caseload
precluded him from providing effective representation to individual clients."[5] An article in the *New York Times* (April 9, 2001) indicated that New
Orleans was not alone in facing a caseload crisis. The article, which was enti-

tled "A Lawyer for the Poor with a Client List of 1600," was filled with numerous examples from New York City's indigent defense services that were equally troubling.[6] Less extreme figures, although still bothersome, were reported by the Bureau of Justice Statistics in the agency's 1999 survey of large counties. They found the average number of cases handled to be 22,300, with an average of fifty-two attorneys, which equates to each lawyer handling 430 cases a year.[7]

Budget figures can be a useful indicator of the overall fiscal health of a public defender program. They may also provide an indirect measure of a community's commitment to indigent defense. Table 2.1 indicates the sources of public defender funding.[8]

The Bureau of Justice Statistics found that more recent trends in appropriation for public defenders have remained static over the past twenty years. Their research disclosed that of all the money spent on criminal justice institutions and programs by federal, state, and local governments—a total of 74 billion dollars—only 2.3% was spent on the public defense of indigent defendants. The police received nearly half of the total, while prosecutors were given more than three times the amount awarded to their adversaries on the defense side.[9] A more recent Justice Department survey showed the one hundred largest cities spending a total of 88 million dollars on public defender programs, which translates into an average of $450,000 per program.[10]

Table 2.1 Sources of Public Defender Funding

	Public				Private	
Percentage of Funding Supplied	Federal	State	City	County	Bar Association	Foundation Grants
0 – 9	6 (8%)	6 (8%)	1 (1.4%)	1 (1.4%)	0	2 (2.8%)
10–19	3 (4.2%)	1 (1.4%)	2 (2.8%)	1 (1.4%)	0	1 (1.4%)
20–29	2 (2.8%)	1 (1.4%)	2 (2.8%)	1 (1.4%)	1 (1.4%)	0
30–39	5 (7.1%)	1 (1.4%)	0	0	0	0
40–49	1 (1.4%)	0	2 (2.8%)	0	0	0
50–59	0	0	0	5 (7.1%)	0	0
60–69	1 (1.4%)	0	0	1 (1.4%)	0	0
70–79	2 (2.8%)	3 (4.2%)	0	1 (1.4%)	0	0
80+	6 (8.5%)	18 (25.7%)	4 (5.7%)	26 (37.1%)	0	0
NR	44 (62.8%)	40 (57.1%)	59 (84%)	34 (48.6%)	69 (98.5%)	66 (98.5%)
NA	17%	28%	8%	41%	1%	5%

NR = No response, NA = National average

Early studies of public defenders by David Sudnow and others described public defenders as being overwhelmed by their professional adversaries and often failing to satisfy their side of the adversarial struggle. Sudnow went so far as to write "The public defender's activity is seldom geared to securing acquittals for clients. He and the District Attorney, as co-workers in the same courts, take it for granted that the persons who come before the courts are guilty of crimes and are treated accordingly."[11] Subsequent research has discredited the somewhat cynical observations of Sudnow. The degree to which a public defender program can successfully wage a credible defense against a prosecutor is influenced by its institutional resources, but today's public defender programs are not inherently flawed in terms of their adversarial contentiousness or competence.

A related concern is the degree of independence and politicization of the office. Many public defender programs attempt to receive their funding from sources independent from the monies going to the prosecutors and judges. New Jersey and several other states have solved the problem by creating a statewide public defender system with regional offices located in each county. Funding for the program comes entirely from the state budget while the prosecutors receive their salaries from the county. Most public defender offices are purposely located outside of the courthouse that houses the prosecutor and judiciary, seeking to establish the appearance of their independence. This is a necessary objective given the suspicious nature of their clients who are fearful of possible prosecutor pressure.

The reputation of a public defender program is primarily based on the perceived competence of its legal staff as well as its adversarial aggressiveness. The more professional and less political, the better the reputation of the public defender program. In California for example, Los Angeles has had a well-established, apolitical public defender program that has earned the reputation of a competent, professional operation. Farther north in the state, San Francisco's public defender program has been tainted by its political linkages. Although its reputation appears to be on the upswing, it is still regarded by many attorneys and defendants with suspicion.[12]

The operating procedures utilized by public defender programs are a final group of variables that can influence the quality of performance. The timing of procedural stages such as how soon a client first meets with his or her defender, the method and thoroughness with which potential clients are screened, as well as whether the office assigns lawyers to a case or a courtroom all contribute to the effectiveness, both perceived and actual, of the public defender program. Many public defender programs organize their office on the basis of envisioning the criminal justice system as a giant assembly line, moving defendants along in a seemingly endless flow of cases. Charles Work, former U.S. attorney for Washington, D.C., described this depressing process as a series of stages, each manned by specialists (prosecutors and defense attorneys) who are responsible for a specific function. Once each specialist's job is completed, the defendant is passed on to the next stage in the process.[13] In recent years many public defender programs have rejected this approach, opting instead for a more verticalized system in which the defendant, once he or she is indicted, will have the same public defender throughout the process until a disposition has been reached. Using basketball terminology, the recent procedure is a man-to-man style of defense replacing the zone coverage previously utilized.

The previous group of institutional, structural, and procedural variables depicts the broad parameters influencing the capability of public defender programs to improve their effectiveness, although they do not capture the presence of a "reform" mentality on the part of the agency leadership. The large majority of defender agencies merely attempt to survive from one crisis to the next, with the defenders doing their best to represent their clients and maintain their sanity and professional reputation. These "traditional agencies" stand in contrast to a minority of reform programs, epitomized by the Essex County regional defender office studied closely in the next four chapters (and the Washington, D.C. agency in the concluding chapter). These traditional programs have been plagued by a diverse group of problem areas including several from the following list.

1. An inexperienced staff that is in perpetual flux. The typical young defender remains with the office less than three years and receives almost no initial training and very little supervision once he or she reaches the courtroom. The problem is compounded by the common feeling of low self-esteem, as the judiciary, local bar, prosecution, family members, and especially the clients themselves denigrate the defender's efforts.
2. Compared with the prosecutor's office, institutional resources such as many more investigators, expert witnesses, and secretarial/support staff are in short supply, severely undermining the public defender's adversarial effort in his or her uphill battle on a very uneven playing field.
3. Inadequate pay and unattractive working conditions also combine to discourage top-quality law school graduates from applying for a position with the local defender agency.
4. Finally, traditional programs are often subjected to outside interference from the judiciary or dominant local political party. Decisions related to hiring, firing, or promotion are influenced by such political actors as the mayor, district attorney, judiciary, or prominent bar association members.

The remainder of this chapter will examine two prominent traditional public defender programs that have been carefully studied since their creation in the 1920s. The two large jurisdictions are New York City's Legal Aid Society and the Cook County/Chicago public defender program. Although both programs have a rich history of legal accomplishments, they clearly satisfy the traditional defender model.

New York and Chicago: Traditional Defender Programs

Although the majority of this book will focus upon the Essex County regional defender office (Chapters Three through Seven will describe its performance and operation in great detail), which is a reform public defender program, most of our nation's urban justice systems operate traditional defender agencies similar to the New York and Chicago model, albeit on a much smaller scale. Studying these two traditional systems first will provide a useful prism by which to gain a better appreciation of the Essex regional office. At several points where the distinction between the New York and Chicago defender agencies are in sharpest contrast with the Essex reform office, a comparison will be noted.

Demographically Newark and Essex County may be much smaller than Chicago and New York, yet all three cities being compared are plagued by similar urban problems such as high crime rates and large areas of poverty, and each also features sizable minority populations. The three cities were chosen in part because of the author's familiarity with their criminal justice systems as a result of previous research, as well as the availability of additional books, journal articles, and newspaper reports on their defense systems.

Cook County/Chicago

Even though Chicago and Cook County are several times larger than Newark and Essex County, they are demographically comparable in many ways. Chicago and Newark are both cities suffering from high crime rates and many families living below the poverty line. The cities are surrounded by suburban communities that become increasingly more affluent and Caucasian as one moves away from the downtown business district.

The primary reason for selecting the Cook County public defender program for comparison with Essex County was an excellent study of its operation by Lisa McIntyre, published by the University of Chicago Press in 1987. Her book *The Chicago Public Defender: The Practice of Law in the Shadows of Repute* is the only other book-length volume on public defenders besides my examination of the Essex County public defenders. The two major findings presented in McIntyre's study were her belief that public defenders labor under the "stigma of ineptitude" and they strive to remain in the "shadows of obscurity" in order to keep the general public from learning of their legal accomplishments. I found that the Essex County public defenders also suffer from a "stigma of ineptitude" in the eyes of the general public and even lawyers unfamiliar with the criminal courts, but, despite their success, they do not concern themselves with making a conscious effort to shield themselves from publicity. In fact, based on interviews with nearly every attorney in the office, they would welcome increased media attention. The explanation for this sharp difference in their attitudes toward publicity will be discussed in subsequent portions of this chapter, although it appears the two most significant factors are the relatively apolitical nature of the Essex defender office and its stable state funding.

An important methodological difference between my Newark study and McIntyre's Chicago book is the comprehensiveness of the two groups of defenders interviewed. Because the smaller Essex office is staffed by only forty-seven attorneys, compared to the more than three hundred employed by Cook County, I was able to interview over 90% of the staff. (In addition to conducting lengthy interviews lasting approximately two to three hours each, all of the defenders were also observed representing clients in the Essex County courthouse.) McIntyre was forced to use sampling procedures because of the size of the Cook County office. She spoke with only twenty active defenders out of the three hundred, although she did conduct brief interviews with another sixty former public defenders who had served in the office between 1960 and 1979. She also attempted to observe the defenders in action in both the office and the courthouse, but it was unclear exactly how much time was actually spent on these observations.[14]

The Cook County public defender program is one of the nation's oldest; it was established in 1930, thirty-seven years before the Essex County office was created as part of a statewide system. The Chicago Bar Association provided the initial impetus for the development of a system of indigent defense for the city. The bar association was especially concerned with the corrupt Cook County criminal justice system as documented in an authoritative study by the Chicago Crime Commission. In response to the report, in 1929 the County Board of Commissioners created and funded a judicial advisory council that was charged with overseeing the operation and improvement of the courts. McIntyre explained that one of their first actions was the formation of a public defender office for the county. The board soon named prominent criminal lawyer Benjamin C. Bachrach to head the office.[15]

Despite the early commitment to a public defender program, the office has had a stormy history, especially in its efforts to weather the omnipresent political pressures so predominant in Cook County. In Chapter Four of her book, McIntyre describes the continual struggle of public defenders to maintain their autonomy while also rising above the recurring scandals plaguing the city's criminal justice system. The 1970s were a critical period in the public defender's fight for independence, as they were forced to combat powerful Cook County Presiding Judge John Boyle. The head of the public defender office at this time was Gerald W. Getty, who had served for nearly two decades with former Chief Judge Cornelius Harrington. Boyle in 1972 found "serious irregularities" in the Getty administration, charging nepotism, financial mismanagement, and improper use of influence.[16] The tensions between the judge and public defender exemplify the presence of hardball politics at every level of Chicago government. McIntyre explains the soundness in the thinking of subsequent public defenders who seek to avoid the pitfalls of being mired in city politics by staying out of the public spotlight. She writes, "[T]he lack of visibility serves in lieu of legitimacy as protection (for the public defenders) against threats from outsiders (the politicians)."[17]

The power of the judiciary to affect all appointments to the public defender office is one of the most unusual aspects of the Cook County justice system. At the time of McIntyre's study (1986), the chief public defender served at the pleasure of the county judiciary. Additionally, the judiciary had control over the appointments of every assistant public defender, who had to be interviewed and then approved by a committee of judges. The delegation of power to the judiciary appears to undermine any attempt to grant the defenders the autonomy needed to remain independent, aggressive adversaries.

Newark and Essex County both have an ongoing tradition of political corruption that on occasion rivals Cook County and Chicago, although the judiciary has fortunately been spared the embarrassment of such scandals. One possible explanation for Essex County's court system's ability to remain relatively apolitical is that the New Jersey state government has been fairly progressive in creating and administering a statewide public defender system with regional offices in each county. There is a clear meritocratic emphasis in most personnel decisions, rarely allowing for the intrusion of local political considerations. The county courts are also carefully controlled by a state agency, the Administrative Office of the Courts, located in Trenton but with representatives, called trial court administrators, in each county. Although many Cook County public defenders are chosen on the basis of merit, political favoritism is still a factor, especially with regard to promotions.

Who works for the Cook County defender office and for how long? Similar to Essex County, the Cook County public defender office has a higher percentage of blacks and females than found in the local bar. There is a striking difference, however, when one compares the two programs. Only 4% of Cook County's public defenders are black, compared to 29% of the Essex defenders. Additionally, the Essex County regional office employed 15% more female attorneys than the Cook County office (36% to 21%).[18]

The most blatant contrast between the two programs was the length of tenure for each attorney. In the Cook County defender office (which is more consistent with national trends) half of the attorneys have been with the office for less than four years, and only 28% have served for more than ten years. McIntyre aptly describes the Cook County operation as a "transit station" for young lawyers on their way to a "real" legal position, gaining useful litigation experience. Young attorneys were similarly attracted to the Essex County office, seeking courtroom experience, but the large majority (88%) chose to remain with the office for more than four years, and 77% stayed on for more than ten years. The Essex figures are unusual compared to national statistics, but they certainly indicate a very stable office.

A major operational difference between the two offices, which may affect the tenure and transience of their respective legal staffs, is the Essex County's "verticalized" system of case management. A public defender is randomly assigned a case immediately after a defendant's initial arraignment and a request for a public defender has been made. Pairs of defenders are assigned to a specific judge for about a year. A defender will remain with his or her client throughout the entire process until final disposition. It is significant that the New Jersey public defenders working out of one of the county regional offices represent only adult defendants charged with indictable offenses. (These are the more serious crimes designated as felonies in other jurisdictions.) The Cook County public defenders are responsible for juveniles in family court. In New Jersey legal representation for juveniles is handled by a separate division of the statewide program.

An equally important difference is the decision by Cook County to organize their case management on a "horizontal" basis, creating an assembly-line process where a defender is assigned to a specific courtroom. These Cook County defenders represent only the indigent defendants who are passing through their courtroom at a designated stage in the proceedings, such as preliminary hearing, grand jury, or arraignment. Recently, the Chicago defender office created a few verticalized units to handle the more serious cases, particularly homicides, but this new system affects only 10% of their caseload.

An interesting by-product of the Essex verticalized process is the early opportunity it provides for its young attorneys to quickly be involved in a serious case, often having a chance to litigate within a month or two after joining the office. Being paired with a more experienced public defender who serves as a mentor, the young Essex attorneys receive the necessary guidance as they plunge into their first trial. Similar to most defender offices, including Cook County, the Essex defenders receive very little training before being assigned to a courtroom with their own trial list. It is a classic example of on-the-job training. The "sink or swim" situation is tempered by the mentoring system, but young attorneys learn quickly whether they are up to the demanding rigors of defending indigent clients in serious criminal matters. Generally, Cook County defenders are developed more cautiously, beginning with assignments in the juvenile division, followed by a stay in the misdemeanor courts. Beginning lawyers anxious to handle more serious cases are often frustrated by the careful pace that reserves felony cases for the more senior attorneys in the office. Their guarded approach may explain why many impatient young attorneys abandon the office after a few years of the tedium of family or municipal court.

McIntyre discovered many Chicago public defenders who enjoyed their jobs but could not afford to remain with the office. They described their experience in the public defender office as interesting and demanding, yet they rarely remained more than four years. Most of the Chicago defenders thought they would only remain with the office for about two years, and the majority followed through on their original intentions. The one aspect of their public defender experience that was most upsetting, as well as surprising, was the lack of respect from clients, judges, and other members of the criminal court work group. Essex County defenders exhibited similar frustrations but were not as surprised as their midwestern counterparts.

The Cook County public defenders were especially troubled by their second-class status vis-à-vis the prosecutors, who received higher salaries and were aided by appreciably larger support personnel such as investigators, expert witnesses, and secretarial assistance. The Essex County defenders, as part of a well-financed statewide organization, were actually paid higher salaries than the local prosecutors who were dependent on county funding. The New Jersey defenders could also rely on support services that equaled, and in many cases surpassed, those of the county prosecutor. The Essex County defenders, who averaged ten years of experience, not only believed themselves the equal of prosecutors but in many instances were confident of their superiority. Adding to their confidence was the nearly constant turmoil in the Essex County prosecutor's office that resulted in a high turnover of personnel, low morale, and uncertain financial support.

Several Chicago public defenders noted that their office was burdened by a number of political appointees from the current Democratic Party machine. This small group was given "ghost" or no-show leadership positions within the defender office. The intrusion of party politics and patronage into their office was dispiriting to most public defenders and was mentioned as another reason for their brief tenure within the office. A few jaundiced defenders believed that assignments and promotions were also influenced by political considerations. By comparison, the Essex County public defender office, as well as nearly all of the regional offices in the statewide system, was operated in an apolitical manner. Only the occasional power struggles at the top of the state defender's office in Trenton when a new leader was appointed by the governor reflected the intrusion of politics. These top-level appointments usually had no direct impact upon the regional offices. Not a single defender interviewed indicated his or her awareness of political influences during the hiring or promotion process. The New Jersey system successfully maintained the ethos of a civil service meritocracy.

The Essex and Cook County defender programs are similar in their lack of initial training as well as the absence of close supervision. Beginning public defenders in both programs disclosed frightening experiences during their first months on the job, although the Cook County defenders were placed in less demanding positions in the family and municipal courts where the consequences of their mistakes were of less magnitude. Most Cook County defenders resigned before having an opportunity to try a serious felony case, the responsibility of the more senior staff attorneys. By contrast, the Essex County defenders were thrust into trials within a few months, although always under the watchful eye of an experienced defender assigned to the same judge.

Even though Essex and Cook County public defenders process cases in a markedly different system—vertical vs. horizontal—both offices are similar in the large amounts of freedom delegated to individual staff attorneys. Essex defenders continually mentioned how important it was for them to be given so much professional autonomy. McIntyre stressed the informal socialization process occurring within the seemingly loose-knit Cook County defender organization. She argues that a myth of competence and institutional structure with adequate supervision is necessary in order to satisfy the constitutional requirement of the Sixth Amendment as well as provide "A psychic haven for public defenders who see themselves as real lawyers operating within a viable bureaucratic organization."[19] McIntyre concludes her analysis of the Cook County defender organizational structure by describing the importance of a "presumption of competency" as an organizing myth for Chicago public defenders. She writes, "[P]ublic defenders have the freedom to act as real lawyers but they pay the price in terms of amount of respect they can earn from others."[20]

Although Cook County public defenders enjoy their autonomy, McIntyre found that they would also like more training and supervision. Six public defenders were so upset over the intrusion of politics into their professional life that they brought a lawsuit in 1983 alleging their denial of equal treatment in promotions, salary, and job assignments based on their race. Three years later a special C.J. Commission recommended that the public defender office needed to be run without patronage or political interference. The commission also called for a clear policy for hiring, firing, and promotions, as well as increased salaries.[21] Fortunately, Essex County has not experienced similar fissures.

It is a shame that McIntyre or others have not reexamined Cook County defenders during the fifteen years following the publication of her book. It would be interesting to learn if the commission's recommendations have been implemented, and if so, what impact they have had upon the defender office.

New York City and the Demise of the Legal Aid Society

New York City, despite being only a few miles across the Hudson River from Newark, operates a system of public defense for indigent defendants much closer to the Cook County office just described. Both New York and Chicago created their respective public defender programs early in the twentieth century, many decades before the *Gideon* decision mandated indigent defense. New York City established its defender program in 1917, fourteen years before Chicago's. The New York City system was initiated by reformers in the city's bar association who wanted to replace the haphazard assigned-counsel system. Representatives from the Legal Aid Society, district attorney's office, police department, and private philanthropists joined together to create the Voluntary Defenders Committee, which would provide legal counsel for indigent defendants in criminal cases. It would soon evolve into a part of the city's Legal Aid Society.[22]

The Legal Aid Society has continued to serve as the city's primary public defender organization, although in recent years it has been embroiled in a protracted struggle with the mayor's office over threatened strikes and better budgetary negotiations. The result of this contentious relationship has been the development of alternative forms of indigent defense, such as assigned counsel (more commonly known by their statutory designation as 18-B lawyers) and, more recently, contract law firms. The 18-B lawyers were initially created to provide representation for indigent defendants who the Legal Aid Society could not defend because of a conflict of interest caused in most instances by multiple-defendant cases. Beginning with threatened strikes by Legal Aid during the Koch administration, and escalating to an actual work stoppage in 1984, New York's public defenders have endured a serious reduction in their caseload as 18-B attorneys and the newly created contract law firms have been given many additional new clients. The Legal Aid Society presently represents less than half of the city's indigent criminal defendants. Its prospects for the future do not appear good.

The roots of the current dilemma date back to 1966, when New York, in response to the *Gideon* requirements, began to enter into a series of annual contracts with the Legal Aid Society to provide representation for the bulk of indigent defendants. The same year, the city's bar association created a panel of lawyers with varying degrees of criminal defense experience to assist the Legal Aid Society by handling a small portion of the indigent defense caseload, primarily conflict-of- interest cases. The city would pay the 18-B panel attorneys on an hourly fee basis with set limits. Cases would be assigned on a random basis. In their authoritative study of the evolution of New York City's indigent defense system, Michael McConville and Chester Mirsky concluded that from its 1966 inception, the bar association plan was flawed because it failed to establish any clear demarcation of cases between Legal Aid and 18-B attorneys. The confusing result was that "the two defense entities functioned without regard either to the contemplated distribution of cases under the plan or to the effect that a departure from this contemplated distribution would have on the quality of indigent defense services in general."[23]

During the mid-1970s and stretching until the Legal Aid Society's strike in 1984, they found themselves facing increasingly greater caseloads. Their city contracts required an unlimited number of cases for a fixed budget, resulting in increasingly greater caseloads for each Legal Aid attorney. The office was forced to develop a horizontal system of case coverage in which attorneys were assigned to a specific courtroom or proceeding. Legal Aid clients would be represented by a series of attorneys, passed along the criminal justice assembly line. The society tried to reduce their growing caseloads by declining representation in homicide and multiple-defendant cases. A third strategy to reduce caseloads and involve increasing numbers of 18-B assigned counsel is described by McConville and Mirsky. "As the relationship between the Society's attorneys and their clients weakened, the proportion of cases referred to the 18-B panel increased. Judges replaced Society attorneys when 'for any reason' the Society's attorneys were not available to undertake case responsibility, instead of requiring an 'appropriate' reason, as the Society contract envisioned."[24]

As their caseloads increased, Legal Aid lawyers had a difficult time offering quality representation. They increasingly relied on referrals to 18-B panel attorneys, although there was very little oversight over their competence by the society. Following a series of staff attorney strikes in the mid and late 1970s, Legal Aid shifted from its horizontal style of representation to a verticalized system where one attorney stayed with a case until its conclusion. Although this change may have improved the quality of defense offered by the society, it necessitated shifting increasing numbers of cases to the 18-B panel. Another strike in 1982, which lasted nearly four months, allowed the 18-B panel to become the principle provider of indigent defense in the city. Even after the strike ended, the society continued to give increasing numbers of cases to assigned private attorneys off the panel list. By 1984 the panel's felony assignments had grown to over 36,000, representing over one-fourth of the total caseload. The city's court administrator released figures for the same year indicating that indigent clients charged with either felonies or misdemeanors were represented by private attorneys in 25% of the cases, while Legal Aid handled 40% and 18-B lawyers handled the remaining 35%.[25]

The 18-B panel attorneys were primarily solo practitioners who were dependent upon criminal case referrals for a major part of their practice. Judges anxious to move cases expeditiously often remove cases from overburdened Legal Aid Society lawyers, replacing them with more-than-willing 18-B lawyers who were continually hustling for cases. This occurs most commonly when a Legal Aid attorney was not in the courtroom when his or her client appeared before the judge. The panel lawyers, despite their availability and keen interest in defending indigents, performed ineffectively according to a 1986 study that concluded they failed to communicate with clients, failed to have an adequate knowledge of the case, and failed to completely represent the client in court. Their primary function was described as "a messenger who relays to the defendant news of his or her fate."[26]

McConville and Mirsky's critical assessment of the crisis in indigent defense in New York from 1966–1984 finds the city's commitment to be primarily "securing social control at minimal expense. . . . A long term consequence of the emphasis on cost-efficient defense has been a gradual but irrevocable loss of legitimacy in adversarial advocacy and an inability to vigorously oppose the state in the arrest and prosecution of indigent defendants."[27] Their report pessimistically concludes that viable reform is unlikely given the objectives of the city and organized bar, which appear antithetical to the needs of indigent defendants.

Between the serious strikes of 1985 and 1994, the Legal Aid Society continued its decline as its relationship with the mayor became further eroded. Prosecutor David Heilbroner describes his adversarial struggle with Legal Aid attorneys in the following quote "In case after case, ancient memoranda filled with outdated case law passed back and forth in the guise of legal argument, and I resigned myself to fighting Legal Aid's boilerplate with ours. It was assembly-line litigation the battle of the forms."[28]

By 1994 the Legal Aid Society, angry over what the lawyers believed were impossible working conditions, demanded a 15% decrease in individual caseloads and a raise in wages. Mayor Giuliani was incensed, threatening to terminate the city's long-standing contract with the society. The mayor also demanded a $16 million retroactive budget cut and warned that any Legal Aid Society lawyer refusing to return to work would be permanently barred from practicing as a criminal defense lawyer—either for the Legal Aid Society or as an 18-B assigned counsel. The lawyer's union caved into the mayor's threats, returning to court. Mayor Giuliani continued to be angry over the society's behavior and when the society's contract came up again the next year (1995), he further slashed funding, necessitating massive layoffs and major reductions in the training and supervision of staff attorneys. Of equal importance, the mayor actively solicited proposals from any association of attorneys who wished to represent a portion of the city's indigent defendants for a set annual fee.

Giuliani's retaliatory actions meant that for the first time in its history, the Legal Aid Society would be facing competition from the newly created contract law firms. Similar contract law firms had been operating in other jurisdictions since the early 1980s. A recent United States Justice Department survey estimated that approximately 15% of all counties with a population of over a million people utilized a contract system, although they have faced persistent criticism for their threat to the quality of indigent defense services. The fear is these associations may compromise their adversarial effort in order to achieve a desirable profit margin. The ABA warned that the contracts should not be awarded primarily on the basis of cost, suggesting "they should be for services which include the terms and conditions designed to ensure quality representation and professional independence."[29]

Several of the city's legal associations, concerned over the possible repercussions from simply contracting with the group of lawyers offering the least expensive indigent defense costs, joined together to recommend the creation of an oversight commission to monitor the new contract firms. The city, supporting Giuliani's position, rejected this proposal. Undaunted, the group, which included the New York County Lawyer's Association, the Association for the City of New York, and the Bronx Bar Association, turned to the state judicial system, which accepted their proposal. An eight-member Indigent Defense Organization Oversight Committee was established with the authority to monitor all defense services in the Bronx and Manhattan. The committee drafted a set of standards and guidelines designed to measure the performance of the various organizations providing indigent defense services in the criminal courts. Failure to satisfy the oversight committee standards would result in the loss of certification as a quality provider. Inspection teams visited defense organization offices. A report was issued in

the fall of 1996 indicating that all three defense organizations met the committee's standards, although they noted that several problems were discovered and if not corrected would seriously reduce the quality of indigent
defense. The Legal Aid Society, in particular, was warned that its caseload
far exceeded the recommended numbers specified by the committee. During 1997 the committee began its second round of monitoring with several
new defense organizations. These included the Bronx Defenders, New York
City County Defenders Service, and the Center for Appellate Litigation.
(They joined Legal Aid Society, the Office of the Appellate Defender, and
the Neighborhood Defender Service of Harlem.)[30]

Moving into the new millennium brought no relief to the plight of the
New York City indigent defendant population. Writing in a three-part investigative series for the *New York Times* entitled "Two-Tier Justice" (from April
8–10, 2001), Jane Fritsch and David Rohde reported on their seven-month
analysis of thousands of criminal cases for the preceding year (2000). The
essence of their lengthy series of articles was that "almost no part of the indigent defense system functioned as it was intended. . . . From the felony
courts to the misdemeanor mills and the parole violation trailers on Rikers
Island, defendants frequently get assembly-line representation from lawyers
who may spend only a few minutes on each case. . . . For their part, the lawyers complain that they are overworked and underpaid in a system under
pressure to produce a high volume of quick guilty pleas. The number of lawyers willing to take such cases has dropped sharply in recent years, and
some who do sign up say privately that they are forced to cut corners."[31]

New York presently (2003) operates a mixed indigent defense system
that employs a variety of approaches to the problem. In contrast to Essex
County (Newark) and Cook County (Chicago), which depend almost
entirely on a public defender system for indigent defense, New York City
uses three types of programs. Their Legal Aid Society has served as the
city's public defender system since 1917, but in recent years has had to
share its responsibilities with assigned counsel from the 18-B panel and,
most recently, with a group of contract law firms. Mayor Giuliani's frustration with Legal Aid has resulted in the agency losing nearly 20% of its
caseload. The newly created contract law firms have picked up most of
Legal Aid's cases, as well as competing for an even greater percentage in
future negotiations.

In the year 2000, 380,000 indigent defendants were charged with criminal offenses. The city spent $125 million for their defense, while the State of
New York contributed an additional $10 million. While Legal Aid attorneys
and contract firm lawyers receive annual salaries, 18-B panel lawyers
assigned to approximately 25% of the cases were paid $40 an hour for court-
room work and $25 an hour for out of courtroom work. The New York pay
scale ranks next to last in the nation—only New Jersey pays less. It is shocking to learn that Southern states with appreciably lower costs of living pay
twice the New York rate. In 2001 New York Governor George Pataki

promised to raise the abysmally low fees, but a year later he reversed himself, citing budget constraints and other fiscal problems resulting from the 9-11 terrorist attacks on New York City. In May of 2002 a frustrated state supreme court justice Lucinda Suarez declared that assigned counsel would receive more than double their current hourly rate. The judge ordered the state to begin paying $90 an hour for both in and out of courtroom work. The judge stated that the state's failure to increase the current pay "has rendered hollow the constitutional and statutory right to counsel and obstructs the judiciary's ability to function."[32]

The series of *New York Times* articles documented the shifting of cases away from the long-standing Legal Aid Society to the recently created contract organizations. Although Legal Aid still defends nearly 200,000 indigent defendants, the contract firms were given 18% of the total caseload, while the remaining 115,000 cases were handled by assigned counsel through the 18-B panel. The large number of cases going to assigned counsel distinguishes New York from most other cities. Essex regional public defenders represent over 90% of the county's indigent defendants facing felony charges, while Chicago's public defenders are responsible for defending over 80% of their city's indigent defendants. Nationally, recent statistics released by the United States Justice Department estimated that large cities with over a million people rely on public defenders for the criminal defense of approximately 80% of their indigent defendants. New York's Legal Aid Society represents barely 50% of these indigent defendants, most of whom are charged with misdemeanors (less serious offenses).[33]

The second article in the *New York Times* series focused on the assigned-counsel system. The authors emphasized the high volume of cases handled by these overworked private attorneys. Given the very low hourly rate of pay, these attorneys must maintain dangerously high numbers of caseloads in order to survive financially. In 2000 one attorney, Sean Sullivan, was appointed to represent 1600 defendants, earning $125,000 from the city. Increasingly, however, private lawyers have declined to participate in the 18-B panel. Despite a rising number of cases during the past twenty years, the number of available lawyers has been cut nearly in half, from 2200 in 1983 to 1150 in 2001. Although the Legal Aid Society, and more recently the contract organizations, are monitored, there is no equivalent system in place for recording how many cases a specific 18-B lawyer has at any given time or any viable review of their competence. The recent *Times* analysis did discover that during 2000 "the twenty busiest private defense attorneys handled more than 9000 defendants whose cases went past arraignment and more who pled guilty on the day they were arrested." The *Times'* seven-month investigation also found that many judges "circumvented administrative procedures and simply assigned lawyers on their own (sometimes drafting any lawyer available in the courtroom)."[34]

The continuing struggle between the Legal Aid Society and Mayor Giuliani may have peaked in 1994, but shortly before he left office in January 2002, the mayor renewed his contentious relationship with the society by trying to eliminate the automatic renewal of its contract with the city, thereby forcing the society to compete with a growing number of other organizations. The society had already lost nearly 20% of its budget since 1995 as its legal staff declined by 180 lawyers; its investigators and social workers were reduced by 50%. Despite these diminished figures, the society represents the same number of indigent defendants as it did six years earlier in 1995. The result has caused two-thirds of the legal staff to have caseloads above the 400-case limit recommended by the National Legal Aid and Defender Association. The difficult working conditions have caused many of the society's lawyers to resign. Many of these attorneys have joined one of the newly created contract firms that offer more reasonable caseloads and improved salaries.[35]

The embattled Legal Aid Society has attempted to reverse the mayor's punitive measures, which its members believe could eventually cause the society's extinction, by challenging him in the federal courts. The society has filed a lawsuit accusing Giuliani of illegally retaliating because of the 1994 strike. They are very pessimistic about their chances for survival as an effective public defender agency representing the city's indigent defendants if they are forced to compete annually for new contracts in each of the five boroughs. The twelve new contracts went into effect in July 2002 and are scheduled to run through 2004. Newly elected Mayor Michael Bloomberg has thus far been noncommittal about his willingness to follow Giuliani's antagonistic policies toward the society. The former mayor was also disturbed by the poor performance of the 18-B attorneys but failed to develop a workable plan for reducing their soaring caseload or improving their faltering performance.[36]

The numerous problems currently plaguing the Legal Aid Society resulting from its continuous struggles with the mayor's office are in sharp contrast with the Essex County public defender office. The Essex office has maintained a remarkably stable defender program by studiously avoiding involvement in local politics at either the county or city level. With adequate state funding, the Essex County regional defender office has been well staffed, including investigators and support personnel. The lengthy tenure of most Essex defenders is reflective of their apolitical work environment. By comparison, the Legal Aid Society appears to be a dispirited, transient, largely inexperienced group of attorneys. The society has had a reputation for attracting high quality, motivated young attorneys, but it is unlikely that this situation will continue much longer. Not only are their working conditions deteriorating and their salaries declining, the newly established contract firms are rumored to be hiring the best of the recent law school graduates.

Another major difference between the New York City and Essex County indigent defense systems is the role played by assigned counsel. In New York the role of assigned counsel during the past 20 years has consistently expanded to where today they represent 25% of the city's criminal caseload. In Essex County private criminal lawyers defend barely 5% of the defendants. The only indigent defendants represented are co-defendants in cases where the public defenders handle one of the clients. There has been no effort by political officials or local bar associations in Essex County to expand the role of private attorneys within the local justice system.

Following their early dominance in the 1960s, the Legal Aid Society has become enmeshed in a three-sided struggle with the mayor's office and the private bar. Without the complication of competitive programs and a plethora of private criminal lawyers seeking 18-B appointments, the Essex County defenders have been able to concentrate on their primary responsibility of providing quality legal defense for their many indigent clients. It is disappointing to find the once highly respected Legal Aid Society of New York reduced to a barely functional legal defense organization. A new mayoral administration may hopefully restore it to its former position as a successful public defender agency.

The Essex County Regional Defender Office: The Evolution and Organization of a Reform Defender System

In response to the plethora of problems and defects plaguing "traditional" public defender agencies, a sizable minority of reform defender agencies have emerged attempting to develop model indigent defense systems. They seek to formulate adequate budgets guaranteeing respectable salaries for staff lawyers and their support personnel. (This has often resulted in the creation of a statewide program with equitable budgets for all jurisdictions.) These reform agencies also strive to maintain a group of experienced lawyers who are willing to remain with the defender agencies for an extended period of time. Additionally, an effort is made to provide "vertical representation," where a lawyer remains with his or her client throughout the entire dispositional process, instead of merely offering assembly-line coverage representing all defendants appearing at a specific stage of the process. Finally, most reform programs emphasize independence from any political or judicial influence. This has had the ancillary effect of reform programs frequently distinguished by strong leadership, merit-based personnel decision making, and a resulting esprit de corps or collegiality that allows employees to survive (and occasionally flourish) in a hostile work environment. The Essex County regional defender office, which will be carefully examined in subsequent chapters, exemplifies such a reform defender agency.

Indigent Defense in New Jersey: A Statewide System

Public defenders in New Jersey are part of a statewide system. The headquarters, located in Trenton, the state capital, administers the regional public defender offices operating in each county or judicial vicinage. The state program began in 1967 in response to the constitutional demands created by the 1963 *Gideon* case that guaranteed state criminal court defendants the right to the assistance of counsel. The state defender program was initially headed by Peter Murray, who was only thirty-two years old. One of his first decisions was to appoint former Essex County assistant prosecutor Leonard Ronco to become the first deputy defender for Essex County.

Murray may have been only thirty-two years old when he assumed his duties as director of the statewide program, but he had been deeply involved in the defense of indigents for several years in his capacity as the pioneering head of the Essex County Legal Aid Society, which in the preceding two years had provided indigent defendants with legal representation. The modest operation handled approximately one thousand clients a year. He first became interested in legal aid for indigent defendants in 1961 when he was working as an assistant prosecutor for Essex prosecutor (soon to be governor) Brendan Byrne. Murray was working in the appellate section of the prosecutor's office when the *Gideon* decision was handed down. In 1965, June Strelecki stepped down as the director of the Essex County Legal Aid program. Murray applied for her position. The office was only two years old and Strelecki was its first director. Murray wanted to play a role in shaping the county's response to the plight of indigent defendants. The old method of assigning counsel to indigents was to simply choose someone from an alphabetical list of lawyers who had volunteered their services. Murray knew that this antiquated system was not adequate for coping with the steadily rising number of indigent defendants in the Essex County criminal justice system following the *Gideon* decision. The old system's reliance on pro bono representation also compounded the problem of getting enough competent attorneys for the state's numerous indigent defendants. Under Murray's guidance the Legal Aid program was credited with many innovations, such as having lawyers who did not want to volunteer to represent indigent clients donate $50 to remove themselves from the list, while young lawyers eager for trial experience collected fees of $50 per week. Essex Prosecutor Byrne, his former boss, praised Murray's administrative skills as he formalized procedures in what was a nascent area of the law. Governor Hughes, in making the appointment, noted Murray's leadership qualities and found him "eminently qualified to carry out the intent of the public defender bill."[1]

Murray was a lifelong resident of Newark, attending St. Benedict's Prep, and graduating from Seton Hall's undergraduate college and law school. He was admitted to the bar in 1960 and served briefly as law secretary to Judge Mark Sullivan in the superior court's appellate division before joining the prosecutor's office. During this period he also served as director of a two-year pilot program providing legal aid to indigent juveniles. In addition, he was a member of the study commission that helped draft the state's 1967 public defender law. Murray was critical in ensuring that the new statewide program for indigent defendants would get off to a good start, but unfortunately his tenure as director was abruptly ended by his death in 1968. Mystery still surrounds his suicide, a rather dramatic jump off the Point Pleasant Bridge.

Peter Murray was succeeded by Stanley Van Ness, former counsel to Governor Hughes. Van Ness took office a month after Murray's death and was soon embroiled in controversy. Typical of many public defender programs during their infancy, the agency came under attack from private attorneys who charged that the defender agency was taking clients who could afford to pay for their own attorneys. In a speech before the Essex County Bar Association, Van Ness complained that several lawyers had been "sniping and yapping at our heels," and requested that the association assist the state agency in fending off such attacks. Jerome Kessler, a private Essex County attorney, responded to Van Ness by charging that the state agency failed to properly screen and then verify the financial capabilities of their clients. This resulted, he said, in "depriving lawyers in private practice of some income." Van Ness, speaking at the bar association's annual criminal law workshop, admitted that mistakes may have been made in not probing sufficiently into a client's finances but asked for understanding during the agency's beginning months as it experienced inevitable growing pains. He confessed "How many people got this service and were entitled to it, I don't know, but the vast majority did need our service. But I do not wish to represent people who can afford counsel."[2]

Van Ness predicted that his office would be able to defend 6,800 cases in 1969. With only twenty-six investigators for the entire state, it would be impossible to conduct a thorough investigation into each client's financial resources. Leonard Ronco, head of the Essex office, supported Van Ness' statements. His office had 3,600 clients in its first year of operation. He thought that only one or two of them were able to pay for their own attorney and invited Kessler to investigate any of the Essex clientele. Kessler answered the public defenders by stating that he did not object to the free service "but when someone deprives the economic life of the bar, then I must rise up and ask that abuses be corrected."[3]

Following the mild commotion over investigating clients' finances in 1969, the state's public defenders under Van Ness's steady guidance quietly established a viable program. Nevertheless, in two years the agency was again criticized, this time for doing too good a job! Governor Cahill established a blue-ribbon Management Commission comprised of business executives to study state government and make recommendations designed to trim unnecessary expenses. The businessmen concluded in a report on efficiency and economy, turned into the governor at the end of 1970, that public defenders had gone too far in their efforts to defend indigents. The commission stated, "It [the public defender agency] is permitted to overemphasize service to indigents and, in some cases, to provide more than adequate legal representation."[4]

The response to the puzzling criticism by the governor's Management Commission was unanimous in its support for the public defenders who were being reprimanded because they were doing too good a job, a job whose level of competence was required by both the state and federal constitutions. Despite the commission's request that the agency's funding be reduced (possibly in hopes of ensuring that their level of performance would decline), Governor Cahill publicly commended the agency's successful defense of indigent defendants and recommended a budget increase in order to permit them to provide quality representation in the face of an escalating caseload. Although the amount of the increase was modest ($300,000), it did mean the agency would be able to hire fourteen new attorneys, along with the requisite support staff. It was estimated that the state's public defenders would be serving 2,500 new clients above the 20,000 who were assisted during the previous year (1970). An editorial in the *Newark Star Ledger* typified the public's reaction to the Management Commission critique. The editorial ridiculed the commission, asking, "What's wrong with emphasizing service to the poor? That's what the defender's service is supposed to do."[5]

Essex County Deputy Defender Leonard Ronco came forward to defend the state's defender agency. His office was handling more than one-quarter of the state's indigent defense cases. Ronco stated that he and his staff of twenty-three attorneys were proud to be chastised for more than "just adequate" representation. He pointed out that according to the 1967 statute that created the agency, public defenders are specifically instructed to treat clients "as though privately engaged by him without regard to the use of public funds." Ronco also commented on their less-than-ideal working conditions. They were housed on the fourth floor of a dilapidated state employment building on Washington Street. The building was infested with rodents, with Ronco fearing the mice were about to take over the library, while cockroaches had long controlled the lunchroom.[6]

In 1971, the state public defender agency was merged into the larger, newly created office of public advocacy, which had broader responsibilities reaching all legal problems involving and affecting indigents. The office was formally divided into civil and criminal components. The former public defender agency assumed control over criminal law cases. It continued to be organized on its county regional basis. In 1995 the cumbersome office was altered to its present form. Its broad, policy-oriented posture as a public advocate was eliminated and the agency returned to its narrow responsibilities as a defender of individual cases restricted to representing indigent defendants. It has been rumored that newly elected Governor James McGreevy has expressed a desire to recreate the office of public advocacy, reinstituting a broader public policy role, particularly in the area of class action suits. Several of the current state-level officials and deputy defenders expressed concern that a change to a more policy-oriented agency might politicize the agency. A new advocacy role would likely complicate their position, undermining their effectiveness as professional defense attorneys and diverting their time and energy away from many of their clients.

As of the year 2000, there were 480 lawyers employed by the New Jersey state public defender agency, although only 263 were assigned to the adult criminal division. The remainder were distributed among the appellate, juvenile, legal guardian, and administrative sections. Recent growth in the agency has been rather slow, with only approximately fifteen new attorneys hired each year. Fortunately the caseloads have not risen markedly in the same period. With a sluggish economy, many staff attorneys are reluctant to leave the security of the state agency.

Statewide, New Jersey public defenders handle approximately 80% of all criminal cases. In urban areas with larger pockets of poverty, such as Newark, Paterson, Jersey City, and Camden, public defenders are defending over 90% of the criminal defendants. In multiple-defendant cases where state rules require the public defender agency to represent only one of the defendants, a pool list is utilized to select private attorneys for additional defendants. These attorneys are paid $25 an hour for out-of-court time and $30 an hour for in-court work. (These amounts are well below national standards as reported by the National Legal Aid and Defender Association.) Administration of the pool list and selection processes vary between the regional defender offices. Figures for the year 2000 indicate that statewide public defender programs opened 88,000 new cases and closed 72,000. Nearly 10,000 were given to pool attorneys. These statistics show that the average public defender was able to close 263 cases during the year.

There does not appear to be a specific state agency or department supervising the public defender organization, although they are technically listed as a branch of the Treasury Department. In the opinion of many public defenders, it is the Administrative Office of the Courts (AOC), which oversees the operation of the entire state court system, that has the most influence over the state defender agency. The AOC implements directives from the chief justice and state supreme court, in addition to supervising nearly every aspect of the state's judicial system. There is much conjecture over how much power the AOC actually possess vis-à-vis the public defenders, although nearly all of the defenders interviewed were in agreement that increased AOC influence was not a good idea and wished to be considered "independent contractors" with the state. Nevertheless, the AOC does require record keeping and reporting by the regional public defender offices, an obligation that only serves to aggravate the tension between the two agencies.

Adding to the strain between the judiciary and public defenders is the defenders' perception that the trial court judges believe that the defenders work for them and are under their control. Public defenders are obviously directly affected by a judge's ruling in a specific courtroom. They can also be influenced by statewide policies and decisions directed by the state supreme court. Despite this accumulation of judicial power, public defenders persist in asserting their independence as a viable proponent of their client's best interests. Defenders are also cognizant of their control over the pace of litigation, thereby allowing them to exert a critical role in reducing the criminal courts' mounting caseload and backlog problems. Any concerted effort by one or more public defenders to engage in a policy of rejecting plea bargains and insisting on going to trial can soon bring a local criminal court to a standstill The judges do not have the power to determine which public defender will be assigned to a particular case. Because judges are under a great deal of pressure from the AOC in Trenton to move cases as expeditiously as possible, there are occasional complaints about lawyer readiness, but these are even more likely to be caused by the prosecution than the defense. The most common cause of slowdowns is the inability of the assistant prosecutor to provide the defense with the required discovery in a timely fashion. Frustrated judges enmeshed in the snail-like pace of litigation may berate both prosecution and defense, but this venting accomplishes very little in the long run.

The head of the statewide public defender agency is appointed by the governor for a five-year term, but realistically serves at the governor's discretion and can be pressured out of office at any time. In the early 1990s Governor James Florio forced Fred Carabello out of the state director's office after a dispute arose between them. Past appointments indicate that governors favor minority candidates, either African-American or Latino, for the top position. Current director Peter Garcia was named to replace Ivy Torres, who died unexpectedly of cancer. Both Garcia and Torres had previously worked together in Camden County.

A related issue involves the relationship between the state public defender headquarters in Trenton and the twenty-one regional offices. As a general principle, the state has the final say in all hiring and firing decisions, although recommendations from regional directors—deputy public defenders heading each county office—carry significant weight. The deputy public defender can exercise direct control over transfers, either into or out of a regional office. Involuntary transfers can only be made for a six-month period, while voluntary transfers can be blocked or rejected by the local deputy director. It is assumed by most defenders interviewed that the state agency in Trenton can override any personnel decision, but in fact they defer a great deal to local regional directors, rarely interfering.

The state headquarters maintains a file on all transfer requests and appears to try to honor them. Given the fixed number of assistant public defenders in each county, it usually requires a voluntary transfer out before a new transfer can be moved into the desired slot. Thus, the transfer process is rather complex and creates a domino effect throughout various regional offices. Involuntary transfers are very rare due to state regulations and are utilized principally as a punitive measure. Firing an attorney is euphemistically termed "separating." It is a difficult, cumbersome process given the defender's union rights as well as the unwanted emotional trauma for both sides. Separation procedures are usually initiated by the regional director, with Trenton maintaining the final say. In the years 1997–2001, only three attorneys were fired statewide, all cases brought to Trenton's attention by a regional director.

With the present instability in the state headquarters due to Director Torres's death and the election of a new governor, it is unlikely that the regional offices will be challenged in the near future. The unionization of nonmanagement personnel (which includes all staff attorneys) has eliminated the necessity for Trenton to become involved in salary disputes. Most staff lawyers interviewed were satisfied with their current union-negotiated salaries. Experienced attorneys who had been with the office for over ten years were making close to $100,000, with an attractive pension plan and medical benefits. Management (i.e., regional directors and their first assistants as well as the Trenton leadership) salaries are controlled by the state. As a result of an agreement reached in the early 1990s devised by Supreme Court Justice Morris Pashman and Attorney General Donald Belsole, there are two public defenders, one investigator, and one secretary for every trial judge. The state's Office of Management and Budget has agreed to follow these guidelines.

The state public defender office has always had responsibility for indigent defendants requiring services at the superior court level. These county trial courts handle serious indictable crimes involving possible state incarceration for over a year. The state also maintains several hundred municipal courts, which are responsible for adjudicating lesser crimes (termed municipal offenses) where the defendant may face up to a year in the county jail. The U.S. Supreme Court's 1972 *Argersinger* decision mandated the appointment of counsel in these cases as well. New Jersey statute 1A currently requires each municipal court judge to assign an attorney to any indigent defendant facing a jail sentence. The judge may establish an assigned-counsel system of operating on a case-by-case basis, or create a permanent staff of available attorneys. The financial costs of either system are to be absorbed by the local municipality although they can charge a defendant $200 to reimburse the town.

Dating back to the 1971 governor's Management Commission report, there has always been concern that the public defender system has failed to carefully verify the indigency of defendants requesting services. The state system uses the federal government's indigency standards. Since 1994 the responsibility for validating the indigency claims of potential clients has been the responsibility of the case manager and his or her staff.

From observations and interviews, it does not appear that a great effort is put into the verification process. The regional public defender offices seem capable of handling their caseload, while most members of the local bar do not appear overly concerned with increasing their involvement in the criminal courts. A calculation is supposedly made to see if a defendant's family expenses are equal to the revenue income being earned. If the income exceeds $150, then a judgment bill is filed. These are sent to the state's

Division of Revenue, which works with a collection agency to try and raise the money. Amounts under $150 are simply recorded on a computerized file so if a defendant has several opportunities to use a public defender, the state will be aware when the $150 threshold is exceeded. The overall success rate of collecting these contribution orders from defendants has been difficult to determine. Since many defendants wind up in prison serving long sentences, it is unrealistic to expect a large return on the efforts of the collection agencies.

All defendants are also expected to pay $50 to cover administrative expenses. The responsibility for collecting these fees has been placed by state headquarters upon the regional offices. Although many regional offices have made an effort to collect these monies, the Essex public defenders, with their immense caseload (equal to nearly 30% of the state total), have been ignoring their collection responsibilities. They argue that being forced to badger their clients for these fees exacerbates their already shaky and contentious relationship. Many defenders noted that not being involved in unpleasant fee collection hassles was one of the main reasons why they joined the public defender office rather than practice privately and collect supposedly more lucrative fees. If the money must be collected, they thought the job should be handled by either the case manager or their investigators and support staff. Trenton has been increasingly insistent upon Essex pulling its own weight on this question, but the staff attorneys are rather adamant in their refusal to become involved in such mundane fiduciary matters.

The state public defender office in Trenton recognizes its responsibilities for pressuring the state legislature for the necessary appropriations to provide effective indigent representation. They do not believe, however, that they should engage in public relations efforts to pressure the legislature. Their stated goal is to simply represent individual clients in individual cases and not be involved in lobbying on behalf of particular legal issues or policy questions.

The delicate balance required in a regionalized statewide defender system between the flexibility needed in local defender offices versus the importance of maintaining a unified, strong whole is an ongoing struggle. With a strong emphasis on success in the courtroom as a prime measure of the defender's effectiveness, the Trenton headquarters' efforts to achieve statewide control is often minimized. The importance of the public defender's ability to provide competent, professional legal representation for the state's indigent defendants is an objective understood by both state and regional leadership.

Creation of the Essex Regional Office

On September 4, 1967, state public defender Peter Murray announced the appointment of a group of deputy public defenders to head a number of the regional offices. Leonard Ronco, a native of Bellville who had spent the past three years as an assistant prosecutor, was named to head the new

Essex County public defender office at an annual salary of $17,000. The Essex office, which includes Newark's crime-infested streets, was expected to be the busiest office in the state. State officials estimated that Ronco's office would have a third of the state's indigent defendants. The forty-two-year-old Ronco had been extremely active in Essex County political affairs since 1961 when he was admitted to the bar following graduation from John Marshall College of Law. State defender Peter Murray declared, "We are indeed fortunate to have a lawyer with Mr. Ronco's experience to head our program in Essex County." Ronco's former boss, Essex prosecutor Brendan Byrne commented "He [Ronco] is the most colorful prosecutor ever to grace a courtroom. He is extremely thorough and we hope he will be an administrator and not only an adversary."[7]

Ronco, as a result of his excellent record as a trial attorney (both with the prosecutor's office and in private practice) and his active role in county politics (as former state assemblyman, confidential secretary to the Essex County Board of Elections, and co-counsel to the County Welfare Board), is known among his numerous friends as the "Duke of Essex." Although the Essex office would be staffed with only a handful of assistant public defenders, the small group included three future judges, a pair of future defenders (Jack McMahon and Roger Higgins), and one of the top trial lawyers in the state, Allen Lowenstein.

In February 1971, during Ronco's fourth year in office, the governor's Management Commission issued a report critical of the operation of the state public defender office. They said the office does not receive proper supervision and "is permitted to overemphasize service to indigents and in some cases to provide more than adequate legal representation."[8] This group of business executives also thought the public defender needed to implement a series of cost-cutting procedures, including improved record keeping, establishing performance standards, and better coordination among attorneys. Their major criticism was to chastise the attorneys for doing too good a job, insinuating that indigent defendants were entitled to only mediocre or average representation. Ronco responded to the commission's report by stating how proud he was of his office's performance, winning 40% of their trials and 60% of their murder cases. His small but enthusiastic team of public defenders was housed in a dilapidated, roach-infested building, but the dismal setting did not dampen their spirits or diminish their courtroom success.

Despite enjoying the challenge of defense work after his prosecutorial experience, Ronco resigned from his position in 1971. The Duke of Essex did not enjoy working with several members of new State Public Advocate (the new title for the top public defender who was also given control over legal services) Stanley Van Ness's staff. When the opportunity to rejoin the Essex County prosecutors' office as chief trial attorney became available, he switched sides. Ronco's career continued to flourish during the next seven years as he was promoted in 1976 by then-Governor Brendan Byrne to become assistant attorney general and deputy director of the state Division of Criminal Justice. In 1977 the governor named him acting Essex County prosecutor. The next year he was appointed by Byrne to the superior court of Essex County. By the time of his permanent retirement in 1995, Judge Ronco had served with distinction on the bench for seventeen years.

The current deputy public defender in charge of the Essex regional office is Mike Marucci, who began working as a public defender in 1971. He worked briefly with the federal defender office in Newark (1974–1977) and also served as deputy director of both the Passaic and Morris County offices. It has been a rewarding experience for him to observe the Essex office grow from eighteen staff attorneys in 1977 to nearly fifty by the start of the twenty-first century. The facilities have also improved significantly from inadequate, depressing buildings first on Washington Street and then an only slightly better location on Halsey Street. The current location on Clinton Street is in a recently renovated twelve-story building offering acceptable working conditions for the growing number of lawyers, investigators, and support staff. What has remained constant, however, is the enthusiasm of the office, which has not perceptibly diminished since the initial stewardship of Leonardo Ronco.

Contemporary Newark: Entering the Twenty-first Century

As Newark enters the twenty-first century, it remains a seriously troubled city, although no longer meriting the title of "worst city in America," which it was given in a 1975 *Harper's* magazine article. Its population has declined from 440,000 in 1950 to 270,000 in the 2000 census, a drop of nearly 40%. Today, as it has been for roughly the past fifty years, Newark is surrounded by a series of concentric rings extended mainly to its northern and western borders. As one leaves Newark following a western route, the neighborhoods become more affluent the farther one travels. Newark may be the governmental and financial business center of Essex County, but over two-thirds of the county's citizens live outside of the city limits, a city whose size was drastically reduced by the county and state during the early decades of the twentieth century. The easiest way to comprehend the difference between Newark and the surrounding Essex County communities is to drive out on one of the broad avenues that stretch from the city's central business district to the farthest edge of the county. Journalist and long-time Newark resident Ron Palumbo describes in graphic fashion his drive to work on Springfield Avenue.

> Springfield Avenue which begins peacefully in the suburbs of Springfield runs through the white retreats of Short Hills, Millburn, and Maplewood and ends seven miles later in a frustrated rage. What was an avenue of transportation ends as a prison winding into Newark's hardcore ghetto, "the Strip" with a string of bars, liquor stores, and

barbecue shops with greasy windows. It perverts, it intimidates, and it finally suffocates those who come in contact with it in a sea of movement, marijuana, heroin, and liquor.[9]

Palumbo's description was written thirty years ago. In an effort to update his depressing picture, I recently took the same route, although I reversed directions, driving from downtown Newark westward. Palumbo's physical description remained fairly accurate. What did appear missing was the pulsating life and raw emotional energy that was so palpable to Palumbo. The streets were still lined with parked cars, garbage spilled into gutters, and every block was dotted with abandoned buildings. The tension and anger observed by Palumbo was noticeably subdued. I did see many children with their mothers, as well as numerous senior citizens engaged in animated conversations. There were also a troubling number of young and middle-aged men leaning against storefronts, staring blankly at the midday traffic. It was interesting to note the subtle changes in the various black communities as one traveled westward from downtown Newark. Moving from Irvington to Hillside to Maplewood, there was a clear socioeconomic progression from underclass to working class to middle class, although all the towns were predominantly black. The appearance of a white middle class was not visible until the westernmost edge of Maplewood.

Newark's current population of 270,000 has remained stable for the last decade but is down more than 100,000 since 1970. In addition to the large number of whites who have fled the city since 1960, middle class blacks have also been migrating to the more popular, pleasant suburban communities such as Montclair, Maplewood, and South Orange. The most discernible recent demographic shift in recent years has been the continued influx of Hispanics, who now comprise over a third of the city's population. Whites have bottomed out at barely 5% living in the most distant sections of the North Ward. (The remaining population is over 60% black.)

The city is divided into five political wards. The North Ward, which had formerly been predominantly Italian-American, is presently Hispanic with strong Puerto Rican and Dominican neighborhoods. The East Ward, known locally as the Ironbound because its borders are demarcated by railroad tracks and elevated highways, is a bustling Portuguese and Brazilian community with well-kept modest row houses. This ward is experiencing an economic revival. Its crowded streets are lined with busy restaurants and stores. It is thought to be the safest section of the city. The Central Ward, where riots erupted in 1967, remains the central business district. It is here that most of the public and private efforts to rebuild the city have been attempted. Recent civic improvements include the opening in 1996 of the New Jersey Performing Arts Center, the return of the minor league baseball team, and the restoration of several downtown office buildings. Many of the ward's high-rise public housing projects have been demolished and replaced by low-rise, mixed homes. The South Ward, once the home to the city's sizable Jewish community, has been a working class black neighborhood since the 1960s. The West Ward, which reaches Irvington and East Orange, is almost entirely black and contains the largest proportion of low-income families.

In 2001 a series of articles in the *New York Times* and *Newark Star Ledger* portrayed Newark as a city that is beginning to make a few modest strides toward stabilization and possibly revitalization. There is a great deal more to be done and serious concerns remain that a large number of the black underclass will continue to be trapped in a cycle of poverty. Sadonna Bryant, who has served for the past five years as the coordinator for the city's Community Development Network, stated in a *New York Times* article that "The city turned a corner in that people are realizing its investment potential both for commercial and housing development. . . . Unfortunately there is resentment by long-term residents. They don't feel that they are necessarily a part of the renaissance because the focus is on downtown."[10]

Popular Mayor James Sharpe is continually boosting the city's safer streets—homicides, robberies, and burglaries are down by 50% since 1996. Community development corporations have received land and money from the city for neighborhood projects. His efforts have also stressed increasing home ownership through obtaining state and federal block grants. Critics of the mayor's efforts point to failure in long-term, systematic planning. Boye Wilson, director of the New Jersey Office of the Regional Planning Association, commented in a May 2002 *New York Times* article that "[T]here has not been a lot of planning at all that considers how to build and sustain a community, how to make Newark viable long-term. . . . That kind of planning demands open space, recreation space, housing that is built to scale, all of which is part of the fabric of a community."[11]

The emerging picture is one of a beleaguered city that has begun to show evidence of improved community pride, as well as isolated success stories pointing toward guarded optimism for the future. While various social and economic indicators such as the crime rate and unemployment figures have improved during the past decade, they are still at unacceptable levels. The city's unemployment rate remains twice the state average at 8.1%, the drug trade continues to snare the young, and schools are still performing well below state and federal standards. Will the city continue to take small steps in its evolution toward becoming a safe, livable community for its 270,000 citizens? Will current efforts result in better schools and housing? Will the county, state, and federal authorities care about the fate of this city and provide the support necessary to sustain its revitalization? Only time will tell, but at least the city seems to be moving in the right direction.

Crime and Justice in Newark: A Historical Perspective

Although Newark is a modest-sized city of 270,000 (and its population has never exceeded 450,000), it has enjoyed a prominent place in the criminal justice annals of our nation, both past and present. Italian and Jewish racketeers thrived in Newark throughout Prohibition. The city's location near the Jersey Shore, close to New York and Philadelphia, allowed it to be a distribution point for liquor smuggled into the mid-Atlantic region. Richie Boiardo headed the Italian organization of the First Ward. He had moved to Newark from Chicago before World War I. He started out delivering milk and soon branched out into the numbers racket nicknamed "The Italian Lottery." It became so popular by the 1940s that it was said you could place bets daily under the dome of city hall. His Jewish counterpart was Abner "Longy" Zwillman who controlled the Third Ward to the south. There was an uneasy peace between them after Prohibition ended; Zwillman believed peaceful coexistence would be better for business than bloody turf wars. Many of Zwillman's businesses were legitimate, as he became a major legal importer of alcohol. Boiardo and his organization continued to provide illegal services for the Newark community. They began with the numbers racket and loan sharking, expanding into drug trafficking during the 1950s, selling heroin in the black neighborhoods of the Central Ward.[12]

By the end of the decade (1950s), Newark had established itself as a major drug distribution point for northern New Jersey, serving part of an East Coast organized crime drug network for both marijuana and heroin. Corruption has been endemic in Newark city government going back to the 1930s when the entire Board of Commissioners was indicted in a bribery scandal. The city has probably had more mayors convicted of corruption, bribery, or extortion than any other major municipality in the country. Among the most prominent recent mayors to lapse into criminal behavior were Hugh Addonizio and his successor, Kenneth Gibson. Addonizio's ties to organized crime figure Anthony "Tony Boy" Boiardo and five of his associates were verified during his trail for extortion and tax evasion.

Probably most disturbing to the city's many law-abiding citizens were persistent instances of police brutality that escalated during and after the 1967 riots into violent racial attacks. As early as 1954 blacks had called upon the city government to conduct a "full scale investigation of the conduct of some policemen who seem to have a sadistic desire to beat citizens of minority groups when making an arrest." Throughout the 1960s, Newark, like many other American cities, tried unsuccessfully to formulate a civilian review board to examine charges of police brutality. The most serious instance of police brutality grew out of the 1967 riots when several policemen were accused of shooting and beating black citizens. Ultimately, five policemen were sentenced, although for less serious crimes than originally charged.

Newark's notoriety as a high-profile crime community is not only based on colorful personalities like Richie Boiardo and "Longy" Zwillman. It is more directly related to the volume of crime generated out of its violent streets. During the 1960s and 1970s, Newark's crime rate was consistently among the nation's highest. The city's drug problems gained statewide attention in the 1980s when an epidemic of crack cocaine use forced the state legislature to enact one of the most severe drug laws in the nation. So many young blacks have been sentenced under this law that the state's prison population has tripled in the twenty years since its passage. During the 1990s Newark again gained unwanted national attention as the media named Newark the "auto theft capital of the nation," and then a few years later added on the title "car-jacking capital." Beyond media hype and hyperbole, the annual state police "Urban Crime Profiles" show a hardly reassuring picture. In 1997, Newark's overall crime index, which is comprised of murder, rape, robbery, aggravated assault, burglary, larceny, and auto theft, totaled 29,713—more than twice any other city in the state and three times every city with the exception of Jersey City.[13] In the year 2000, the Essex County criminal courts handled 16,235 cases. Ninety percent of these cases involved indigent defendants represented by the Essex Regional Office of the State Public Defender.

Essex Regional Public Defender Office

Structure and Organization

The Essex regional public defender office is located in downtown Newark approximately a mile and a half from the county courthouse with its adjoining jail, which houses most of the defendants unable to make bail. The public defenders who are responsible for representing all indigent adult defendants charged with indictable offenses occupy three floors of a twelve-story, nearly fifty-year-old building that was recently renovated. The appellate and juvenile divisions of the state defender agency are also housed in the building, which dominates a narrow side street stretching one block between the major thoroughfares of Broad and Mulberry Streets.

The seventh floor houses the Essex deputy director's office as well as most of the more senior staff and their secretarial support staff. There is a modest kitchen and a fairly large, open room serving as a law library as well as a lunchtime gathering spot. The larger offices reserved for the deputy director and his first assistants are located in the four corners, although none of the offices could be considered much more than functional. The remainder of the staff attorneys are found on the sixth floor along with a skeletal secretarial staff and twenty investigators. There is a large conference room in the center that can be used for the rare (usually semi-annual) staff meeting and can accommodate twenty-five persons around a large table. The room is also occasionally used by lawyers and investigators for discussions with clients and/or witnesses. The fifth floor houses the case files and the support staff who are responsible for filing and keeping track of the thick case folders. It is from here that new cases are brought up to the assigned attorney; it also serves as the permanent repository for the files once a case has been closed. In addition, there is a row of small conference rooms where for security reasons attorneys can interview defendants rather than in the attorneys' offices on the sixth and seventh floor. Most clients, however, are reluctant to visit the Clinton offices, preferring to simply talk with their attorney in a private corner of the county courthouse after their court appearance.

The defenders all have individual offices equipped with a fairly new computer, desk, and at least one wall of bookshelves. A bland institutional gray is the predominant color scheme although a few of the attorneys have made an attempt to enliven the otherwise lifeless atmosphere by decorating the walls with their children's artwork or African decorative reproductions. All of the rectangular offices are located off of a hallway that forms the perimeter for each floor. There is a large airshaft running through the center of each floor although none of the offices have windows facing out toward this dreary open space.

Access to the public defenders on all three floors is restricted. To gain entrance one must either have a special plastic card or knock very loudly on the door. Despite this pretense to security, it is fairly easy to enter the offices because the doors are often not completely closed or a passerby roaming the halls will often allow one inside. There are no internal stairways connecting the floors, so one must go outside and use the fire stairs. According to the regional director, this seemingly minor inconvenience creates a significant obstacle to the ability of the attorneys to interact and communicate with one another. This type of segmentation was avoided in their former office, which also occupied several floors but had internal stairways.

Most of the staff appear satisfied with their modest accommodations, or at least there was very little grumbling during the interviews. Since the defenders spend so much time in the courthouse, the condition of their offices does not seem to warrant much concern. Several of the senior attorneys did comment that they missed their previous building even though it was decrepit and infested with cockroaches and other vermin. They grew nostalgic over the older building, crediting it with contributing to the office's sociability and warmth. Older defenders reminisced about regular Friday afternoon parties that often spilled over into McGovern's, a convivial Irish pub near the office. The bar's welcoming ambience allowed the staff to wash away the depressing memories of a difficult week. Although the new offices are four blocks away, the older defenders still patronize McGovern's, consuming pints of Guinness with filling corned beef sandwiches. Today the bar stands isolated on an abandoned street, a forlorn reminder of better days.

Relationship with the State Defender

As the Essex regional public defenders go about their busy responsibilities representing the county's indigent defendants, it is easy to forget they are part of a larger statewide system. The state defender agency is headquartered in Trenton and maintains control over the budgetary, personnel, and operating procedures that can directly impact each regional office. Nevertheless, it is apparent that the regional offices have been granted a significant amount of autonomy and discretionary power. What emerges is a delicate balancing act orchestrated by the leadership in Trenton's and Newark's regional offices, which preserves the unified strength of the whole with the necessary flexibility granted to the regional staff. Based upon interviews and personal observations, the difficult relationship between state and regional offices appears to be working, although it is an uneasy peace with both sides cautious and protective of their perceived prerogatives.

The Essex regional public defenders are appreciative of the effective lobbying efforts of the state defender office in Trenton in procuring adequate budgets. They take advantage of the state's benevolence that allows for the defenders to attend seminars and conferences around the country at state expense, contributing to their professional development. They also recognize the importance of being able to receive office support in utilizing expert witnesses and other specialized requests related to their lawyering efforts. They noted in interviews their belief that their state support exceeds that which is afforded local prosecutors who are dependent on county funding. Salaries and benefits for assistant public defenders are negotiated with the state through their union. Interviews with the public defenders indicated a fairly positive acceptance of recent union efforts. There was an underlying acknowledgment that one should not expect significant monetary rewards for being a public defender, although they did have to survive and take care of their families. Relative to other public servants—particularly lawyers— working for the government, nearly all of the defenders felt that their financial package was acceptable.

A good example of the complex balancing act between comprehensive state policy and regional flexibility involves hiring, firing, and transfer of personnel. The majority of public defenders recently hired in the Essex region were initially interviewed and recommended by the Newark office. The job candidates had chosen the Essex office because of its heavy caseload of interesting, serious cases, many of which may lead to challenging trials. The reputation of the Essex office as a collegial environment staffed with high-quality, experienced attorneys also served to attract numerous applicants. Following a thorough interview with the regional deputy director and several of the top assistants, a recommendation is made to Trenton requesting that the candidate be hired. Trenton, however, has the final say in granting regional requests as well as determining exactly when the new lawyer can begin work. Even attorneys who first applied directly to Trenton for a job within the state defender office will eventually be interviewed by a regional office. Given the rather static nature of the number of public defenders (who are legislatively controlled by the number of judges in a particular county), the state must carefully maintain a broad overview of the various regional offices. A similar interaction between regional recommendations and state confirmation is maintained for all personnel decisions— firing, promotion, and transfers. State control is especially necessary for transfers between regional offices, which can have a domino effect on a number of counties.

There appears to be little tension between the Trenton headquarters and the Essex regional office. The Essex leadership states that it is in everyone's best interest to have open lines of communication and comply with the state agency's directives. Several of the assistant public defenders were not so positive about Trenton. They thought that the state headquarters acted as if the regional offices existed merely to justify them. Further, they characterized the state defender agency as a group of bureaucrats whose primary function should be to provide the money and support services necessary for the regional defenders to maximize their efforts. Officials in Trenton responded by declaring that it is only through their ability to present the state's public defenders as a competent, unified whole that they can effectively lobby the legislature to provide the necessary funds for the statewide program.

The most irritating aspect of the state agency's oversight responsibilities affecting the Essex regional office involves their obligation to collect money owed by indigent clients as required by state law. Although New Jersey public defenders represent indigent defendants, this does not mean their legal assistance is offered completely free of charge. Each client is required to file a financial form with the office indicating assets and net worth. The state can then order the defendant to pay a portion of his legal expenses. Since 1994 the Administrative Office of the Courts (AOC), through their various regional case managers, has the responsibility for verifying the indigency status of each defendant applying for representation by a state public defender. Following the completion of a case, the public defender office is required by state statute to bill the defendant, who hopefully will pay the state a portion of the amount depending on his or her financial capabilities. The amount of the bill is determined by the number of hours devoted to the case calculated at $30 per hour, as well as any additional expenses resulting from time spent by investigators and special witnesses or scientific tests. They are also charged with a flat fee for discovery by the prosecutor's office. Liens may be filed against the defendant. The responsibility for collecting the total figure presently rests in the hands of the state Treasury Department, who has subcontracted it out to a private collection agency (who can retain a portion of the collected monies for their services). Nearly all of this paperwork is meaningless since the State rarely collects anything from the defendants who are most likely either incarcerated or unemployed. Neither situation presents the client an opportunity to accumulate the funds necessary to repay the state.

The absurdity of the contrived arrangement only serves to make the Essex public defenders less willing to be active participants in the state's collection scheme. An additional annoying feature of the program is the growing pressure from Trenton to have regional offices collect a $50 fee from every client to help pay for the administrative costs of operating the verification and collection programs. This token contribution was to be collected by assigned public defenders as part of the closing of a case file. It was disclosed at a recent staff meeting that the Essex regional defenders could no longer ignore the state's requests for this money. Every other regional defender office had made an effort to collect the fee while only Essex had stubbornly refused to cooperate. What made its position even more tenuous was that because of the size of the Essex caseload—by far the greatest in the state—it was turning its back on thousands of dollars. It was equally embarrassing to have the state's largest county, with the largest and arguably the most competent regional office, refuse to comply with Trenton's requests for cooperation. Ideally, the state hoped that Essex would set a positive example for the other counties instead of dragging its heels.

The state agency that the Essex regional office has the most trouble with is the AOC, which it derisively characterizes as "bean counters." The AOC serves as the administrative arm of the state supreme court overseeing the operation of all levels of the judicial process: municipal, county, and appellate. The management of these various court systems is the responsibility of the AOC's county trial court administrators and their staff. Although the AOC's county trial court administrators assisted by their criminal case management teams cannot exert direct pressure on regional public defenders, they can nevertheless influence judges and prosecutors who in turn can affect local public defenders. Because of Essex County's prominence within the state's criminal justice system, they are frequently in the spotlight. This appears to have exacerbated the tension between the AOC and the Essex regional office.

Representatives of the criminal case manager's office interview all defendants at the earliest stage of the process, as they are brought to the courthouse for their initial appearance. Their fact-finding includes the application for a public defender as well as information necessary for determining a defendant's pretrial status, such as requests for release on recognizance. Although their impact upon the Essex public defenders appears to be minimal, there is a mutual distrust that colors any interaction between the two organizations. The public defenders perceive a clear prosecution bias as well as an unhealthy closeness in their relationship with superior court judges. A number of the public defenders thought several of the county judges were in awe of the AOC's links to the chief justice and the supreme court whose directives could directly impact their professional lives through transfers or promotions.

Leadership Structure

The Essex regional office is headed by deputy defender Mike Marucci, who has been a public defender since 1971, with a brief hiatus of two years with the federal defender's office. He served briefly as head of the Passaic regional office from 1990 to 1993 when state defender Zalema Farber brought him back to head the Newark office. Although a large part of the deputy's job involves handling personnel issues within the Essex office, an equally important responsibility is serving as a liaison between the Trenton and Newark offices. The regional director must ensure that state policies and directives are implemented by the local office while also keeping Trenton apprised of local developments. The previously noted tension between the state and Essex over the collection of fees epitomizes the difficult position of the regional director as he tries to appease both groups.

The regional defender is aided by four first assistants who serve as team leaders supervising approximately ten lawyers, as well as having additional specialized responsibilities. One of the first assistants, John McMahon, is designated chief trial attorney. All of the cases requiring a public defender come first to him. Most cases are distributed randomly among the team leaders, but murders are assigned to experienced attorneys. McMahon, who is recognized as one of the best criminal lawyers in the city, is permitted to occasionally select one of the more challenging murder cases for himself. Deputy Director Marucci also has a sterling reputation as a trial attorney, but unfortunately his weighty, time-consuming administrative responsibilities preclude him from returning to the courtroom except in the most extreme of cases. McMahon is the highest-ranking first assistant. He is not only second in command but his office is located adjacent to the director's, facilitating communication between the two leaders.

John Mask, another first assistant and team leader, brings a great deal of experience to his position. He served for many years in the Hudson County regional office before coming to Newark. In addition to his supervisory duties as team leader, Mask is also responsible for overseeing the operation of the three pre-indictment courts each staffed by a pair of public defenders: the Central Judicial Processing Unit (CJP), which performs the initial intake for all defendants; the Pre-Indictment Disposition Court (PDC), which takes early pleas in less serious felony cases; and the remand court, which disposes of Newark cases reduced to municipal offenses. Each court utilizes experienced public defenders who handle a large number of cases every day. Another responsibility given to this first assistant is administering the wide range of personnel problems generated by the forty-seven Essex attorneys. This job mainly involves overseeing the twice-yearly staff evaluations as well as the scheduling of vacations for the entire office.

The third first assistant is Al Kapin, also an experienced public defender with over twenty years of service. In addition to his supervisory responsibilities as a team leader and participating in an occasional trial, he is in charge of training and resolving client complaints. Most of the initial training is presently performed in a three-day session in Trenton, but additional seminars and conferences are also available for the professional development of all attorneys. He makes himself available to the young attorneys for mentoring and advising.

Yvonne Segars is the fourth first assistant. She is responsible for the pool list that is utilized in selecting private criminal lawyers for multiple-defendant cases. All of the attorneys on the list have volunteered for service, but she must be careful of not over-matching an inexperienced attorney in a serious or complex case. She oversees all operational issues with the office secretarial support staff. Her final task, which probably is the most important of her responsibilities, is helping to run the drug court with the assistance of another public defender. This specialized court will be discussed in detail in Chapter Five, but it is important to note that Ms. Segars has emerged as a nationally respected leader in the drug court movement. She is frequently brought to Washington by the U.S. Department of Justice to speak, as well as traveling around the nation assisting in the establishing of drug courts in other jurisdictions.

Joe Krakora is the fifth and final lawyer designated as a first assistant although he is actually a specialist in handling death penalty cases throughout the state. He is housed in the Newark office because he previously worked there for three years and lives in fairly close proximity. His unique talents and excellent trial record appear to have earned the respect of his Essex colleagues although he is often away from the office for lengthy periods of time.

All of the first assistants downplayed the importance of their position in the office hierarchy. They acknowledge during interviews that they do fill out semi-annual evaluations of all team members as well as try to make themselves available for assisting and supporting all attorneys assigned to their team. The first assistants also serve as a useful buffer between the staff attorneys and the regional director. Without these team leaders absorbing a wide range of miscellaneous administrative responsibilities ranging from client complaints to the scheduling of vacations, the director would be mired in a plethora of minutiae, unable to devote his energies to more important problems. Freed from these tedious tasks, he is available to observe his staff perform in the courtroom, focus on resolving serious personnel issues, and communicate effectively with his superiors in Trenton. The first assistants, however, did agree that these teams are an organizational mirage, designed primarily to placate state headquarters, giving the appearance of a viable organizational structure in accordance with the concepts of bureaucratic theory. In reality, the staff attorneys function independently, hardly aware of the invisible lines separating one team from another. Team leaders and public defenders understand the permeable nature of the four groups, and the legal staff is encouraged to seek advice from any attorney whom they respect and with whom they feel comfortable. All of the staff appreciates the freedom of independence granted to them. The result of this flexible, trusting system is an office distinguished by effective communication and blessed by collegial staff who generally respect one another.

In comparison to most large law firms and governmental agencies, the Essex regional office barely resembles one's conception of a bureaucratic organization. Yet the office does have over a hundred employees when one combines lawyers, secretarial staff, and investigators. Several of the Essex public defenders commented that it was naïve to think that the office was not without some bureaucratic patterns of behavior. Merely because the regional office is not driven by a bottom-line or profit motive, it is still an integral part of the Essex County criminal justice system as well as under the control of the statewide defender agency. The convivial nature of the Essex regional office and the relaxed leadership style of the director and his first assistant camouflage the unpleasant aspects of its bureaucratic reality. There are discernible limits that even the most freewheeling senior attorneys are unable to escape. If they refuse to work within these loose guidelines and fail to carry out their professional obligations to their clients, they know they will be disciplined. A few attorneys test the limits of this tolerant organiza-tion, but they are reined in and made accountable for their transgressions.

Intake Procedures: Caseloads and Assignments

The Essex regional office has the responsibility for representing all indi-gent defendants charged with indictable offenses–any serious crime which could result in a state prison sentence of a year or more. These cases are first processed by the Central Judicial Processing Unit of the Newark Municipal Court and then referred to the Essex County Superior Court (Criminal Divi-sion) where a grand jury will decide if a defendant should be indicted. Fol-lowing arrest, all defendants are given the opportunity to fill out form 5A requesting a public defender. The defendant must also demonstrate his or her inability to afford an attorney. The state public defender estimates that they defend 80% of all indictable cases in the state. They also note that in urban areas such as Newark the percentage of representation usually reaches approximately 90% to 95% of the defendants. After a year of observing the Essex County courts, I estimate that at least nine out of ten defendants are represented by a public defender (or assigned counsel in a multiple-defendant case).

The criminal case manager has responsibility for handling the intake paperwork for all the defendants as well as verifying the claims of indigency by those requesting a public defender. The consensus of Essex County crim-inal justice officials interviewed is that not much effort is put into the verifi-cation process. If someone wishes to have a public defender instead of a private attorney, it is assumed that this individual has no choice and is not trying to "beat the system." It is believed by all that if money were available, he or she would surely opt for hiring a private attorney. Thus, when a defen-dant requests a public defender, this is tantamount to establishing one's indi-gency. Occasionally a public defender will suspect that his or her client is gainfully employed and could have possibly paid for private counsel but nothing is done. One public defender disclosed in an interview that he once had a client who turned out to be an airline pilot. He notified the deputy director, but was allowed to continue with his representation without protest from the private bar or comment from the bench.

Following completion of the paperwork, the defendant is brought into the Central Judicial Processing Unit of the Newark Municipal Court where a request for indigency can be made. The completed forms are next sent to the fifth floor of the Clinton Street offices of the Essex regional office where a clerk opens a file for the new client. At this time, the clerk checks to see if the defendant is already being represented by a public defender in another case which is still pending. A final, careful review of the client's application is made to ensure that he or she is not using an alias or has used one in the past. Once satisfied, a letter is sent to the client requesting that he or she come to the Essex office for an interview. For those defendants who could not make bail and are detained in the county jail, their assigned public defender will visit them. It usually takes several weeks before the clerks have completed their reviews and forwarded the case file up to the seventh floor where it will be assigned to a particular attorney. The assignment of cases is made randomly, with the exception of murder cases, which are reviewed and distributed personally by first assistant John McMahon. It is not unusual for McMahon to keep several of these serious cases for himself, in his capacity as chief trial attorney. McMahon also often consults with Deputy Director Marucci over the specific assignments of these homicides.

Statistics from the state public defender office indicated that during the year 2000, their office opened 88,000 new cases statewide, 10,000 of which required a private attorney from the pool list. During this year, state defenders were able to close 72,000 cases. Their figures indicated that the average public defender was able to close 263 cases during the year. With Essex County encompassing high crime areas such as Newark, East Orange, and Irvington, their average caseload was significantly higher than the state average. Interviews with the Essex regional defenders estimated that at any one time they had approximately one hundred active cases. These cases were divided between sixty in the pre-indictment stage and forty in the more critical post-indictment period. Several defenders commented that if they did not make a diligent effort to close cases, they would soon be overwhelmed. Because the average time from arrest to disposition in Essex County stretches beyond a year, and many cases languish in the usually dormant pre-indictment period for at least four months, it is common for defendants out on bail awaiting trial to get into trouble with the law before the original case is concluded. Thus, public defenders often find themselves defending a client at his or her parole violation hearing, which usually means that he or she has a new charge pending, and before these matters can be resolved a third problem arises. One attorney has seen her caseload rise to over 200, with 150 pre-indictment cases and another 75 in the post-indictment stage. She stated that she was presently representing one highly active client in his fourth trial within a two-year period of time. All of the cases were serious, including several armed robberies and a pair of drug distribution cases.

For those more senior attorneys (in addition to the chief trial attorney) who handle murder trials that can commonly take several months, efforts are made to protect them from accumulating too many new cases. Most attorneys noted the cyclical nature of the caseload, which can rapidly jump from a calm, manageable number to a seemingly overwhelming number of clients. These cyclical trends also seem to occur in terms of clients wishing to go to trial. The public defenders working in tandem with the special pre-indictment courts (remand and PDC) have unique responsibilities in these high-volume, fast-paced courts, which can drive up their caseloads into the hundreds. Fortunately for them, nearly all of their cases are quickly resolved through non-trial dispositions. One of the senior attorneys working in the PDC courtroom noted that when the assigned prosecutor is feeling the pressure of an escalating caseload, they could easily negotiate 200 plea bargains in a month.

The most unique feature of the assignment process utilized by the Essex defender office is that the choice of a particular defender determines which judge will hear the case. Public defenders are assigned in pairs to a specific judge (usually a senior defender works in tandem with a younger, less experienced defender) for a period from twelve to eighteen months. During this period every new case assigned to a public defender will follow him or her into the courtroom of the judge to whom he or she has been posted. This is the reverse of the more common assignment procedure that will direct a case to a specific judge.

Nearly every public defender agreed that the most difficult and often frustrating aspect of their job was being able to bring a case to closure. This occurs when the court has reached a disposition and the defendant has been sentenced. If the sentence is suspended, however, and the client placed on probation for a period of time with certain specified conditions such as completing an anger-management class, returning to school, or submitting to weekly drug testing, the case cannot be closed until the defendant has completed the probationary period. Because this probationary period is often several years, it provides most defendants the chance to get in trouble again, which will reopen the client's file for an even longer period of time until the newest problem has been resolved. This process inevitably results in a seemingly endless series of legal problems for one's client. It can also give the assigned public defender an ulcer, much angst, and a growing pile of cases that never appears to recede.

Training and Professional Development

Even though nearly all the attorneys hired by the Essex regional office are just beginning their professional careers, the state public defender provides very little formal training. All new hires are given a three-day training session in Trenton, but it is offered sporadically. Several of the recently hired younger attorneys were on the job several months before they were able to attend the training session. Al Kapin, the first assistant responsible for training, usually participates in the sessions, which are primarily a series of exercises where the young attorneys work through hypothetical cases. The sessions also utilize videotapes to teach trial techniques. Nearly all of the Essex public defenders thought that their real training began once they began working in the courtroom. The office carefully pairs young attorneys with more experienced ones who can serve as their mentors. It also allows for the beginning lawyer to be eased into more complex cases and trial situations. The senior attorney is able to step in and assist whenever the new public defender is faltering. It was noted it was important not to jeopardize a client's case for the sake of a learning experience.

This trial-by-fire method of on-the-job training succeeds because of the commitment of the more experienced attorneys to assist their partners or any other new hire. The Essex office does offer an annual in-house training day, but all of the defenders interviewed agreed that their education began when they first engaged in formal conversations with their more experienced colleagues in the courthouse hallways, lunchroom "bull sessions," or simply whenever a handful of attorneys were conversing. As one young attorney stated, "There is an unlimited potential for learning." As one roams the sixth and seventh floor hallways of the Clinton Street office, there is a constant exchange of information between attorneys with continual encouragement and mutual support. With a staff top-heavy with experienced attorneys having over fifteen years of service, there are abundant mentors available. The entire office clearly subscribes to this informal socialization process that encourages younger attorneys to seek out advice, so no one ever feels totally alone or afraid to ask a question because they appear it will make them appear stupid or silly. The director and most of the first assistants set the tone for this smoothly functioning support system. Whenever one of the younger attorneys is in trial they drop by the courtroom to show their support and be available to give advice if requested.

The state defender in Trenton and the regional Essex office were equally committed to the professional development of their staff. This went beyond the initial education of young attorneys to the even more critical task of stimulating the experienced attorneys, keeping them motivated and aware of the latest in trial techniques or most recent appellate decisions. There was money available to send interested lawyers to seminars and conferences around the country. One attorney who had recently returned from a seminar deeply appreciated the opportunity to stimulate his intellectual interests and sharpen his trial techniques. After nearly twenty years with the office, he believes that his drive for excellence as an effective litigator is directly related to his opportunities to attend these seminars. He especially enjoys his mentoring role, sharing his knowledge and trial experiences with the office's younger attorneys. (At times he almost appears as a frustrated law professor.) It was interesting to observe at a staff meeting one of the most respected senior defenders reporting on a seminar he had recently attended. He offered to share with his fellow attorneys "cutting edge" developments in criminal law on such topics as new techniques in discrediting expert witnesses on fingerprint reliability to the latest psychological studies challenging the validity of confessions. Most of the defenders found their teaching responsibilities to be one of the more enjoyable aspects of their job, rather than an annoying digression from more important work. The educational process went far beyond simply relating "war stories" to the passing along of briefs and motions that might prove helpful to the beginning attorneys. Several of the older attorneys added a cautionary note as to how far this mentoring process could go in one's professional development. They agreed that it was important to ask questions and observe, but in the end, each attorney had to formulate his or her own unique approach. They warned that one needed a good portion of humility combined with a healthy dose of paranoia to survive as a criminal defense lawyer. It was important to maintain a skeptical eye in order to preserve that necessary "edge." Several of the experienced lawyers warned that much of what constitutes a successful criminal lawyer cannot be taught; it is simply related to one's personality. One of the most respected senior lawyers even went so far as to state "trial lawyers are born, not made. The good ones are good immediately. It is like the gift of bullshit for the natural born salesman!"

In conclusion, the education and professional development of the Essex regional staff succeeds not because of the abbreviated, sporadic training opportunities but rather because of the presence of a large, committed group of experienced attorneys who are willing participants in the socialization process that has produced not only competent attorneys but an exceedingly hospitable work environment. The tone is set from the deputy director down to the most recent recruits who have bought into the program.

Personnel Decisions: Hiring, Firing, and Promotion

The general principle governing personnel decisions within the statewide public defender system is that the regional office may make recommendations, but the state defender in Trenton has the final word. Turning first to the hiring process, lawyers initiate their request for a job at the state headquarters where they may be interviewed and directed toward a regional office that has a vacancy. Approximately one-third of the recent hires in Essex County began their job search in this manner. They then visited the regional office with the vacancy and were interviewed by the local staff who decided whether or not to request that the applicant be hired. Because of Essex County's reputation as a professional operation with excellent, experienced attorneys and an abundance of challenging cases, most applicants choose the Newark office over competing vacancies in other regional offices. The majority of applicants, however, first visit the Newark office for an interview after learning of a vacancy. The deputy director may then send a positive recommendation to Trenton, requesting permission to hire the individual. The interviews, whether conducted in Newark or Trenton, followed a similar pattern, with the candidate being examined by a number of senior staff attorneys who presented a number of hypothetical cases designed to test one's legal acuity as well as the ability to think quickly under pressure. Several of the most recently hired Essex regional public defenders were former law clerks for superior court judges. There also appeared to be a trend during the past decade of hiring an increasing number of women, although this could be a function of many more women graduating from law school during this time compared with earlier years.

With the authorized number of public defender positions governed by the number of judges in the county or vicinage (an old-fashioned term for a New Jersey judicial district) and the bureaucratic paperwork progressing at a snail's pace, young lawyers must be very patient waiting for their positions to be officially granted. In Essex County, in order to assist a young lawyer who has been requested and approved by the state, the regional office is allowed to issue the attorney a temporary contract, which usually lasts for three to six months. During this time, the "public defender to be" is assigned clients and paid on a per-case basis, although he or she is not allowed to receive benefits.

Similar to hiring procedures, all promotions and demotions must be finalized by the state defender agency following a recommendation by the regional deputy director. There was a general consensus among staff attorneys that promotions were made on a merit basis. In contrast to a place like Chicago, where political considerations can play a major role in all personnel decisions, they appear to be nonexistent in Essex County. Several of those interviewed noted that politics did influence appointments in Trenton at the highest level and occasionally in the selection of a regional director, but below that it was not a factor.

Because of the way regional offices are structured there are few opportunities for promotion during a public defender's career. Assistant public defenders are classified into three grade levels, beginning with level three and advancing to level one. Each level has several steps that are achieved after a number of years of service earning the defender an increase in salary. The next step after reaching the first level assistant public defender is to become first assistant, of which there are only four. This is a significant jump because as a first assistant and team leader, one is now part of management, and no longer a member of the union. The salaries of first assistants and directors are determined by the state defender in Trenton.

The theoretical basis for promotions of assistant public defenders is their semi-annual evaluations by team leaders. Most of the staff, however, discounted the importance of the evaluations, finding the promotion process to be rather haphazard, and not always related to one's ability as an attorney. The move up to a management-level position as a first assistant or deputy director was even more difficult to predict. Such moves were also rare because there were so few opportunities for advancement. The organization was consistently described as static with almost no room at the top.

Turning to negative personnel decisions–demotions–these occurred rarely, were judged to be nonpolitical, and were based upon reasonable judgments. Most defenders agreed that young staff attorneys usually resigned before they were fired. These decisions were usually made a year or two after joining the office, the young lawyer and his or her team leader mutually agreeing that it had been a bad fit. No one in the office remembered anyone who had actually been fired or forced to resign from the office against his or her wishes.

Demotions typically involved transferring an individual from a trial court to one of the three pre-indictment courts, although most of the lawyers currently working in these busy, tedious courtrooms were placed there because of a health problem, that is, heart condition, hypertension, or the general malaise caused by burnout. Two of the non–health related demotions were caused by ineffective courtroom performance. Another attorney was demoted from first assistant back to staff attorney (assistant public defender). This decision was caused by a shakeup in the office resulting from the arrival of a new deputy director who wanted to bring in a new group of first assistants. Overall, there was very little griping over personnel decisions although one senior attorney with thirty years of experience expressed frustration over his failure to become a team leader. He theorized that some people in management (most likely in Trenton) thought that he was a bad influence on younger lawyers, showing them shortcuts and how to avoid being tied down to the office. Early in his career he was described by several other senior attorneys as being a feared adversary, but presently he was content to operate on the fringe of the office although remaining an effective counselor for his clients.

Transfers are the most frequent yet most complex type of personnel decision. They can be either voluntary–requested by an attorney wishing to move to another regional office–or involuntary. Anyone who is involuntarily transferred has the option after six months of returning to his or her original office. (This policy was created so that transfers could not be used punitively.) Public defenders wishing to transfer send their request to Trenton, usually with the approval of the regional deputy. These requests are kept in a master file in Trenton. Before a request can be granted (requests are usually made for a specific regional office), either a vacancy must occur or an additional position is created by the appointment of a new judge. It is not unusual to wait several years before a request is granted. Once a vacancy is available and one individual moves, it creates a domino effect, causing vacancies to open around the state as the Trenton office controls the series of transfers. During the eighteen months spent observing the Essex office, only one transfer was made. It involved a fifteen-year veteran who had recently moved a great distance from Newark into the rural northwest corner of the state about thirty miles away. His transfer request, which was a result of his wish to avoid a commute of more than an hour, took nearly a year before it was granted.

In contrast to private law firms where much attention is paid to salary and promotion, especially the move from associate to partner, the public defenders are minimally concerned with these issues. When money matters do become significant, such as the impending birth of children, having to buy a larger home, or sending a child to college or private school, the defender looks toward moving to a position in the private sector rather than remaining and complaining about his or her finances. (The same scenario applies to lawyers frustrated by a lack of promotion or having transfer requests denied.)

Office Leadership

The Essex regional office is blessed with excellent leadership. The first deputy director in 1967, Leonard Ronco, set a high standard, and with one possible exception, this position has been filled with competent individuals. The current (2002) deputy director, Mike Marucci, was brought into the office in 1973 after a three-year stint as the head of the Passaic County regional office. He first joined the public defenders in 1971 and has remained with the program since then with the exception of a two-and-a-half-year hiatus with the federal public defender office in Newark.

Marucci spends roughly half of his time talking with his legal staff discussing cases. He can also be found in the Essex County courthouse most days observing his staff in action. He also devotes a surprising amount of his remaining time on personnel issues, which include defenders' complaints as well as having to deal with resignations, illnesses, and a diverse range of other problems growing out of a staff of nearly fifty attorneys, an equal number of secretarial and clerical staff, and twenty investigators. When he is in his Clinton Street office, Marucci's door is always open. He appears to always be accessible as he roams the hallways engaging in friendly conversation. His openness is especially apparent during the lunch hour when he frequently joins the staff in the law library joking, gossiping, or simply listening to his fellow attorneys.

Another concern of the regional director is to insulate his staff from Trenton, continually maintaining the office's autonomy that is critical in preserving its morale and courtroom effectiveness. Marucci's reputation for fairness combined with his integrity and intelligence have allowed him to become an effective buffer between his staff and the state office in Trenton. He has earned the trust and respect of both sides despite the numerous inherent points of conflict. Marucci is also concerned with outside pressure from the judiciary, county prosecutor's office, trial court administrators, and multitude of unhappy clients. Despite all of these outside groups pressuring his office, Marucci makes it very clear that his primary responsibility is to his staff.

During the year spent observing the Essex regional defender office, a number of incidents occurred that exemplify the style and character of the director's leadership. The first was observed during a visit by Marucci to the courtroom where a young assistant public defender was trying her first murder case. He entered the small courtroom midway through her direct examination of the primary witness and sat quietly in the second row. During a recess in the trial, he rose and the young attorney came over. He spoke softly to her, giving her encouragement and emotional support. Marucci's words had an obvious calming effect for the young attorney, as she resumed her questioning with energy and confidence. Although this may have been a minor event in and of itself, it was repeated numerous times in other courtrooms, forming a persistent pattern of encouragement that the staff could always rely upon.

A second example of Marucci's style of leadership was seen during his convening of one of the office's rare staff meetings on a late October afternoon. About three quarters of the legal staff gathered in the sixth-floor conference room that was barely adequate for the semi-annual meeting. Half of the attorneys present sat around a long table in the middle of the room while the remainder sat on folding chairs against the wall or stood by the door. Although the meeting was scheduled to begin at four o'clock, it took fifteen minutes for everyone to drift in while the director stood patiently at the head of the table, coatless with his sleeves rolled up, waiting for everyone to quiet down.

Although I have never attended a partners' meeting at a large law firm, I cannot imagine that it in any way resembled the somewhat chaotic scene unfolding before me in the Essex regional defender office. Among the more striking differences were the style of dress, degree of levity, level of candor, lack of decorum, and relaxed style of leadership exhibited by the director. Turning first to the absence of sartorial concern, it was abundantly clear that the office failed to observe any dress code. The button-down shirt and three-piece suit, the recognized uniform of the corporate lawyer, was worn by only a few attorneys. Although the lateness in the day accounted in large measure for the informal mode of dress, there is generally little attention paid to clothing. A few of the more flamboyant or rebellious attorneys showed up sockless, tieless, and in jeans and a knit shirt, eschewing the somber tones of gray and black for the multicolored diversity of the rainbow.

The degree of levity was also surprising. The badinage and joking produced loud belly laughs, not the wry smirks and soft chuckles found in the more carefully calibrated exchange of corporate jocularity. Also driving up the decibel level was the "I bet I can top that one" competition between several of the more senior attorneys, although all joined in when the punch line was delivered. A great deal of the humor was directed at themselves, but an even greater amount was targeted toward the judges, prosecutors, and court clerks who could make their lives miserable. Their irreverence spared no one, including nearby attorneys who were only too ready to shoot back an acerbic rejoinder.

Once the meeting began there was only a slight decline in the levity as most comments were made with a startling degree of candor. As the director moved through his agenda, the staff discussed each issue in an aggressive, often combative style. Contentious points were argued loudly, yet the verbal jousting was obviously good-natured. Despite the lack of respect shown to colleagues, no one seemed to take personal offense. Other than trying to strike back with a deftly aimed retort of their own, the sharp comments were like verbal "love taps" delivered with both gusto and warmth.

Overseeing the somewhat chaotic scene was the director, apparently enjoying the verbal warfare transpiring in front of him. Calmly smiling, he would permit the staff to vent their emotions to a point at which time he would bring them under control. The ease with which the director manipulated the staff, moving gently toward a new point or away from a raucous argument was impressive, illustrating the esteem in which he was held by the rest of the office.

The first item of business this day was a plea from the chief of their twenty-person investigative team asking the attorneys to try and be more reasonable when making last-minute demands. The chief investigator related several occasions where her staff felt slighted and inconvenienced by what they thought were unreasonable public defenders who were making last-minute changes contradicting earlier requests. Several of the attorneys responded to the criticism by defending their ill-timed requests as necessitated by the frequently changing demands of prosecutors and clients. They exhibited little sympathy for the investigator's concerns. At this point the director stepped in and reduced the tension by urging the attorneys to be more sensitive to the investigators, by trying to be as clear and timely as possible. The director's conciliatory efforts ended the discussion and prepared the group for the next order of business.

Without reading too much into the heated discussion, there did appear to be a palpable animosity between a small group of lawyers and investigators. Although both groups acknowledged that they are both working toward the same goal—trying to uncover the facts in a case—the differing professional demands and time constraints of each group tend to heighten their mutual frustrations. Several of the lawyers were rather outspoken in their negative opinion of the investigators, describing them as slow and unresponsive to their requests. The investigators, on the other hand, were upset over the lack of respect and appreciation for their job, which is often difficult as well as dangerous.

It appeared to be an ongoing problem that the director must continually mediate. His mild-mannered, unflappable style of leadership is well-suited toward resolving such persistent personality conflicts between two groups of well-intentioned professionals frustrated by the annoying behavior of members of the Essex County criminal justice system.

The second item discussed was a brief report from one of the senior attorneys who had recently attended an interesting seminar covering several of the most recent developments in defense strategy focusing on the reliability of fingerprints and confessions. Following the report, the director encouraged the staff to attend similar seminars, noting that he had money available from the state for any interested attorneys.

The third point on the agenda was a welcome bit of news. The director announced that the office had finally worked out an agreement with the county to allow the attorneys free parking in the public lot located directly behind the courthouse. The news caused loud cheering among the staff, taking the director several minutes to calm everyone down. Because the courthouse is half a mile up a steep hill from their offices through a depressing downtown shopping area, most of the staff preferred driving, but the parking proved to be prohibitively expensive. With the new arrangement the attorneys will be able to save their money while also avoiding the discomfort of walking in inclement weather.

The final topic of the day would result in a heated and lengthy discussion, lasting nearly an hour. It grew out of the failure of the attorneys to collect a $50 fee from their clients for administrative costs. The state agency had been after the Essex staff for some time to collect the money, but the lawyers had stubbornly ignored their requests. The fee was originally collected by another state agency but had been shifted to the public defenders. A few of the attorneys pointed out that in other counties the fee was collected by the investigators or secretarial staff, but Director Marucci explained that because the lawyers in Essex County conduct the initial intake interviews at the CJP, they are obligated to carry out this annoying responsibility. The idea of having to confront their clients and extract these administrative fees from them was unanimously rejected as repulsive. One lawyer explained emotionally that he became a public defender so he would not have to be involved in such "money grubbing unpleasantries." Another stated that forcing them to become involved in clients' financial problems would create another reason for the defendants to distrust them.

The director tried to calm the attorneys down by saying he was well aware of their distaste for being dragged into the collection process. He explained that he had been shielding the Essex office from threats from state headquarters but the pressure was currently being increased to the point where he could no longer ignore their persistent demands. He articulated a recent state report showing collection figures for the past year. It showed in embarrassingly clear terms how unresponsive their regional office had been. Even though Essex was by far the largest and busiest office in the state, they had collected only a solitary fee during the past year, whereas all of the other regional offices had complied with Trenton's wishes. Counties one-fifth the size of Essex had collected twenty times the number of fees.

Even in the face of such incontrovertible evidence, the Essex County attorneys continued to object. The director shared their frustration, stating he would work with them to try and develop a more acceptable collection procedure. He hoped someone could come up with a creative solution but implored them to begin to make a good faith effort to collect the fees and get the state agency off their backs. The staff appeared resigned to their fate, acquiescing to their director's reluctant yet reasonable request.

The staff meeting was my first opportunity to meet the attorneys that I would be interviewing and observing over the next eighteen months. The director introduced me as the meeting began. He encouraged them to cooperate in my research project, a request that was deeply appreciated and proved instrumental to the success of the project. Overall, I was greatly impressed by the director's leadership abilities. He had used a combination of patience, intelligence, and humor to guide his outspoken, strong-willed staff. Speaking in a reasonable, soft-spoken fashion, he was able to gain their grudging acceptance on several important issues. The Essex public defenders were ready to follow their director's lead, "pulling the wagons in a circle" if need be, in order to fend off the aggravating intrusions from prosecutors, judges, "bean counters from the AOC," or even their own headquarters in Trenton.

The director's leadership style was especially appropriate to a regional office top-heavy with so many senior attorneys with many years of experience. As several of the older lawyers commented, "the office runs itself." Their observation is a subtle and somewhat paradoxical compliment to Director Marucci. Given the number of strong personalities in the office, most of whom have been accustomed to having a large degree of independence, it is amazing that the director, in a seemingly effortless manner, has been able to operate a smoothly-running, extremely collegial defender office. The entire staff, without exception, had only complimentary words for their boss. Comments such as "He's a great friend and boss," "I'd do anything for him," and "He is a wonderful human being" were echoed by nearly every attorney. Most categorized him as the best deputy director in the state. They deeply appreciated his willingness to grant them a great deal of autonomy while always being supportive. His advice could be relied on for its compassion, intelligence, and fairness. In closing, Mike Marucci's leadership is probably the most important factor shaping the Essex office, allowing the staff to perform at such a high level of competence, professionalism, and commitment.

Support Staff and Resources

Public defenders are rarely able to match the resources available to a prosecutor's office.[14] The prosecution is usually able to hire expert witnesses, forensic scientists, or pay for any other assistance necessary in their effort to protect society. Conversely, the public defenders almost always have to worry about financial considerations in their attempt at competent representation of indigent defendants. Fortunately for their indigent clientele, New Jersey's statewide public defenders are one of the rare exceptions to this rule. Because each county is responsible for the local prosecutor's operating budget, the state-funded public defender regional office in a financially limited county such as Essex, with a depleted tax base, is in an advantageous position. The Essex defenders are able to rely on the fiscal commitment of the state in their legal defense of indigent clients. Several defenders commented that no questions are asked for any reasonable request for research or resources on behalf of one's clientele. One experienced defender noted "the only limit is the aggressiveness of the attorney." A few years ago when he was involved in a complex double murder case, he had to spend $30,000 for expert witness testimony that the state paid without question.

Both the Essex regional deputy director and high-ranking members of the state defender's office reiterated in interviews a strong commitment to quality defense, supported by adequate funding. The state defender agency maintains a list of experts with comments on their demonstrated competence and performance record. They have regular consultants for drug and ballistic tests as well as their own team of polygraphists. One state official stated that the policy to honor all lawyer requests is directly related to the goal of providing whatever experts are necessary so that clients cannot charge a public defender with failure to raise issues or pursue avenues of defense. Thus far the strategy is working in Essex, where there have been very few instances of indigent defendants charging the public defenders with failure to provide a competent defense as required by the Sixth Amendment. One older defender even conjectured that the state provides more money and better resources than most private criminal lawyers would spend. He explained that a private attorney, concerned about being reimbursed by clients, would compromise his or her effort if a client could not afford the services of an expert witness who usually costs several hundred dollars an hour.

The defender office's support staff, comprised of secretaries, receptionists, and file clerks, is another important resource related to providing effective representation. The secretaries and receptionists on the seventh floor who assist the attorneys were thought to be competent by nearly everyone, with very few complaints. Because so many lawyers use word processors and computers for tasks that were formerly done by secretaries, this support staff has not been overtaxed and has sufficient time to assist in the drafting of letters and documents when their assistance is requested. Nearly all of the attorneys did complain, however, about file clerks on the fifth floor who maintain all case folders. They are responsible for processing and developing case files when they first come in as well as terminating the file when the case has been concluded. These clerks were characterized as painfully slow, disorganized, and occasionally uncooperative. A major problem was the delay in receiving a new file. It was not unusual for the assigned defender to not have the case file until a month after the client had been arrested. For defendants unable to obtain pretrial release, this delay meant they would be unable to see their lawyer for four to five weeks, waiting anxiously in the crowded and dangerous county jail. This unfortunate situation did not help the already strained defender-client relationship once the defender finally appeared.

Investigators

Another advantage held by most prosecutors but not found in Essex County is the number and quality of investigators available to their attorneys. Although the Essex County prosecutor's office did have a few more investigators, the public defenders agreed that they were convinced that their twenty investigators were superior to their adversaries' investigators.

The primary job of an investigator is to assist the attorney in preparing a case. Their work usually includes visiting the crime scene for evidence, interviewing witnesses, and any other tasks requested by the attorney. The investigators are also frequently involved in obtaining important information from the police and prosecutors required by the New Jersey discovery requirements. This task is one of the most demanding because of the dilatory tactics commonly enjoyed by the prosecutor, unwilling to share evidence that might prove exculpatory. Their job can also prove dangerous because of the unsafe, high-crime neighborhoods they are required to visit.

Each public defender decides how to use his or her investigator. A small minority of the defenders preferred to do most of the preparation by themselves without the assistance of an investigator. These attorneys explained that this was due to a combination of not having much confidence in the investigators as well as their belief that the attorney was the only one who could be relied upon to do a competent job. The large majority of lawyers, however, had a positive impression of the quality of investigative work and utilized investigators on a regular basis. The defenders were cognizant of variations in the abilities of the investigators, but their overall level of performance was consistently better than their prosecutorial counterparts. The attorneys found them especially helpful in cases involving Spanish-speaking clients and witnesses. Seven of the twenty investigators are Hispanic and more than half are bilingual.

The Essex regional office investigators are organized similarly to the legal staff. They are both under the state Civil Service Commission, with regional offices in each county. The director of state investigative services is headquartered in Trenton and is aided by two assistant directors, one each for the northern and southern regions of the state. The Essex regional office is directed by a chief investigator with twenty years of experience. The investigators are divided into three teams, each led by a senior investigator. The office is divided between thirteen men and seven women and is balanced ethnically between eight blacks, seven Hispanic, and five white investigators.

Following state civil service requirements, job openings in the regional offices are posted on a state Web page. All applicants must take an exam with a special test for candidates wishing to demonstrate fluency in Spanish. Following an interview with the local office, the state will contact the person, conduct a background investigation, and finalize all of the necessary paperwork. Occasionally when there is a job freeze, the regional office is given permission to hire someone temporarily on a per diem basis without benefits.

One of the most frustrating aspects of an investigator's job is having to deal with the police and prosecutors. Public defenders often need the arresting officer's initial report as well as any additional information turned over to the prosecutor such as the names and addresses of witnesses. Most of this information will eventually be available to the defense through discovery, but this might not occur for several months. The defenders use investigators to try and pry loose this information earlier in the process. It is a challenging task. The investigators frequently must resort to finesse and deception in their attempt to obtain the important information from the prosecution. Their efforts can backfire, causing a protracted, embittered confrontation between the two offices, often forcing the public defenders to go into court seeking a subpoena.

Once the chief investigator receives a request for one of her staff from a public defender, she randomly assigns it to one of her team leaders who then chooses a specific individual. Homicide cases are the sole exception. The chief will personally select a qualified investigator for these serious cases. Even though the investigators must go into some of Newark's roughest neighborhoods, they are not allowed to be armed. They are encouraged to visit these dangerous areas early in the day, always traveling in pairs. As an investigator gains experience, he or she recognizes a threatening situation, sensing when to be aggressive and when to back off. During the chief's long tenure with the office, they have been fortunate not to have anyone seriously injured.

The relationship between the investigator and public defender can easily become strained when the investigator believe that his or her efforts are not appreciated. This can occur when an investigator has worked diligently, spending many hours on a case, and the lawyer does not even take the time to inform him or her of the outcome. A simple "thank you" would go a long way toward improving the situation, but some attorneys are insensitive. Several defenders are also accused of being thoughtless, making last-minute demands on an investigator who is working on several cases at the same time. From the defender's perspective, the investigators are merely a resource, a support staff gathering reliable, useful data. There is no need to thank them for doing their job. During a recent staff meeting, the regional director communicated a series of complaints from the chief investigator to his staff attorneys, cataloguing a number of recent incidents where attorneys made unreasonable demands and were insensitive to the heavy workloads of her staff. Several of the defenders quickly responded that some of the investigators were slow and unresponsive to their demands. Because Deputy Director Marucci appears sympathetic to the investigators' plight, the chief investigator remained cautiously optimistic that the tensions could be reduced as communications improved. The defenders recognize the inevitable variation in ability and effort between the investigators, but when an attorney is stuck in a difficult case, he or she may take frustrations out on the support staff. As the chief investigator noted, "The main thing one needs to survive in this job is a good sense of humor and a strong measure of perspective." A number of defenders did admit that the investigators are a fearless group who are willing to go into places where they themselves would be afraid to go. In closing, the overall consensus was that investigators have a challenging yet thankless job where ultimately their personal satisfaction comes from doing a good job.

CHAPTER FOUR

The Staff Attorneys: Background and Career Patterns

In the spring of 2001 the Essex County regional public defender office employed forty-seven attorneys. Their primary responsibility was to defend all adult indigent defendants charged with indictable offenses (felonies) by the county prosecutor. Because of the extreme poverty found in Newark and several adjoining towns (e.g., Hillside, Irvington, and East Orange), the Essex public defenders represented over 90% of all defendants in the county's superior criminal courts. What type of lawyer chooses to work for the local defender agency? The position ranks near the bottom of the legal profession in terms of status and monetary rewards. The general public and even their clients hold them in low regard. This chapter offers a detailed group portrait of the Essex regional defenders, describing their personal and professional backgrounds as well as tracing their varied paths to the office. Interviews with 95% of the staff attorneys (forty-four out of forty-seven) uncovered not only the different reasons that lawyers joined the office but also the equally interesting question of why they stayed, and, in a few instances, why they are planning to leave.

Demographic Background

The general perception of a public defender is that of a young attorney recently graduated from a second-rate law school. It is thought that the inexperienced attorney will only work as a public defender for a few years in order to gain the litigation experience that will make him or her more attractive to a law firm that will offer a lucrative salary in contrast to the amount earned as a public servant. It is also common to think that the young lawyer was forced to begin his or her legal career as a public defender because it was the only job available. These negative assumptions will be challenged throughout this chapter, especially in the review of the demographic and educational backgrounds of the public defenders.[1]

In sharp contrast to the public's belief that public defenders are usually under thirty years of age, over half of the Essex regional office's attorneys were between forty and fifty. Only three of the lawyers (6%) were under thirty and a small number were under the age of thirty-five. Although there has been a tightening of the state budget in recent years, a more reasonable explanation is that there are few vacancies for new attorneys because so few of the staff are departing. As noted in Chapter Three, the size of the staff is legislatively regulated by the number of superior court judges in the county, and this figure has barely changed during the past decade.

Logically, having an older, experienced group of defenders is viewed as a positive. Clients should have better representation with an attorney who is familiar with the local court system, including the idiosyncrasies of particular judges and prosecutors. Unfortunately, there may be a point of diminishing returns when a defender office lacks new blood and is dominated by an older staff that has lost their combative edge. This does not appear to be the case in Essex County, although there are a handful of older attorneys who do fit into this troubling pattern. The state and regional leadership are aware of the potential problems raised by an aging, tired staff. These older attorneys, especially those with health concerns, were placed in less stressful, pre-indictment courts where they would not face the debilitating pressure of litigation. The large majority of senior attorneys over fifty, however, remained energetic and committed to providing quality representation for their clients. They also served as knowledgeable mentors for the younger attorneys in search of professional guidance. To define the demographic portrait further, it is necessary to examine the number of years an attorney has served as a public defender. These figures include not only the years with the Essex office but the total number of years spent working within the statewide system, including serving in other regional offices. Only ten of the forty-four attorneys (23%) interviewed have been with the office less than ten years while nineteen (44%) have served for more than fifteen years. Examining the extremes, only five lawyers (14%) have worked for less than five years while ten have been public defenders for more than twenty years. These figures take on added significance when compared to other defender programs across the country. In Cook County (Chicago), Illinois, for example, Lisa McIntyre found that over two-thirds of the public defenders had been with the office less than four years—a figure six times as great as the Essex office! At the opposite end of the tenure spectrum, Essex had five times as many experienced attorneys with over fifteen years of service than the Cook County office.[2] National trends closely approximate the Cook County figures.

It is reasonable to conclude that after ten years of experience, a public defender has comprehended the local legal culture as well as fundamentals of criminal law. The Essex County office is therefore fortunate to have 78% of its attorneys who have accumulated this level of experience.

In viewing the age and tenure of the Essex regional public defenders, a generational divide exists between a small group of attorneys who have been with the office less than four years and the majority of the attorneys who have served more than fifteen years. After many months of observing the Essex office, the more senior attorneys cluster into three categories. The first group is the "Bridge Group" that has been with the office for between five and ten years. These five lawyers serve as mentors for the youngest attorneys who are most uncertain about whether they will become career public defenders. Several are already considering leaving if a good job opportunity comes along in the private sector. They are unsure of their lawyering skills and wish to have the chance to try a few serious cases before beginning their careers in earnest. Three of the five enjoy their defense work a great deal but question whether they can afford to stay another year or two. The remaining two have simply been with the office for too short a period of time to make any conclusive judgments about their future. The Bridge Group is amenable to teaching the young lawyers the basics of survival in the Essex County courthouse, as well as useful legal strategies for a criminal defense attorney. The Bridge Group recognized, however, that several of the younger lawyers lacked the strong commitment so prevalent among the senior staff. One Bridge lawyer clarified this sentiment by commenting that the newer attorneys "are too self-contained. They don't ask for help like we did. Maybe they are afraid to look incompetent. They must remember this isn't just a job!"

A second group of experienced defenders has served between ten and twenty years. These twenty-three attorneys comprise the heart and soul of the office—most of the top lawyers in the Essex office come from this age group. A large percentage have decided to make the defense of indigent clients their life's work and will likely remain with the Essex regional office until their retirement. Most have been able to maintain their passion for indigent defense while improving the quality of their lawyering skills. They frequently are given the most difficult cases. The first assistants with supervisory responsibilities are all chosen from this age group.

The third and final group is made up of the most experienced lawyers who have been with the office more than twenty years. Several have begun to lose a little of their earlier compassion and competitive edge as they anxiously await retirement, which will be within the next five years. Summarizing the feelings of the whole group, one lawyer stated, "We're ready. We have paid our dues." Several members of this group have developed serious medical problems, which has necessitated their being placed in special pre-indictment courtrooms. Although they are spared the rigors of intense litigation, their administrative responsibilities are nevertheless rather taxing as they churn through each day's busy docket of thirty to forty cases.

Gender and racial statistics are more consistent with national defender trends, which show a much larger proportion of black and female attorneys than is found among the private bar.[3] White males have traditionally dominated the practice of law in the United States. It has only been since the feminist movement of the 1960s and 1970s that women have begun to make noticeable strides in the legal profession. Consistent with national trends, women and racial minorities have disproportionately preferred employment as lawyers within the public sector rather than with law firms in private practice or as legal counsel with corporations. More than a third of the Essex County defenders are women. A nearly equal percentage (35%) is African-American. There is only a single Hispanic attorney, which is surprising given Newark's fairly sizeable Latino population (36%). The investigative staff closely reflects Newark's racial and ethnic profile, with two-thirds made up of Hispanic and black employees.

With an overwhelmingly black clientele, the high percentage of black public defenders can be a positive force in developing improved lawyer-client relations. Although nationally blacks make up only 5% of the legal profession, they account for 30% of the Essex regional defenders. It is also noteworthy that two-thirds of the office's black attorneys are women, an even greater disproportion relative to national statistics.

Why are black and female lawyers more attracted to public service in agencies like a public defender office? The lawyers interviewed in the Essex regional office thought these two groups would be less likely to experience discrimination in a public agency. A few of the attorneys who had worked briefly in the private sector preferred the relaxed atmosphere and reduced pressure of the public defender office. A second theory offered was that black and female attorneys were attracted philosophically to public service, finding the defense of the underdog to be especially appealing. Several viewed their job as aiding the client beyond the courtroom, trying to assist these beleaguered individuals in putting their lives in order. This quasi-social worker mentality was most common among female attorneys, both black and white.

Consistent with studies of solo practitioners by Carlin, Wice, and others, the Essex County public defenders come mainly from working- and middle-class families.[4] Only 28% of the Essex attorneys were from professional backgrounds while more than a third had working-class parents and 40% had middle-class roots. Only three of the forty-four Essex attorneys interviewed had a parent who was an attorney. Nearly three-fourths of the public defenders came from New Jersey with one-third of them raised in Essex County. Another 20% grew up in a neighboring Middle Atlantic state, leaving two attorneys who were from California and another who was from Georgia. This high degree of localism is also consistent with Carlin's findings. Another explanation, however, might cynically note the negative stereotype of New Jersey. Thus, one would not expect many people to flock to the Garden State to seek employment, especially trained professionals such as attorneys. It was interesting to discover that one young attorney who had recently joined the office had come from California to New Jersey specifically because of his desire to work in the state's public defender system, which he thought was one of the nation's finest.

Table 4.1 summarizes the demographic background of the Essex public defenders. Overall, they are middle-aged lawyers who have worked in the office for approximately ten years. They come from middle-class families, raised either in New Jersey or a nearby Middle Atlantic state. There is an unusually large percentage of women and blacks in comparison to national percentages for the legal profession. Their age and experience are most noteworthy when compared to public defenders across the country.

Educational Background

The Essex regional public defenders received their undergraduate and legal education from a wide range of academic institutions ranging from prestigious Ivy League schools to lower-status local public and private institutions. In contrast to the educational background of lawyers working in large corporate law firms, most of the public defenders attended institutions of regional notoriety. For example, twenty-three, or slightly half (53.5%), went to either Rutgers or Seton Hall law schools, both located in Newark a few blocks from the public defender office as well as the criminal courthouse. Only four graduated from prestigious law schools—Georgetown, Cornell, and Duke. At the other end of the spectrum, nearly 30% went to lower-quality law schools outside of New Jersey. Table 4.2 indicates that nearly 20% attended high-quality private undergraduate institutions while an additional 42% graduated from highly regarded regional universities such as Rutgers and New York University. The prestigious undergraduate schools included Princeton, Brown, Williams, Cornell, Colgate, Colby, and Lafayette. Many of the public defenders who attended high-quality private colleges returned to New Jersey (their home state in most cases) where they either went directly to law school or took a few years off before entering Rutgers or Seton Hall.

Aiding in the recruitment of high-quality law school graduates to the New Jersey public defender system is the respectable annual salary and attractive benefits package, including a medical plan and pension equal to many private law firms. The recent unionization of the staff attorneys is credited with sustaining the decent salary and benefits in recent years. Compared to the Essex prosecutors, who are dependent on county funds, the public defenders receive their wages from the much more solvent state treasury. Essex County, especially in recent years, has had serious revenue problems and the salaries of their employees have suffered accordingly. Thus, the Essex regional office is in the unusual position vis-à-vis most public defender programs of being able to offer attorneys a more lucrative initial salary than their adversaries in the prosecutor's office. Nationally, prosecutors are paid appreciably more than their counterparts in the public defender office.[5]

Table 4.1 Demographic Background of Essex County Public Defenders

Demographic	Percentage in Office	Number in Office
Age		
Under 30	7%	3
31–40	23.5%	10
41–50	48%	21
Over 50	21.5%	9
Tenure		
Less than 3 years	11.6%	5
4–10 years	11.6%	5
11–15 years	32.5%	14
16–20 years	21.5%	9
Over 20 years	23.5%	10
Race and Gender		
White	71%	32
Male	53.8%	24
Female	17.8%	8
Black	29%	14
Male	9.9%	5
Female	19.1%	9
Parents' socioeconomic status		
Working class/blue collar	30%	13
Middle class	41.8%	18
Professional (upper middle class)	28.2%	12
Hometown (where raised)		
Newark (NJ)	9.3%	4
Essex County *	32.5%	14
North Jersey**	51%	22
Central and South Jersey	21.5%	9
Middle Atlantic state	18.6%	8
Other U.S.	7%	3

*Includes Newark
**Includes Essex

Table 4.2 Educational Background of Essex County Public Defenders*

Undergraduate	Percentage	Number	Law School	Percentage	Number
Prestigious	18.6%	8	Prestigious**	9.3%	4
Quality regional	42%	18	Quality (non–New Jersey)	9.3%	4
Public university (modest ranking)	7%	3	Rutgers	28%	12
			Seton Hall	25.4%	11
Lower prestige	32.5%	14	Lower prestige (non–New Jersey)	28%	12
public	16.2%	7			
private	16.2%	7			

*Rankings are based on the author's 30 years of experience as a pre-law advisor as well as consulting *U.S. News and World Report, Coleman Report,* and *Princeton Review* annual assessments of undergraduate and law school programs.
**Georgetown, Cornell, and Duke

The large number of Essex public defenders receiving a legal education at local institutions–Rutgers and Seton Hall–is the product of several factors. First, there are only three law schools in the entire state (the third being Rutgers-Camden) so there are simply few choices if one is contemplating studying law in the Garden State (obviously, one's choices expand greatly if one is willing to consider studying in New York City, which has nine law schools). Second, because nearly all of the public defenders come from middle- or working-class families, monetary considerations likely played a part in their decision. Rutgers offers a reasonable tuition as a state institution, and both law schools permit students to live at home thereby offering even greater savings. Third, Seton Hall and Rutgers law schools emphasize public service. They both have established poverty law clinics as well as internship programs with several public agencies, including the public defender and county prosecutor offices.

A large number of the public defenders interviewed, most of whom have been with the office more than ten years, described their law school experiences in realistic terms. It was an obligatory professional hurdle to their ultimate objective, which was to litigate or engage in public service work. Law school was rarely discussed in terms of the intellectual challenge or as a stepping-stone to financial security, more common goals among the larger lawyer population.

Career Patterns Prior to Joining the Office

It was surprising to learn that so many of the Essex public defenders did not target their professional goals after law school. A large number did indicate an early and persistent interest in litigation. Many in fact began their professional careers as prosecutors, their interest in litigation outweighing any ideological commitment to the defense side of the adversarial struggle. The overwhelming majority of public defenders were motivated by pragmatic considerations rather than a compelling philosophical position. Nevertheless, many of the public defenders who began professional life as prosecutors discovered that within a year or two they preferred the defense position and switched sides.

Only a handful of attorneys came directly to the public defender office following law school graduation. Most of these were recent hires who were forced to work as "contract lawyers" for several months before becoming official, full-time employees. Public defender offices are permitted to select qualified lawyers on a regular basis for defendants who would normally be assigned an attorney from the "pool list"—a group of experienced defense attorneys who volunteer to serve as counsel in multiple-defendant cases where the public defender is restricted to a single defendant because of conflict-of-interest consideration. Lawyers working on contract will be paid on a per diem basis but do not receive any medical benefits. This procedure is used to assist young attorneys who have been selected to join the office but who are awaiting a vacancy or official approval from Trenton. Rather than losing a desirable candidate to another office, they award a temporary contract that will soon lead to another position. Three of the last four attorneys hired in the Essex County office were initially granted a temporary contract. Even these recent hires did not indicate any long-standing desire to become public defenders. They did generally possess a strong desire to litigate but were not interested in joining a large firm or achieving financial security through a commercial practice.

One-fourth of the public defenders joined the office after serving as law clerks to a judge for the required year. Although a few clerked at the federal level, most worked for superior court judges in Essex and surrounding counties. Nearly all worked for judges in the criminal trial division. These clerkships were a traditional path to either the county prosecutor office or public defender office. Obviously, a recommendation from a superior court (county) judge would have great influence with both the state and regional defender offices. Not only would the judge be able to offer a knowledgeable evaluation of the clerk's intellect and diligence but would also be appreciative if his or her recommendation was followed. It therefore provides the public defender agency a rare opportunity to get on the good side of a judge. Finally, in practical terms, after working for a year behind the scenes of a criminal courtroom, the young lawyer leaves the clerkship with an invaluable introduction to the real work of the criminal courthouse and its local legal culture.

The prosecutor's office served as an apprenticeship for one-fourth of the public defenders. The county prosecutor provides the invaluable opportunity to try cases. Because of its highly politicized nature as well as low salaries, the Essex prosecutor's office is plagued by a high turnover in personnel, creating continuous vacancies for entry-level staff attorneys. Several public defenders who had begun their careers as prosecutors were turned off by the overzealous pursuit of convictions as well as the haunting specter of political machinations at the supervisory level of office administration. Everyone had to be aware of the political and legal implications of every decision. They felt as if they were on a short leash, with almost no independence or creativity in their professional life. In contrast, these former prosecutors enjoy the greater discretion granted to public defenders by their supervisors. They also noted that the defense position was more intellectually challenging. The prosecutor is required to defend police actions as well as parrot arrest reports and crime scene observations. Public defenders, they argued, had greater freedom to creatively devise strategies designed to undermine the state's case, discrediting their key witnesses.

It was surprising not to hear any of the public defenders commenting on the professional and personal implications of winning nearly all their cases as a prosecutor—an overwhelming percentage of guilty pleas and a sprinkling of convictions, with few dismissals and an even smaller number of acquittals—compared with the frustrating losing record of public defenders who rarely are able to gain acquittals or dismissals for their indigent clients. It appears that one's self-image as a successful defense lawyer is not based merely on winning percentages but on the more nebulous concept of performing competently. The ability of public defenders to redefine their meaning of courtroom success given the inherent difficulties of having to defend so many clients with little chance of victory will be discussed more fully in Chapter Seven.

In addition to clerking positions and the county prosecutor office, law firms of varying size also provide about one-fourth of the public defenders with their initial professional experience. The law firms range from the large corporate firms employing more than fifty attorneys to mid-size and smaller firms employing five to twenty attorneys. The larger firms, often located in metropolitan areas, have corporate clients with complex financial problems while the smaller firms handle smaller businesses as well as individual clients. The latter group often specializes in a particular area of the law such as tax, commercial transactions, negligence, or matrimonial.

The larger firms offer lucrative salaries, glamorous working conditions, and prestigious clients. In exchange for the extravagant salaries, these firms demand long hours in a high-pressure environment. In the highly competitive struggle to make partner, young lawyers often become disillusioned, even burned out, and seek employment in a less intense setting. Public defenders who began their legal careers working in private law firms describe their early professional experience in similar terms. They complained of being trapped in law libraries, doing "grunt work," writing memos, and doing research for senior partners. They found their corporate clients involved in boring, even trivial, cases. Most frustrating was their inability to litigate. For those defenders who began work in smaller civil practice firms, they quickly became disinterested in commercial issues. They especially disliked the humbling tasks of hustling for clients and collecting fees.

Four of the Essex public defenders became solo practitioners immediately after graduating from law school. Inexperienced and unknown, these young lawyers scrounged up cases wherever possible. They were often dependent on referrals from more established attorneys, being given the cases no one else wanted. After a year or two the idealized life of the solo practitioner vanished into the reality of long, lonely hours waiting for a client to appear, as well as the steadily rising pile of unpaid bills.

Approximately 20% of the defenders followed a rather erratic and tortuous path before joining the Essex regional office. This group of young attorneys jumped from a series of temporary positions, many having only a marginal relationship to the law. It was not uncommon with this unlucky group that on occasion economic necessity drove them to jobs completely unrelated to the law. Several worked as bartenders, schoolteachers, and accountants while waiting for bar exam results or riding out a hiring freeze at local law firms or public agencies. In a few instances these initial jobs were inspired by the draft laws and the looming Vietnam War. Several young attorneys opted to continue the political and social activism that had inspired them during law school. These jobs included working for a civil rights organization, providing legal advice for the homeless, becoming a community organizer, raising funds for a world hunger group, and working for the New Jersey Casino Control Commission.

It is somewhat surprising given the diverse career patterns experienced by the Essex defenders prior to joining the office that more than half remained with the office for more than a decade. Most from this group stated that they have chosen to remain public defenders for the rest of their professional lives, barring some unforeseen health or economic emergency.

Reasons for Becoming a Public Defender

Most individuals are drawn to the legal profession for its lucrative salaries, its glamorous lifestyle, its interesting clients, and the opportunity to become a major player in the worlds of politics and business. It is therefore somewhat puzzling why a law school graduate would choose to become a public defender, with its modest wages, grimy work environment, ungrateful clients, and generally low status. The answers to this question given by the forty-four Essex public defenders interviewed for this book are both reasonable and rational, yet in many instances quite surprising.

The primary motivation for a young lawyer to become a public defender is the love of litigation. Well over half of the defenders interviewed stated that the great joy derived from trying cases was not only what motivated them to become public defenders, but what has remained the basic reason for staying with the office. By having the opportunity to continually try cases, these attorneys realize they are doing something they truly love but in all likelihood would not have the chance to do in private practice, particularly in a large corporate firm. The defenders are able to sharpen their litigation skills because of their recurring trial opportunities. Additionally, the regional office, with assistance from state headquarters in Trenton, encourages the development of trial techniques and strategies by sending staff attorneys to professional conferences and teaching seminars around the country.

Although litigation is a specialty occupying only a small percentage of the legal profession–most attorneys spend the majority of their time advising clients, drafting documents, and negotiating settlements–it is nonetheless the layman's persistent idea of a lawyer at work. Working within the adversarial system of justice, the trial attorney, presiding judge, jury, and packed courtroom embody the heroic quintessence of the profession. The Essex public defenders, similar to private criminal lawyers interviewed twenty years ago, spoke in excited tones of the adrenaline rush produced by a dramatic cross-examination or a closing argument. The combination of challenging intellectual issues, having to think quickly before a difficult judge, and performing before an intent, sometimes hostile audience continued to motivate all of the defenders regardless of the length of their tenure with the office.

The added enjoyment of having the state as one's adversary was another important reason given by many public defenders who enjoyed litigation. Casting themselves as underdogs in an imagined David vs. Goliath scenario, public defenders found honor and meaning in battling the powerful prosecutor's office. Many defenders stated that because of their race, gender, or religion, they could empathize with their clients' struggle against an imposing adversary.

It is somewhat paradoxical that the defenders emphasize their love of litigation as the primary reason for joining the office because in actuality they have very few trial opportunities, settling at least 90% of their cases through plea negotiations. The defenders estimated that they were usually involved in only ten to fifteen trials a year, although it appears that this is sufficient to satisfy the need for courtroom drama. Although trials may be separated by many weeks of paper shuffling and plea negotiations, the excitement of litigating a case easily surmounts the large amount of time spent on the more mundane aspects of their job. When one of the defenders is trying a case, many of their colleagues will often pop into the courtroom to see how the trial is proceeding and provide emotional support. Back at the regional office, usually at lunchtime when many attorneys gather in the law library, recent courtroom victories, successful trial techniques, and the relating of amusing anecdotes about recent courtroom miscues (both by defenders and prosecutors) are the constant topic of noontime discussions.

A second reason for becoming a public defender–given by a third of the lawyers–was disinterest in private practice, especially having to hustle for clients and grovel for fees. As defenders they received a guaranteed annual salary and an endless flow of clients. They could then concentrate on the intellectual challenges continually arising in the more difficult cases as well as awaiting the next opportunity for a trial. Most of the defenders soon became bored with the range of issues raised in civil cases–negligence, matrimonial, real estate, and contractual–particularly those involving financial institutions and businesses. Cases almost never went to trial; instead they were buried in paperwork and depositions. They rarely felt empathy or concern for their faceless clients. Several of the defenders who began their legal careers with civil law firms found themselves involved in situations raising troubling ethical issues and grew uncomfortable having to work in a gray area of morality. The advice from their more senior associates at the firm was not to worry about "crossing the line" because it was "only money at stake." As public defenders, however, they found that their ethical behavior had to be on a higher plane because their clients' personal freedom was on the line.

Approximately one-third of the public defenders (and more than three-fourths of the female attorneys) were pleased to discover that the job was strictly from nine to five. This granted the staff the flexibility and time to have a normal family life. In contrast to the extreme demands of the larger law firms who expected seventy- and eighty-hour workweeks, public defenders, several who were single parents, appreciated the normal hours and supportive attitude of the office. Even though they probably could double their annual salary at a law firm, most of the defenders characterized their wages as adequate, especially when one also considered the pension and benefits package. Recent unionization was viewed as a positive development for insuring that their wages would continue to rise in the future.

Select members of the office gave an interesting array of additional reasons for becoming public defenders. A few enjoyed the opportunity to take on the powerful legal establishment of the State as represented by the prosecutor's office. This group was also motivated by the intellectual challenges raised in difficult cases when the prosecutor appeared to be "holding all the cards." One cynical public defender commented (somewhat sarcastically) that on occasion his office offered professional shelter for attorneys who were unemployable elsewhere. He made specific reference to a period fifteen years earlier when the state headquarters in Trenton had the chance to expand rapidly, creating numerous staff positions within a short timeframe before the budgetary year expired. It was apparent that the Essex office did have a handful of lawyers whose personalities and abilities would seriously limit job opportunities in the private sector. A few attorneys were retained despite medical problems that limited their effectiveness, but it was also clear that the office would not tolerate incompetence that would compromise a defendant's freedom.

At least ten of the lawyers had no specific reason or strong motivation for joining the Essex public defender office other than it appeared to be a decent job with an acceptable salary; most importantly, it was available. Once hired, the office frequently appeared to grow on people. The longer an attorney was with the agency, the more satisfied he or she was with the decision to become a public defender. This might be explained as the attorneys simply rationalizing earlier decisions, but there was a palpable sense of camaraderie and pride among the more senior attorneys.

It is important to note that many of the attorneys were specifically attracted to the Essex office and their positive feelings about remaining public defenders are related to that particular office. It has long had a reputation as the office that handles the most difficult cases and maintains the highest caseloads in the state. It is in the major leagues of criminal defense, handling the same type of serious cases found in New York, Chicago, or Washington, D.C. Several of the defenders fled more suburban regional offices handling less violent crimes for the opportunity to be "where the action is" in terms of heinous criminal activity. Even though Newark and its environs are rarely considered desirable locales, nevertheless a half dozen of the attorneys were born and raised in the area. They maintained a strong commitment to serve their much-maligned hometown. This group watched the city burn in 1967 and observed its continued downward spiral since the riots. Their hope is to be part of a possible rebirth, or stated more realistically, to help the city get off its knees, using their legal skills to assist their clients in becoming more productive members of the local community.

Career Patterns within the Office: A Brief Overview and Discussion

Once the Essex regional office has decided to hire an attorney and has received the approval of Trenton, the individual is quickly assigned to a specific judge and courtroom where he or she will work in tandem with a more experienced second attorney who can serve as a mentor. The pair will remain with the judge for twelve to fifteen months; at the end of this time period they will be reassigned to another judge. With the exception of the eight public defenders assigned to specialized pre-indictment courts and the four senior attorneys serving supervisory functions, all of the remaining attorneys are relegated in tandem to a specific criminal court judge. The majority of attorneys will spend their entire career as a public defender working in one of the assigned courtrooms. The only apparent manifestation of seniority or status is the size of one's office.

Nearly all public defenders who become dissatisfied with the job leave the office within two years, usually of their own volition. Of the four most recent departures all but one left for financial reasons, moving on to a mid-sized law firm. Rising fiscal pressure caused by growing families was a factor in two cases. The sole attorney who left for non-monetary reasons was described as a bad fit for the office and the practice of criminal law. Both she and the office realized a mistake had been made shortly after she tried her first case.

Two public defenders had the unusual, yet telling, experience of leaving the office for a better paying job, but they soon returned. The first attorney left for a more lucrative position but returned sheepishly one day later realizing she had made a mistake. She was welcomed back by the regional director who had warned her about private practice but failed to utter a single "I told you so." The second attorney's departure lasted longer, but he also returned to the good graces of the office. After graduating from a prestigious Ivy League law school, he initially worked in a large firm specializing in civil litigation. After three years he decided he wanted to try criminal cases and joined the public defender office. He worked his way up to first assistant during his twelve-year tenure but his growing family necessitated his return to his old firm, which offered a significant increase in salary. He lasted only three years back in civil practice before being drawn back to the defender office, this time hired as a special first assistant specializing in death penalty cases.

The career path for most public defenders is a slow, smooth one with few twists or turns. The only major adjustment in a public defender's career is most likely to be transferring offices. A third of the Essex defenders transferred in from another county office elsewhere in the state. As previously noted, the Essex region has been traditionally viewed as the busiest and most challenging area for public defenders. Public defenders wishing to escape the boredom of a slower criminal docket in a suburban or semi-rural region of the state eagerly seek the opportunity to come to Essex where the action never stops. Nearly all the attorneys, particularly those with children, live far outside the Newark city limits, yet they are willing to endure a brutal commute rather than settle for the less challenging criminal caseloads of a suburban regional office.

Future Plans: Staying or Leaving

It is commonly assumed that young lawyers become public defenders in order to obtain sufficient trial experience, enabling them to join the litigation section of a law firm with a sizeable increase in pay. The Essex public defenders do not, for the most part, conform to this pattern. As indicated earlier in this chapter, the overwhelming majority of Essex defenders have been with the regional office for more than ten years. What does this group think about their professional futures? Why have most opted to stay with the office? Why has a sizeable minority been considering leaving the comfortable confines of Essex for a more lucrative or challenging position in the private sector?

Most of the defenders are satisfied with their annual salaries and benefits. Backed by an effective union, their financial packages have continued to improve. A number of attorneys commented that after ten or more years they could not afford to leave the office. Many law firms prefer to hire less experienced recent law school graduates and would have a difficult time matching these more experienced attorneys' salaries. Given the weak job market for lawyers in the Northeast, these experienced defenders thought it too risky to leave the office. Additionally, a number of attorneys had spouses who were also professionals earning salaries. With combined earnings, they had established a comfortable lifestyle. For the more senior lawyers who had been in the office for more than fifteen years, several stated it would be foolish for them to leave when they had so much already vested in their pensions. Underlying these sentiments, it should be remembered that many of these lawyers joined the office initially out of an interest in litigation or criminal law rather than any overriding concern for financial gain.

A second reason for remaining with the public defender office that was mentioned by nearly every attorney was the love of litigation. The enjoyment derived from performing in the courtroom and defending a client against the prosecution provided sufficient reason to remain a public defender despite the many frustrations inherent in the job. Even though they would try only a handful of cases each year, plea bargaining over 90% of the immense caseloads, these few courtroom experiences would satisfy their professional appetites.

Another important reason for remaining with the office, particularly among the more senior attorneys, was the strong sense of collegiality that permeated the office. The camaraderie created a hospitable ambiance that was difficult to abandon. The emotional support, professional assistance, and genuine affection were acknowledged in almost every interview. The closeness of the staff was most apparent at the aforementioned lunchtime discussions. Later in the afternoon, the conversations would resurface as attorneys would return from the courthouse and drift into their colleagues' offices. Once the attorneys left the courthouse and settled back into the friendly confines of their offices, they began immediately to relax, the tension visibly draining from their bodies.

A fourth reason given by many of the female defenders was the flexibility and time to care for their families their position granted them, in contrast to the almost unlimited time demands of larger law firms, especially during the early years as an associate trying for partnership. The public defender office operated from nine to five, similar to any governmental agency. As a public institution, the defenders were not beholden to a bottom-line mentality where one's professional status was measured almost entirely in number of hours billed. In the manic competition among associates and junior partners, eighty-hour, six-day workweeks were not uncommon. Family life was sacrificed for six-figure salaries and the possible security and prestige of senior partnership. Single mothers, committed fathers, and most of the married staff were appreciative of the reasonable approach taken by the Essex regional deputy director Mike Marucci. He was perceived as willing to accommodate the needs of his harried staff as they tried to balance professional and personal obligations. The staff showed their appreciation for this humane leadership style by performing diligently and without complaint throughout the workday—it is also reflected in the lengthy tenure of so many Essex defenders, influencing their reluctance to leave. Despite the positive sentiments expressed by most of the attorneys in explaining why they chose to stay with the office, there was also a significant minority who were unhappy or frustrated and were planning to leave. Many members of this dissatisfied group had been with the office between two and six years. They thought that with a private law firm they could easily double their salaries. All cited the experience of peers who had recently left the office and were now earning comfortable salaries. Given the cost of living in the New York metropolitan area as well as the encumbrances of unpaid law school loans, young defenders felt they could not afford to stay. A number commented that if they dragged their heels much longer, becoming too entrenched and complacent as an Essex defender, opportunities would pass them by, unlikely to reappear. They sensed a brief window of opportunity during the first two to four years as a defender. After the fifth year the opportunities would begin to substantially fall off.

A few of the younger lawyers were troubled by the repetitive nature of many of the cases, believing they could not sustain the commitment to high-quality defense. This attitude was exacerbated by the belief that most of their clients were both ungrateful and guilty. For these attorneys who were highly competitive, it was especially frustrating to lose so many cases. This combination of factors depressed several lawyers who said that it was only a matter of time before they burned out. They wanted to leave before that occurred. Short of a burnout, several of the younger attorneys sensed they were becoming stale, their commitment to their clients on the decline. Most of this group had been with the office less than five years. They were already mentally preparing for their move, and a few had begun making inquiries in the private sector.

Since over three-fourths of the attorneys had been with the office for more than ten years, their future plans contrasted sharply with those of the younger attorneys with less than five years of service. Citing the attractive pension plan that would be available in twenty-five years, several attorneys looked forward to retirement at an early age with a chance to still practice privately. One attorney candidly admitted that he would work five more years until he would be eligible for retirement, but he was running out of energy. He stated that defending indigent defendants is "a demanding job, a young person's business. The older you get the more you see. You become callous and cynical. The passion drains away." Nearly all of the lawyers with fifteen to twenty years of service stated that they would stay on until retirement. Most had a rough idea of what they would be doing once they had left the office. A handful wanted to open up their own storefront practices while several others thought they would like to teach. A small group were troubled by the prospect of having to plan for retirement. They were ready to retire but had little idea how they would spend their time.

Personality Patterns

It is a common belief that certain professions attract, demand, and even develop identifiable personality types. Lawyers, especially litigators, have been described as aggressive and competitive, driven by strong egos. These character traits are necessary for attorneys required to face unsympathetic and at times antagonistic judges, outwardly hostile prosecutors, and an audience of intent, often critical jurors carefully observing their every move. Additionally, criminal lawyers must be able to think quickly on their feet and develop empathetic relationships with their clients that will inspire trust and cooperation. What emerges is a complex individual who must be able to combine the seemingly contradictory traits of idealism and cynicism, as well as display bravado and intelligence.

The development of this modal personality type was based on a 1978 study I conducted while serving as a Scholar in Residence with the U.S. Justice Department. The purpose of my research was to describe the professional life of private criminal lawyers. I traveled to nine major cities, interviewing nearly two hundred lawyers. In many ways, this study of public defenders parallels the earlier research into the private defense bar, despite its more intensified local focus and reduced sample of attorneys. Both groups of criminal lawyers share many personality traits. They were drawn to the criminal field by a love of litigation, relishing the time spent in the courtroom before judge and jury, passionately arguing their case, trying to poke enough holes in the prosecutors' cases to create a credible, reasonable doubt. Moving beyond my previous work on private criminal lawyers, I have identified a group of character traits that combine to describe the professional personality of an Essex County public defender. Each trait should be understood conceptually as operating on a continuum, from high to low. The four traits to be discussed are compassion, intelligence, combativeness, and perspective.

Compassion is an important trait for an attorney who desires to build an effective working relationship with his or her client. Many public defenders found it difficult generating the necessary empathy and concern to win over their clients. This was especially true when the defendant was a recidivist such as the multitude of drug offenders that they must represent. Compounding the problem is the large number of clients who are brazenly disrespectful. An even greater number refuse to trust their public defender, lying to him or her with the same facility with which they try to deceive police and prosecutors. Fortunately for their clients, most public defenders appear unaffected by the attitude of these defendants. A few of the defenders were concerned with becoming emotionally involved in a case and made a conscious effort to distance themselves from their clients. The lawyers who were most compassionate viewed their clients as being trapped in a broader social context, refusing to focus only on the immediate offense with which they were charged. For these defenders, their clients were not inherently venal individuals, but unfortunate men and women who lived very different lives and sometimes committed stupid, immature acts. They were basically decent people but plagued by bad judgment and low intelligence. As a general theory, the public defender's compassion tended to wane the longer he or she was with the office, although there were several notable exceptions. The years of frustration and defeat had drained whatever benevolent feelings were present ten or twenty years prior. It simply became increasingly difficult to ignore the hostility, stubbornness, and mendacity of the clients.

Intelligence is a difficult trait to conceptualize and measure because it encompasses so many shades of meaning. This is clearly the case as it is applied to lawyers. A lawyer may be extremely cerebral in drafting motions or uncovering tax loopholes, while another attorney's intelligence may manifest itself in thinking quickly on his or her feet, exhibiting intuitive, creative flashes of brilliance before a jury. Most of the public defenders regarded as the most effective litigators in the Essex office were able to blend their native intelligence, or "raw brain power," with innate common sense, reinforced by street smarts. The Essex defenders exhibited a wide range of intelligence among the various meanings of the term. A small group of experienced defenders were regarded as the intellectual elite. In addition to their native intelligence, they had accumulated valuable lessons over the years in effective trial and plea bargaining techniques. Their colleagues frequently observed their courtroom performances and sought their advice during lunch or visited their offices in the late afternoon.

Without combativeness or the willingness to become an aggressive adversary for one's client, an attorney could not be an effective public defender. This personality trait was present in all defenders although to varying degrees. It also manifested itself in different forms. Some defenders quietly fumed while others were more vocal, sharing their emotions with everyone in the courtroom. The more experienced lawyers were able to control their aggressive behavior, bringing it to the surface only when necessary. It was not unusual, particularly during a trial, to observe a defender's anger and hostility toward a prosecutor, police officer, or even a judge rise to the surface, apparent to everyone in the courtroom. Defenders were most commonly angered when they believed the prosecution was not playing by the rules. Problems in obtaining important documents during discovery was the most common source of tension. Police and prosecution witnesses lying on the stand was another factor triggering a defender's combativeness. Several defenders in the Essex office maintained a persistent, simmering hostility toward the prosecution that was easily ignited, energizing their adversarial aggressiveness.

Maintaining one's perspective is the fourth and final character trait to be discussed. It is essential if a public defender plans to remain with the office for a long time without suffering from ulcers, hypertension, or some other debilitating condition. Most defenders stated that they made a conscious decision to try and leave their sometimes-chaotic professional life behind them once they left the office. They did not want to involve their families, especially their children, in the violent, frightening world of urban crime. The public defenders frequently used humor, albeit dark and perverse, to emotionally distance themselves from the human tragedies that enveloped them on a daily basis. Like the doctors in a military MASH unit who joke while performing life-and-death operations, humor is used to protect raw emotions and sensitivities. A number of public defenders used other psychological defense mechanisms, such as cynicism and self-deprecation, to protect their vulnerable psyches.

It is important to acknowledge that the Essex office, especially its leadership, was extremely tolerant of the staff's varied and occasionally idiosyncratic personalities. The overriding principle was that an attorney's lifestyle or mode of dress did not matter as long as he or she competently defended each client. The regional director's open-mindedness and tolerance exemplified this attitude. The staff appeared greatly appreciative of their personal freedom, a working environment rarely found within bureaucratic organizations and even more unusual in law firms that demand strict conformity to office rules (ranging from dress codes to permissible after hours pursuits). It is likely that the senior partners of large corporate law firms would look disapprovingly at what they would probably term the unprofessional behavior of public defenders. Yet I believe that without this grant of personal freedom and self-expression, the spirit, energy, and competence of the Essex public defenders would certainly diminish. This freedom creates a critical escape valve permitting the inevitable accumulation of pressure and tension during their intense workday to be siphoned off. Otherwise, wear and tear on the nervous systems can easily undermine performance as a defense attorney and appreciably shorten a career.

The Essex office not only tolerated diverse personality types but appeared to genuinely embrace the wide range of unique individuals. Observing the defenders outside the restrictive confines of the courthouse in the more relaxed atmosphere of their Clinton Street offices, their differences were even more obvious. Many dressed informally in jeans, without jackets or ties on days when they did not have to appear in court. The following were among the more unusual characters working in the Essex Regional office.

- An older attorney who grew up in a tough Newark neighborhood and never lost his inner city bravado and speech patterns. He described himself as a lifetime "rock and roller."
- A young black woman who was an ardent member of an evangelical Christian sect. She spent most of her free time in the office proselytizing

and trying to convert her co-workers or anyone else she came into contact with.

- A middle-aged attorney who was the phantom of the office. Suffering from a series of maladies, no one had seen him for several months.

Although the personality traits of the Essex public defenders were similar to those found in my study of private criminal lawyers in 1978, are they also found throughout the entire legal profession or even in other specialists such as tax or divorce attorneys? Unfortunately, no research has been done on this issue. Another related issue that has also failed to interest legal scholars or psychologists is whether the character traits identified with the practice of criminal law are developed once the individual begins to practice this legal specialty or caused by a self-selection process. The answer to this conundrum appears impossible to solve with any degree of certainty. It is plausible that there are elements of truth in either possibility. As I concluded in my book on private criminal lawyers "Lawyers with strong egos and competitive drives are naturally attracted to trial practice, of which criminal law is the most dramatic. Once in criminal law, however, one's ego and aggressiveness must be raised to a higher level . . . if courtroom success and professional recognition are to follow."[6]

CHAPTER FIVE

Procedural Issues: Processing and Litigating Cases

The Essex public defender office is responsible for representing all indigent adult defendants arrested and charged with an indictable offense. In New Jersey, there are two basic categories of crimes. The first is a disorderly persons offense that falls within the jurisdiction of the state's nearly 400 municipal courts. The maximum penalty for a disorderly offense is a year served in a county jail. The second category is an indictable offense, which is a more serious crime. These are handled by a county superior court. Defendants charged with an indictable offense face the possibility of serving a year or more in the state prison system. During the year 2000, ending on June 30, the Essex County superior court received 16,140 new cases while disposing of 15,235. According to these statistics gathered by the Administrative Office of the Courts, Essex County is the busiest jurisdiction in New Jersey, processing 5,000 more cases than any other county in the state. In addition to Newark's well-publicized crime problems (the city is referred to as the auto theft and carjacking capital of the country), the adjacent municipalities of Irvington, Hillside, and East Orange also suffer from high crime rates coupled with a high percentage of their populations living in poverty.

The state public defender office estimates that approximately 90% of the defendants charged with indictable offenses in Essex County are indigent and therefore require the services of the office.[1] This chapter will examine the various stages through which a criminal case proceeds in Essex County, with special attention paid to the responsibilities of the public defender. The entire process can be a lengthy, drawn-out one frequently lasting a year or longer. The serious backlog problems and heavy caseloads plague nearly all jurisdictions throughout the state but reach their apogee in Essex County. In the year 2000 the average time for a case from the defendant's arrest to final disposition was nearly eight months or 221 days.[2] Ten percent of the cases take over a year to be resolved.[3]

The simplest way to comprehend the New Jersey criminal court process is to envision it as a two-stage operation divided into pre- and post-indictment components. The pre-indictment stage begins with the defendant's arrest and concludes with the superior court deciding whether or not to indict. In Essex County the first and only court decision made during the pre-indictment period is made by the Central Judicial Processing Unit of the Newark Municipal Court, which is housed on the fifth floor of the county courthouse. This proceeding occurs soon after the defendant is arrested and transported to the county jail adjacent to the courthouse. Defendants arrested during the weekend may have a lengthier wait before appearing in court when it reconvenes Monday morning. The pre-indictment period is controlled by the county prosecutor's office, which can decide whether the case should be downgraded to a disorderly persons offense and remain within the jurisdiction of the municipal court or be bound over to the county superior court's grand jury for a possible indictment. During the 2000 calendar year, 51% of all defendants arrested in Essex County had their cases downgraded to a disorderly persons offense while another 9% were dismissed. As in most other New Jersey counties, Essex does not utilize a preliminary or probable cause hearing after the Central Judicial Processing Unit has conducted its initial arraignment. The next scheduled event for cases still designated indictable offenses occurs in three to four months when the grand jury decides whether or not to indict. As will be shown in the first section of this chapter, which reviews the pre-indictment period in greater detail, there is a group of important court proceedings such as the remand court, pre-indictment disposition court, and drug court, as well as important decisions concerning admission into one of the pretrial intervention programs. The outcome of these various decisions can be very significant for indigent defendants, particularly the large percentage who are unable to make bail and must spend their time in the county jail.

The Pre-indictment Period

Essex County defendants are brought before the Central Judicial Processing (CJP) Unit as soon as possible following their arrest. Defendants arrested in Newark are brought directly to the county jail for processing and can appear before a CJP judge the same day, or, more likely, the next day. Defendants arrested in other county municipalities beyond Newark are first taken to the local police station where they are temporarily detained before being transported to the county jail. Several municipal police departments prefer to interrogate defendants in the intimidating confines of their own lock-up or detention facilities. Once the defendants are taken to the county jail, the prosecutor takes over the case and controls the investigation. It is not unusual for defendants in East Orange or Hillside to be kept in the local lock-up for several days while the police complete their investigation. Defendants in these towns are often delayed a few days before their first court appearance and may not have the opportunity to meet with a representative from the county public defender's office. Without the intrusion of the public defenders at the local police stations, the police believe they can more easily obtain confessions from defendants.

Representatives of the criminal case manager's office interview all defendants just prior to their appearance in the CJP. They obtain background information that is useful in determining the defendant's pre-trial status and bail amount. They also have the defendant complete Form 5A, which indicates indigency and a desire to be represented by a public defender. Once the form is completed a copy is sent to the Essex defender office on Clinton Street where file clerks on the fifth floor begin to compile a folder that will be sent to the deputy director, who will have one of his first assistants randomly assign the case to one of his team members.

It does not appear that a viable effort is made to verify the defendant's proclaimed indigency status. When queried as to why no effort was made to verify the financial information, all of the officials agreed that if a defendant wanted a public defender instead of paying for a criminal lawyer, that was his or her choice. They reasoned that if one had the financial resources, it was highly unlikely that someone would try to deceive the state just to save a few dollars, risking one's long-term freedom. The crushing caseload sometimes united all members of the courtroom workgroup to work together to expedite their disposition. The judge and his clerks often became visibly annoyed when a private attorney would raise petty objections or posture in front of the court in order to impress his or her client.

Following their interview with the criminal case manager, the defendants are brought up to the CJP. The court is presided over by a Newark municipal court judge despite the unit's physical location inside the county courthouse. Two county prosecutors are paired with two Essex public defenders. The court, which convenes daily around 10:30 A.M., handles approximately forty cases a day. Most of the defendants are brought over from the county jail. Wearing their county-issued orange jump suits, the defendants appear before the judge handcuffed, in groups of three or four at a time.

The fast-paced proceeding moves along with prosecution and defense alternating cases. One reads the upcoming case folder as the other addresses the court in the immediate case. The average time for each case is between two and three minutes. Each defendant learns of the charges against him or her, has bail clarified, and states his or her need for a public defender. The prosecution is usually armed with a statement of the defendant's past criminal record as well as the police arrest report that will indicate the strength of the state's case. Several cases were observed where the public defender challenged the bail amount recommended by the prosecution, requesting either a reduction or a release on the defendant's own recognizance if he or she had strong ties to the community and the charges were not too serious.

Once the small group of defendants have completed their cursory appearance before the judge, they are shuttled out of the courtroom by the bailiffs who quickly replace them with another orange-clad quartet. A handful of defendants who have raised bail sit at one of the rows in the back of the courtroom waiting for their case to be called.

All members of the courtroom workgroup—judge, prosecutor, public defender, calendar clerks, and bailiffs—worked, in syncopation, toward the singular goal of getting through each day's onslaught of cases. The only hint of an adversarial proceeding occurred when the issue of bail and pretrial release was raised. The presiding judge with many years of municipal court experience was officious, moving quickly and confidently through the pile of cases. The two prosecutors, however, were quite young,—most likely recent law school graduates working their first courtroom assignment. The public defenders by contrast were middle-aged, both having more than twenty years of service. Given the tedious and somewhat unchallenging nature of CJP, it was puzzling to find two such experienced attorneys. It was subsequently learned that both of the lawyers were in this courtroom for a reason. One had not proven to be an effective litigator but had willingly joined CJP as a comfortable place to ride out his time until his retirement. Although he had been mired in this courtroom for a long time, he did not appear affected by the repetitive, mundane nature of the job as he methodically plodded through each case. The second attorney was also a victim of burnout but was not nearly as accepting of his boring assignment. He referred to the courtroom as a penal colony. He stated that he had been banished to this "legal gulag" by the regional director because he had no longer proven to be an effective advocate. He was clearly embittered by his assignment, trapped in a bureaucratic nightmare, impatiently waiting for retirement that "could not come soon enough!" Traditionally, the defender office had limited assignment to CJP to a six- to twelve-month period because of its mind-numbing, assembly-line nature, but the current pair, because of their unique situations, would be serving a much longer period of time.

Every defendant processed by the CJP Unit is provisionally eligible to receive the assistance of a public defender. Estimates by court officials as well as my own observations over a six-month period place the percentage of defendants receiving representation by the Essex regional public defender office at over 90%. The overwhelming number of defendants are black and Hispanic young males charged with drug-related offenses. With the completion of the initial court appearance before the CJP Unit, each defendant now has an attorney, his or her bail has been set, and the charges against him or her have been presented. A tentative date for the grand jury hearing in the superior court has been determined but that is several months off and subject to change. The defendant will meet with his or her assigned public defender in a few weeks.

At first glance, the pre-indictment period appears to be a rather moribund phase of the criminal court proceedings. Yet upon closer examination, there are many critical decisions that are made during this lengthy period that will affect many defendants. One positive option available to a select group of defendants is to be admitted into a diversion program. In Essex County the primary diversion program is pretrial intervention (PTI). It is restricted to defendants charged with less serious crimes, usually property offenses. Most defendants gaining admission into this program are young first offenders. Less than 1% of the defendants brought before the CJP Unit were admitted into the program while another 1.6% were granted PTI status following indictment by the superior court. The prosecutor is the primary gatekeeper for the PTI program, although the judge's approval is also required. The program requires the defendant to plead guilty to the offense. The defendant is next placed on a two-year probationary period, and if he or she does not get into further trouble the case is taken off the docket and the defendant's record expunged. In effect, the program places low-risk defendants into a pre-sentence probationary period, removing the case from the system at a fairly early time in the proceedings. In some New Jersey counties PTI is used in more than one-fourth of the cases, but Essex County relies on other means for reducing its caseload.

Public defenders all agreed that it was very difficult to place a client into the PTI program. It must be a very compelling case before the prosecutor will grant his or her approval. The prosecution will normally deal with weak cases by dismissals, downgrades, or early benevolent plea bargains. Essex County has created a remand court to review pre-indictment cases that should either be dismissed or downgraded to a lesser charge, from an indictable offense to a disorderly persons charge. The remand court is located in the county courthouse but is run by a municipal court judge. Two prosecutors as well as a pair of public defenders are also in the courtroom to assist the judge. The decision as to which cases are to be downgraded to a disorderly persons offense, thereby falling within the jurisdiction of the remand court, appears to be made solely by the prosecution. Public defenders interviewed were unsure exactly what factors were considered in making a decision to downgrade. The decision is usually made within a few weeks after arrest. Half of all cases beginning as indictable offenses are downgraded, so this special pre-indictment court serves as an important mechanism for dealing with court backlog. Public defenders are pleased with the frequent use of the remand court. It serves as a reasonable means of dealing with less serious cases, particularly those involving young adults who have made mistakes and first-time offenders. It is especially useful in dealing with the thousands of drug cases that under New Jersey's extremely harsh laws would result in lengthy prison sentences if the cases remained within the jurisdiction of the superior court. The drug laws are particularly severe when sales are made within 1,000 feet of a school or 500 feet of a public building. Given the abundance of schools and public buildings in the Newark area, as well as the minimal amount of drugs necessary to qualify for "intent to distribute," nearly every drug arrest falls within the law's strict penalties.

Presiding over the remand court is an experienced municipal court judge. The two representatives from the public defender office are also veterans of the criminal courts, each with more than twenty years of service. They have both been at the remand court for four years. They were placed here because of serious medical problems—one had had a heart attack and the other suffers from hypertension. It is likely that they will remain in this court until retirement, which should be in less than five years. In striking contrast to the two public defenders going through the bureaucratic motions of the CJP Unit, the remand court defenders have excellent professional reputations. In the year 2000 they were responsible for resolving several thousand cases, although the majority were settled by guilty pleas. There are a few non-jury trials. The court is aided by a representative from the probation department, which can begin to work with the numerous defendants who will be assigned to this department. Beyond the multitude of less serious drug cases (possession for personal use), the court also handles a plethora of simple assaults, probation violations, and trespassers. The defendants are brought to the remand court within one or two weeks following a CJP appearance, although it is not unusual for a few cases to stretch to forty days.

The prosecution views the remand court as an excellent opportunity to "dump its garbage cases." With only a perfunctory screening during the CJP proceedings and the absence of a probable cause hearing prior to indictment, the remand court is the only option for discarding the many weak cases brought by the various county municipal police departments. The high percentage of downgrades in Essex County is consistent with the state's other urban/suburban counties although the split between downgrades and dismissals (51% to 9% in Essex) is extreme. Overall, the court performs the necessary function of weeding out the large number of defendants in custody who have been overcharged and who do not present a threat to society if placed on probation.

During several months of observation, the remand court judge maintained firm control over the courtroom, moving cases along in a no-nonsense manner that nevertheless permitted a focused and careful resolution of each matter. The twin pairs of prosecutors and defenders worked smoothly in tandem, alternating cases. The public defenders in particular paid careful attention to the needs of each client, refusing to speed through the proceeding simply to satisfy the judge who occasionally became irritable if the pile of cases was not reduced with the desired speed. There were always a large number of cases where the judge reviewed the progress of defendants enrolled in the various drug rehabilitation or anger management programs. Each defendant was required to bring a letter from the program attesting to his or her attendance. The judge would either chastise or congratulate each defendant depending on his or her progress. (For those successfully completing these programs, the judge could dismiss the charges.) The majority of the cases involved defendants pleading guilty to the lesser, downgraded disorderly offense, after receiving a few weeks in jail and one or two years of probation. A sizeable percentage of the cases were probation violators who drew the judge's wrath. They were usually given one more chance with a stern warning that the next violation would result in immediate incarceration with revocation of probation. Trials, which were a rarity, lasted approximately two hours.

A second type of diversion program, used even more selectively than PTI, is the Essex drug court. Public defender Yvonne Segars with her associate Wanda Moore were instrumental in developing this treatment-oriented reform. The drug court employs a non-adversarial, holistic treatment approach. With the prosecution and judge controlling the selection process, the drug court works with non-violent defendants charged with drug-related crimes and offers them treatment instead of incarceration. The treatment team consists of the presiding judge as well as representatives from the prosecutor's office, the Essex regional defender office, the probation department, and a relevant drug rehabilitation program. The drug court's supervision includes:

1. Regular status hearings before the judge to monitor treatment progress and compliance with the drug treatment programs
2. Increased defendant accountability through a series of gradual sanctions and rewards
3. Intensive probation supervision
4. Mandatory urine monitoring three or four times a week

The Essex County drug court began operating in 1997. In order to participate in the program, a defendant must plead guilty to the drug-related charges. The participant is placed on probation for a period ranging from eighteen months to a maximum of five years. As of 2002 there were 125 defendants enrolled. The program has been fairly successful, with a recidivism rate of only 30%, which is remarkable for a clientele with a history of serious drug addiction. The court convenes each Thursday. In the morning session the presiding judge and treatment team discuss fifty to sixty people who will report to the court in the afternoon. The program graduates approximately twenty people a year. About half of the participants are in some type of treatment program while the remainder are either working or in school. A major strength of the program is the strong commitment of the judge, who maintains high expectations for the program. He appears to take it personally when a defendant "screws up." The defendant is made to understand that the judge is deeply concerned with the defendant's progress and is closely monitoring his or her behavior.

Public defenders view the drug court positively, wishing it could serve a greater number of defendants. The low number of participants is the result of a very cautious selection process by the prosecutor's office. (Less than 0.5% of indicted defendants are admitted.) Several public defenders were critical of the program, and reluctant to have a client apply for admission.

They thought that the odds of being placed in the program were so slim that it was not worth the effort. Even more troubling was the required admission of guilt. Additionally, if a client "flunks out" of the program, his or her earlier guilty plea will often require immediate incarceration. A final problem is the program's refusal to admit co-defendants. A number of the public defenders expressed a preference for trying to get their clients into Delancey Hall, a recently established private treatment facility. Although only in operation for a year and housed in a large warehouse, several Essex defenders thought it was at least an improvement over the county jail. Despite the skepticism of a number of defenders, the majority found the drug court to be a valuable treatment alternative, especially for those defendants with serious addiction problems that would soon destroy them if they did not receive help.

The final proceeding available to a defendant during the lengthy pre-indictment period is the Pre-Indictment Disposition Court (PDC) created and designed by Essex County superior court judge Phillip Freedman in the early 1980s. It handles mostly third- and fourth-degree (less serious) offenses, but can theoretically handle any crime of any degree. In reality, the bulk of their cases are drug or victimless offenses committed by young or first-time offenders. The PDC proceeding usually occurs two or three weeks after the defendant's arrest. As with most of the pre-indictment proceedings in Essex County, the prosecutor controls its utilization. Cases selected for the PDC have a strong presumption of non-custodial sentence. After PTI and drug court defendants have been selected, the prosecutor decides which defendants will be offered an early plea bargaining opportunity. Public defenders and their clients accepted roughly half of the pleas offered, which amounted to about thirty per week. If a public defender rejected one of these early plea offers, it indicated that either the offer had not been good enough or the defendant had decided to go to trial. The latter choice also meant that the client wanted the problem to go away, hoping that during the eight months before trial, the case might fall between the cracks of the justice system. Perhaps evidence would become lost or a critical witness would disappear.

Similar to the remand court, the Essex regional office placed two experienced public defenders in the PDC. Their adversaries were a pair of young prosecutors, barely thirty years old. The public defenders were both in their mid-fifties. One defender thought he had been stuck in the PDC for nearly seven years because of his overly aggressive nature, independent posture, and acerbic, sarcastic manner of speaking to his superiors. The other defender was a highly respected member of the office with nearly thirty years of experience. He conjectured that his selection to the PDC was because of recent health problems and the perception that he was on the verge of burning out as he closed out the twilight of his career. In sharp contrast, the inexperienced prosecutors frequently had to ask the presiding judge permission to recess so they could contact their superiors. Both of the young attorneys appeared to be always looking over their shoulders, afraid to make an error. If in doubt, they would reflexively take a hard-line position. The veteran public defenders with a combined fifty years of experience (more than ten years in the PDC alone) reacted quickly and decisively to each new problem as it arose.

The PDC was presided over by an experienced judge who processed the cases—nearly all of which involved plea bargains—in a careful yet expeditious manner. He relied heavily on the assistance of his court clerks and public defenders. In the year 2000 the PDC was able to obtain over 1,500 pleas, saving the Essex County court, particularly the grand jury section, a great amount of work. The PDC was similar to an administrative tribunal that effectively processed the plea bargains. The judge, defendant, public defender, and prosecutor all knew their assigned roles as they went through the all-too-familiar incantations whenever a plea was accepted by the court, certifying that the defendant understood what he or she was doing.

The PDC public defenders explained that they would reject a plea offer in cases they thought they had a good chance of winning. They also were cognizant of many future opportunities for plea negotiations with the prosecution and therefore felt little compunction to resolve a case at the first opportunity. Also complicating early plea negotiations for the PDC was the problem of defendants in denial of their guilt or the strength of the prosecutor's case. They would wish to put off their incarceration for as long as possible, irrationally hoping their legal problems might magically disappear. The following is a series of representative case summaries from the PDC. All defendants were represented by public defenders.

1. A black male in his early forties rejected a plea offer in a case involving child endangerment. The defendant had been in jail for eight months. The judge ordered the prosecutor to investigate why the case had not been brought before the grand jury after so much time.
2. A black male in his twenties had been in jail for 120 days and was about to be sentenced. He spoke on his own behalf and pled to receiving stolen property. He had three prior convictions, was on probation when arrested, and had a serious drug addiction problem. He was sentenced to three years and placed in Talbot Hall (a frequently used rehabilitation facility) because of his drug addiction.
3. A black male in his early twenties was being sentenced as part of a plea bargain. He admitted to possessing drugs (cocaine) with intent to sell. This was his first arrest as an adult. He was sentenced to a two-year probationary term, including a required drug evaluation. If he violates parole, he will be sentenced for up to five years.
4. A black male in his forties was sentenced following a plea in a spouse assault case, including making terroristic threats. It was his first felony conviction. He received a three-year probationary sentence with a strongly worded restraining order that would result in his incarceration if violated.

The PDC offers defendants who are unable to make bail and are awaiting trial in the county jail an early opportunity to extricate themselves from this difficult situation with minimal damage. The judge and prosecution both benefit from the PDC by being able to move many of the less serious cases from the clogged calendar. The defendants– who usually receive probation, rarely serving additional time in jail–are able to get on with their lives.

Legal Triage: The Allocation of Cases

Public defenders receive a new case from their team leaders a few days after a defendant's arrest. The only meaningful action taken during the first month by the public defender is an attempt to get the client out of jail. This necessitates filing a motion for reduction in bail or a request for the defendant to be released on his or her own recognizance. Some of the defenders made an effort to visit their clients if they were in jail to reassure them that they had not been forgotten. The majority of the defenders stated that they did very little work on a case for the first two to three months because the prosecutor's office would soon decide to downgrade half their cases to the remand court, dismiss another 10%, and refer an additional 10% to 15% to the PDC. (Only if the public defender in the PDC decides to reject a plea offer will the case be returned to the initially assigned defender.) Thus, a public defender can expect to lose nearly two-thirds of his or her cases as a result of prosecutorial decisions to downgrade, dismiss, or plea bargain during the pre-indictment period.

For those unfortunate clients whose cases were not downgraded or dismissed, the public defender devotes his or her efforts to trying to get them out of jail. The defender will carefully evaluate all of his or her cases in an effort to identify those that need the fastest resolution. The defender will also decide whether the client should apply for PTI or the drug court. Given the tight control over these programs by the prosecutor, who allows only a handful of defendants admittance, it is a rarely used option. Defenders are also reluctant to use these programs if they believe they have a strong case or, conversely, the prosecution has a weak one.

The pre-indictment period, which usually lasts for close to four months, is a fairly quiet period for both prosecutor and defender once the downgrades and dismissals have been made. The public defender tries to prod as much discovery material as possible from the prosecutor during this time, but it is usually restricted to the initial crime scene police report contained in the case folder. A defender's success in obtaining additional information, such as lab reports and statements from witnesses collected by the prosecutor's investigators, is dependent upon the two adversaries establishing a reasonable, cooperative relationship. Such a fortuitous relationship does not develop very frequently. The defender usually must wait until after arraignment (which occurs several weeks following the grand jury indictment) before the prosecution is required to share discovery information. Once the weaker cases have been dismissed or downgraded and the remaining cases are headed toward the grand jury, the prosecution becomes less interested in sharing information.

With the exception of occasional visits to those clients who were unable to gain their pretrial release and remain in jail, public defenders have minimal contact with their clients during the lengthy pre-indictment period. It is office policy to send a letter requesting defendants who are out of jail to come down and visit their recently appointed defender, but the majority of clients choose to ignore this request. They clearly prefer to enjoy their pretrial freedom as long as possible without being reminded of their impending doom. The public defenders generally do not begin their active investigation of the case until the post-indictment period, when they can count on new discovery materials as well as the greater cooperation of the defendant who has finally been forced to become involved in his or her case.

Multiple-defendant Cases and the Pool List

In cases involving multiple defendants, the public defender is prohibited from representing more than one of the defendants because of possible conflict-of-interest problems. In many multiple-defendant cases, each client may reach a different decision regarding possible cooperation with the prosecution in exchange for preferential treatment such as a reduced charge or even outright dismissal. Therefore, with each defendant maneuvering to minimize his or her involvement while placing blame on others, each must have his or her own independent counsel. One public defender described the typical behavior of defendants in these cases as "watching rats racing up the courthouse stairs." In order to provide alternative representation for these defendants, the Essex regional public defender office maintains a "pool list" of private attorneys who have volunteered their services. They are paid according to New Jersey's miserly rate of $20 per hour for out-of-court time and $30 per hour for in-court work. (The state has been embarrassed by the parsimonious fees, which are among the lowest in the nation, and presently has been trying to raise them statewide.) The pool list appointees may request the assistance of public defender investigators as well as the use of approved expert witnesses. The defender office tries to accommodate as many requests as possible. An estimated 10% of all public defender cases involve multiple defendants. The office monitors the vouchers submitted by the pool attorneys, especially if special requests are made.

The Essex regional director said that his office tries to recruit quality private criminal attorneys for the more serious cases. He indicated that they have been fairly successful in the endeavor because the private bar enjoys working with the experienced senior public defenders who have established reputations in the courthouse. The director also noted that some of the older Essex County private attorneys enjoy doing pool work as a change of pace from their more mundane civil practice. The majority of the pool attorneys, however, were evaluated as being of modest capability and frequently inexperienced. The lower hourly rates fail to attract the higher quality, experienced local private attorneys. The major frustration for defenders representing clients in multiple-defender cases is the difficulty of coordinating the work of attorneys who have different personalities and work habits, and, most critical, clients with divergent self-interests.

Plea Bargaining and Other Post-indictment Activities

It is noteworthy to find that during the three- to four-month pre-indictment period, only six public defenders working in tandem in the three specialized courts—CJP, PDC, and remand—are able to dispose of over 60% of all indictable cases, while the nearly forty remaining Essex public defenders operating in nineteen courtrooms are responsible for handling the 40% of the cases that reach the grand jury. In absolute numbers, in the year 2000, nearly 10,000 cases were disposed of during the pre-indictment period, leaving slightly less than 6,000 cases for post-indictment disposition. Once an indictment was handed down by the grand jury, the vast majority of cases (70%–75%) were settled by plea bargains. Only 5% of the cases went to trial, leaving 2% to 3% placed in the PTI program and nearly 20% being dismissed.

Essex County operates an unusual system for the distribution of cases following indictment. Each case is first assigned randomly to a specific public defender shortly after the defendant's arrest. After indictment, the case will be directed to a specific judge and courtroom to which the public defender has been assigned for a twelve- to eighteen-month tour of duty. The prosecutors are likewise assigned to specific judges for approximately the same period of time. Once the public defender has been assigned a case, he or she will be responsible until its final disposition. The system of defense is referred to as verticalized case management, or man-to-man coverage. All post-indictment proceedings in the case should be before the same judge. Most urban criminal justice systems utilize a contrasting system characterized as horizontal case management, or zone coverage. In these systems, the case moves through a series of pre- and post-indictment proceedings with a different public defender (and in most jurisdictions a different prosecutor) in each courtroom presided over by a different judge. It is only when a case is scheduled for trial before a specific judge that the assigned public defender will remain with the case through pretrial motion hearings, the trial itself, and the sentencing hearing.

Within a few weeks after the grand jury has indicted the defendant, the public defender and his or her client will appear at the arraignment. The defendant is required at this point to either plead guilty or state that he or she is preparing to go to trial. All discovery must be completed within two weeks of arraignment. (Discovery is the required sharing of information between the prosecutor and defense, although the state is obliged to produce much more data, exculpatory as well as damaging to the defendant's case.)

This process is extremely important for the defense because it allows the public defender to intelligently evaluate the strength of the prosecutor's case. Defenders quickly learn not to rely solely upon the client's prejudiced and self-serving version of the incident that led to arrest. Once the public defender becomes convinced that the prosecution has an unbeatable case, meaningful plea bargaining can rapidly proceed.

Essex public defenders state that they often receive the police arrest report as part of their client's case folder following his or her appearance before the CJP Unit. In many cases the initial police description of the events that transpired at the time of arrest will prove useful to the defender, permitting an informed judgment about the case. In more serious cases, however, as well as cases where the facts are incomplete or in dispute, additional discovery materials are necessary. The defender will also have to use an investigator to check out the missing or questionable information, verifying what the police have written. The new information may include an updated list of prosecution witnesses, lab reports (ballistics and drugs), and any reports on the case or the defendant from other law enforcement agencies (such as the state police, drug enforcement agency, FBI, and U.S. Attorney's Office). The Newark police as well as the Livingston, Hillside, and East Orange departments all have bad reputations for fabricating evidence, hiding exculpatory evidence, and conducting sloppy forensic investigations. It is, therefore, imperative for the public defender to carefully review the original crime scene reports as well as all subsequent prosecutorial investigations that may revise or discredit the arresting officer's initial description of the incident. Defenders frequently complain that it is difficult to pry this information loose from the prosecutor's office, which feigns ignorance or shifts the blame to uncooperative police officers. Several public defenders stated that the accessibility and comprehensiveness of critical discovery material is the result of two factors: (1) the seriousness of the case, and (2) the reluctance or combativeness of a particular assistant prosecutor. In serious cases such as homicides or rapes, prosecution is more likely to refuse to cooperate than it is in the thousands of drug-related cases flooding the Essex criminal courts. Although most prosecutors were characterized as reasonable and professorial in terms of turning over documents, there was an annoying minority described as hard-nosed, abrasive, and belligerent.

A number of public defenders commented that discovery is almost entirely dependent on the individual prosecutor. Even the prosecutors complain about inconsistencies between the police arrest reports and dispatch records, realizing that these documents can provide an excellent opportunity for creating reasonable doubt by challenging the credibility of police testimony. It was also noted by several public defenders that on many occasions prosecutors are not intentionally hiding information—they simply have a difficult time locating items that the police persistently misplace. This situation forces public defenders to go to the prosecutors requesting that they contact the police and provide the missing information. It is not unusual for critical pieces of information to be turned over to the defense at the latest possible date or most inopportune time. Another prosecution tactic is to turn over the information in bits and pieces, dragging out the process and confusing the defense. One public defender grew so accustomed to these delaying tactics that he developed a "boilerplate" motion form for requesting discovery information (see Figure 5.1.)

Probably the easiest way to prevent this delay and distortion of the discovery process would be to require it to occur earlier, possibly during the lengthy pre-indictment period. Presently, with no sanction and little incentive for prosecutors to release important discovery documents until two weeks after arraignment, public defenders are forced to remain in the dark for nearly five months.

For the defendants pleading not guilty at their arraignments, a trial is scheduled in about two months, preceded by a series of "status conferences" designed to resolve all pretrial motions. The number of plea bargains increases as a case moves closer to the trial date and important motions are decided, such as the suppression of evidence or a confession. As noted earlier, three-fourths of the indicted defendants will eventually plead guilty and only 5% of the cases will go to trial. After several status conferences, a plea cutoff date will be established and both sides realize that they must prepare for a likely trial.

In Essex County, as throughout the state, plea bargaining is the primary mechanism for disposing of cases. Guilty pleas are exchanged for a reduction of charges that will inevitably produce a lighter sentence. The defendant spares the state (prosecution) the time and expense of a trial and is rewarded with a reduced sentence. Both sides achieve hollow victories, frequently complaining about the flawed nature of the criminal justice system. The prosecution is assured of a conviction without risking the time and expense of a trial, the outcome of which can never be certain given the unpredictability of juries. The downside for the prosecution is its failure to punish the defendant to the full extent of the law. This can result in the nagging feeling that the defendant "got away with something." On the other side, the defendant is required to admit his or her guilt in open court, albeit to a less serious crime than originally charged. As one experienced public defender concluded, "There is very little satisfaction in plea bargains. Your efforts are rarely appreciated no matter how good a deal is worked out."

Hopefully, the public defender, as a result of receiving timely, reliable discovery material as well as relying on his or her office's investigation of the case, can make an intelligent decision about whether to go to trial or negotiate a plea arrangement. All of the more experienced Essex public defenders stressed that the most important skill they have developed over the years is the ability to make this decision. They term it as the key to a successful practice as a public defender. Great emphasis is placed on their ability to obtain critical information through discovery. The defenders unanimously agreed

Figure 5.1 Boilerplate motion form requesting discovery information.

State of New Jersey
OFFICE OF THE PUBLIC DEFENDER
Essex Adult Region

JAMES E. McGREEVEY
Governor

YVONNE SMITH SEGARS
Public Defender

MICHAEL J. MARUCCI
Deputy Public Defender
31 Clinton Street, 5th Floor, P.O. Box 46010
Newark, New Jersey 07101
Tel: 973-648-6200 • Fax 973-648-7790; 973-648-7098
E-Mail: TheDefenders@OPD.STATE.NJ.US

, Esquire
Office of the Essex County Prosecutor
New Courts Building
50 West Market Street
Newark, New Jersey 07102

Re: State v.
      Indictment #
      Prosecutor file No.

Dear

Please be advised that after reviewing the discovery in the above matter, the following items were not included in the package:

1)   An updated criminal history record for   ;

2)   Any property evidence report

3)   Any laboratory reports, including but not limited to certificates of analysis, requests for examination and resume of the person who conducted the examination;

4)   Any expert report that the State may rely on to prove possession with intent to distribute and the resume of the person who reached the opinion.

Your prompt attention to this matter is appreciated.

Very truly yours,

, ESQUIRE
ASST. DEPUTY PUBLIC DEFENDER

New Jersey is an Equal Opportunity Employer

that the client is not a reliable source of useful information. Public defenders understand that the client does not fully trust them and is frequently embarrassed by his or her behavior, often slipping into total denial. Rather than trying to browbeat the facts out of an already recalcitrant client, it is less stressful for everyone to use the information obtained through discovery to educate the defendant as to the strength of the prosecutor's case as well as incontrovertible evidence that cannot be ignored. The defense attorney must be convinced that there are enough weaknesses in the prosecutor's case to risk going to trial where, if convicted, the defendant will be facing a maximum penalty. Gaining confidence and wisdom in making this decision is the quintessence of the public defender's job.

Beyond the evidence, another important factor influencing the wisdom of a guilty plea is the particular prosecutor that a defender is facing. All of the defenders interviewed stressed the importance of the prosecutor's personality in the plea bargaining process. Of course, the prosecutor's perception of the public defender is also a critical factor in the equation. An experienced public defender with a successful trial record and an aggressive demeanor may intimidate younger, inexperienced prosecutors into opting for a plea rather than risking humiliation in a trial. Because of the rapid turnover in prosecutors during the past ten years compared to the relatively stable Essex regional public defender office, there is an abundance of experienced, highly qualified public defenders. A major frustration plaguing the large number of inexperienced prosecutors is their office policy requiring them to first receive approval from a superior before accepting a plea. Public defenders are given much more autonomy. They almost never go to a team leader for advice or approval before entering into a plea arrangement for their client. The short leash limiting assistant prosecutors produces delays and occasionally short-circuits the negotiation process as they constantly look over their shoulders for approval. One public defender caustically commented on the situation by stating, "The control freaks in the prosecutor's office frustrate everyone. Being difficult is not the same as being in control." A second member of the courtroom workgroup who can also influence the defendant's decision to plead guilty is the judge. In Essex County, the nineteen superior court judges in the criminal division vary significantly in their style and degree of involvement in the plea bargaining process. A sizeable minority are recognized by the public defenders as actively encouraging plea bargains in order to manage their oppressive caseloads. They believe, in the words of one defender, that "Every case can be settled!" These judges apply pressure on both the prosecutor and defense counsel to reach a plea agreement. Public defenders are warned of the dire consequences facing their client if he or she is convicted after a trial. Without a clear-cut policy governing the proper role of judges in plea negotiation, each judge has developed his or her own style and degree of involvement.

The defendant is clearly the most critical person in the plea bargaining process. Without his or her consent, the case must go to trial. The public defender's job is to evaluate the relative strength of the prosecutor's case and advise the defendant accordingly. Some defendants must trust their lawyer's judgment, acceding to the defender's recommendation. The Essex public defenders disclosed that most defendants are skeptical, requiring their attorney to convince them of the wisdom of a negotiated plea. A third group of defendants, a sizable minority, are in denial of their criminal behavior, possibly too embarrassed to admit their transgressions. This final group poses the most challenging problem for a public defender because of the professional and constitutional limitations on how forceful the attorney can be in coercing a guilty plea from a reluctant client. These defendants either wind up going to trial or pleading guilty at the last possible opportunity, often after the trial has already commenced. Plea bargaining at this late date is only minimally advantageous for the defendant since it saves the prosecution so little time.

Most public defenders agreed that the most opportune time to plea during the post-indictment period was just before trial, during the series of status (motion) conferences that follow arraignment. One defender explained "It was a product of both sides starting to see reality." The defense had finally completed discovery, while the prosecution had finished their assessment of the credibility of critical witnesses. Judicial rulings on key suppression motions had also been made that further contributed to the clarity of the available evidence. The period between the arraignment and trial was acknowledged by all of the public defenders as their most active period, with frequent interaction with their clients. It is when most of their post-indictment cases are resolved. After a few status conferences, the defender must sign a plea cut-off form indicating the case is now set for trial.

There is universal agreement among the public defenders interviewed that in recent years the number of pleas has increased while the number of trials has declined. In the year 2000, there were only 370 trials, while nearly 17,000 defendants were charged with indictable offenses and 6,400 defendants were ultimately indicted. The public defenders all credited the state's recently enacted harsh sentencing laws, particularly regarding drug cases, with causing this increase in plea bargains. The defenders all stated that their clients are simply terrified of going to trial and facing the possibility of such severe sentences.

In addition to the large amount of time public defenders expend on plea negotiations and discovery during post-indictment, they must also devote their energies to prepping a case that might go to trial. The public defender, with the assistance of an investigator, tries to locate witnesses who can corroborate the defendant's version of the incident or refute the prosecution's claims. This task often becomes one of the most frustrating aspects of a defender's job. Working with the supposed assistance of his or her client, the public defender and investigator try to locate and interview witnesses. They are often inhibited in their efforts by inadequate information such as erroneous or missing telephone numbers, street addresses, and names. A large percentage of witnesses are never located. Adding to the frustration, once the defenders do locate someone who might prove helpful to the case, the potential witness often fails to show up for the scheduled appointment. Tracking down these missing elements can be a dangerous proposition since so many of the witnesses live in high-crime areas. Most public defenders expressed a reluctance to go to the crime scene, although a number of the seasoned veterans do so regularly, with or without the accompaniment of an investigator.

Even after locating and speaking with a defense witness, the defender is never certain if the witness will appear for trial or be able to withstand the forceful cross-examination of the prosecutors. Many potential witnesses who might support a client's case often have criminal records and are fearful of implicating themselves further by becoming involved. The safest place for many is as great a distance from the courthouse as possible, even if their absence proves harmful to a friend or relative's defense. Defense witnesses who are currently on probation are especially vulnerable. The majority of witnesses observed testifying in trials were family members or close friends of the defendant. Prosecutors have a fairly easy time discounting the credibility of these witnesses before a jury, thereby diminishing their impact.

In addition to investigating a case and prepping witnesses, defenders also devote a great deal of time to preparing motions for the status conferences preceding the trial. Successful motions can eliminate important prosecutorial evidence such as confessions, improper identifications, and, most commonly, illegally seized evidence. Once the judge has resolved these critical issues, both defense and prosecution have a clear sense of each other's case. This is the time when the adversaries are most prepared to settle the case through plea negotiations.

Public defenders also spend an inordinate amount of time in courtrooms trying to close out a case after the defendant has already been sentenced but was brought back before the original judge because of a probation violation. (The defender remains responsible for a case until the defendant has completed probation.) These transgressions by the defendant may be as mundane as failing to meet a restitution payment, missing an anger management class, or failing to meet with his or her probation officer. A common, more serious problem is when the defendant is rearrested for a new crime. The annoying, seemingly never-ending problems of one client had a public defender muttering to himself, "Some of these clients just won't go away!" This sentiment epitomizes the public defender's major frustration in not being able to gain closure in a case in a timely fashion before moving on to the next client's crisis.

Trial Performance

Even though criminal trials are a statistical rarity in the Essex County superior court, they remain the focal point for public defenders, prosecutors, and judges, as well as the general public. It is the quintessence of the professional lives of all members of the criminal court workgroup. The major reason given by every experienced public defender for their lengthy tenure was their love of litigation, the opportunity to try a case before a judge and jury. These public defenders acknowledge that they may only try eight or ten cases a year, but it remains the primary reason they stay with the office. As one senior defender commented, "The trials are both the most demanding and satisfying part of our job. It is why I am here."

Several public defenders, some who had worked briefly as prosecutors, declared a preference for the defense because it presented many more opportunities for creative lawyering. The prosecutor's primary responsibility is to present the evidence in a manner that convinces the jury of the defendant's guilt. They are limited in most cases to police reports, lab reports, and eyewitness testimony. Because the prosecution has the burden of proof, the main job of the defense is to poke holes in the prosecution's case to create sufficient doubt in the minds of jurors. If a single juror is not convinced of the defendant's guilt beyond a reasonable doubt—a formidable as well as ambiguous standard—the public defender will have succeeded. The defense is under no obligation to prove the defendant's innocence by providing an alternative theory of who committed the crime. Public defenders are quick to explain that they are not concerned with the guilt or innocence of a client, but only whether the prosecutor can present a strong enough case to convince the judge or jury of a client's guilt beyond a reasonable doubt. Theoretical ideals of truth and justice are irrelevant to the American justice system with its adversarial process governing all cases. The prosecution and defense must limit their labor to the pragmatic question of whether the lofty standard of proof has been met.

Several senior defenders explained their basic strategy in the courtroom as simply "just keep pounding the prosecutor." These defenders suggested that the two most important character traits for a successful criminal defense lawyer are a strong competitive drive and a large ego. These dual characteristics allow the attorney to stand in a crowded, often hostile courtroom facing an unsympathetic jury, a skeptical judge, and a belligerent prosecutor. Armed with self-confidence and driven by competitive instincts, the defense attorney is able confront the intimidating power of the state as it tries to punish his or her client. Public defenders take pride in these David versus Goliath confrontations. The metaphor, however, does not seem applicable to Essex County where experienced, confident public defenders take on the younger, nervous prosecutors. Although all of the public defenders agreed that each attorney had to develop his or her own unique courtroom style and persona, there were nevertheless certain guidelines that should be followed in order to maximize one's chances for victory. It was extremely important to be in command of the courtroom. Discrediting a prosecution witness through a rigorous cross-examination, remembering to keep the witness on the stand, developing a feel for the jury, and conducting the trial through innuendo are a group of defense strategies that must be mastered.

Because Essex County public defenders and prosecutors are both assigned to the same judge and courtroom for at least a year, their combative trial behavior can undermine and complicate their day-to-day professional relationship. Most public defenders commented that they made a conscious effort to defuse the frequently bitter adversarial tension that can accumulate during a trial. Once the jury returns with its verdict, it is important to forget about what was said in the heat of a courtroom battle and attempt to renew a cooperative, reasonable relationship. This return to normalcy is necessary in order to dispose of the multitude of cases that must be resolved through shared discovery and mutually acceptable plea negotiations. Harboring resentment lingering from a recently completed trial creates an unhealthy work environment, undermining one's effectiveness as an advocate.

All of the Essex regional defenders agreed that success in the courtroom was heavily dependant upon the lawyer's understanding of the jury's psyche, hopefully shaping them into a sympathetic group who believe the client has been "screwed by the system." The defenders admitted that juries are often difficult to comprehend, rejecting the arguments of both defense attorney and prosecutor. The Essex defenders did think they had a slight advantage because many of the jurors from the Newark area were willing to question the testimony of police officers, rarely giving them the benefit of the doubt. In contrast, jurors from the county's outlying middle class, predominantly white suburban communities (i.e., Millburn, Caldwell, Montclair, and Livingston) assume that the police are honest and unlikely to lie on the witness stand. These suburbanites have infrequent contact with the police whom they rely upon to keep their neighborhoods safe. Several public defenders described this group as naïve, their perception of the police formed almost entirely by television shows. The residents of Newark or East Orange experienced frequent interaction with the police, often under emotionally strained conditions, which may either humanize or demonize the police who are also trying to survive on these "mean streets."

The selection of sympathetic jurors was believed to be a critical stage of the trial according to most public defenders, although a sizable minority thought jury selection was overrated as a determining factor in the outcome of a trial. They found jurors a challenge, but were not overly concerned with what type of individuals constituted a jury. Most defenders had theories about what type of person would be ideal for the defense. As a general rule, public defenders preferred minority, inner-city residents although some defenders refined the equation by including wealthy, liberal suburbanites who might overcompensate for their backgrounds. Upwardly mobile black professionals were to be avoided because of racial embarrassment or role distance from young black defendants. Asians and middle-class corporate types, scientists, and engineers were also suspect from the defense perspective.

Given Essex County's demographics, public defenders can count on facing juries that are at least half black. Their propensity for skepticism toward police testimony, occasionally feeling empathy for defendants, as well as generally being street-wise has given local juries the nickname of "not guilty Newark." Personal observations combined with statistical evidence indicate that this grossly simplified designation is an inaccurate exaggeration. Sixty percent of the trials result in conviction. Yet, public defenders find that jurors are often open-minded, even sympathetic, as the defense is able to cast doubt on prosecution witnesses. I was impressed after observing juries for over a nine-month period. They usually made a sincere effort to reach a proper verdict, paid careful attention to the testimony, and tried to apply the burden of proof standard in an intelligent manner.

I also found that trials seemed to bring out the best in the public defenders on both personal and professional levels. This was not surprising given the great importance and deep enjoyment each public defender derived from this litigation experience. For nearly every attorney interviewed, the trial was the primary reason why they remained with the office. Defenders who were fifteen- and twenty-year veterans disclosed that they were still unable to sleep the night before a trial. Each remained a nervous wreck until the jury returned with its verdict. Once the trial was completed the defender looked forward to returning to the office to receive either congratulations or condolences from colleagues. Trials also gave a public defender the opportunity to shelve for a week the growing pile of case folders requiring mind-numbing attention.

After a public defender has been successful at trial, he or she will be aware of several interesting changes. First, he or she will begin to receive more and better plea bargains from prosecutors who do not wish to confront the defender in the courtroom. One public defender with five years of experience stated that only in the last year, after he had won two difficult cases, was there a perceptible increase in favorable plea offers and no more trials. Prior to his recent success, prosecutors almost seemed to dare him into a courtroom challenge. A second trend is that word of a defender's success spreads quickly through the jail and the defendant grapevine in the courtroom, and he or she begins to be requested. Although most requests are not honored, it is still ego-inflating to have defendants seek one's services, especially in earshot of other attorneys.

Although trials may appear to isolate the public defender into the insular experience of performing in the courtroom alone, trials, in fact, offer an opportunity to observe the camaraderie and spirit of the Essex regional office in action. Whenever an Essex public defender is at trial, especially if he or she is relatively inexperienced, numerous colleagues will drop by the courtroom to offer encouragement and advice, if solicited. Deputy Director Marucci and one or more of the first assistants will make periodic appearances, sitting quietly in the audience until a break in the proceedings gives them a chance to come forward to see if they can be of any help or simply to give the defender a pat on the back.

Not all trial experiences are positive. Being forced to try a case that is an almost certain loser is one of the most upsetting aspects of the public defender's job. Often referred to as "paper bag" cases—the defender being so embarrassed by having to argue a case that cannot possibly be won that the defender would like to wear a bag over his or her head to avoid recognition—they represent failed efforts to convince the client to accept a reasonable negotiated plea from the prosecution. It is not uncommon for a defendant to be unable to objectively analyze his or her chances of acquittal. A defendant described as being in deep denial of the reality of the situation is emotionally unwilling to face the facts and make a rational decision to plead guilty. The defendant may be embarrassed, overly distraught, or simply stubborn, but will force the defender to represent him or her to the best of the defender's ability.

Another type of defendant who also insists on a trial presents an even more serious emotional conundrum for the defender. This is a statistical rarity: the innocent client. Public defenders dread having to represent this type of client because it exerts so much pressure on them. In most cases, the public defender can rationalize after an unsuccessful trial or a disappointing plea bargain that these results are not so catastrophic since the defendant was guilty anyway. However, with an innocent client, the public defender cannot hide behind this cynical justification. The consequences of a wrongful conviction where an innocent client will be incarcerated for a lengthy period of time only intensifies the pressure.

A third category of defendant insisting on a jury trial is anyone charged with a heinous crime who faces the likelihood of a lengthy sentence. The defendant simply has nothing to lose by going to trial since even a plea bargain will result in a long period of incarceration. In kidnapping, murder, and violent sexual assault cases, particularly where there has been media attention, it is unlikely that the prosecution will be offering much of a reduction of charges. The defendant's only hope may be for a hung jury or some other courtroom miracle. As noted earlier, jury behavior can be unpredictable so the defendant is willing to "roll the dice" since there are so few options available. These cases often fall into paper bag types of litigation, providing public defenders with their most challenging, and frequently embarrassing courtroom experiences.

Given the abundance of difficult, even unwinnable, cases that public defenders are obligated to defend, experienced attorneys advise recent additions to the office (also possibly trying to convince themselves) that good lawyers should not worry about the results of individual cases. Working as a public defender means a career filled with "loser cases," and, conversely, very few winning cases. As one highly respected senior defender stated, "Ninety-five percent of the cases try themselves, so there is not much you can do. The main thing to remember is that good lawyers don't worry over results." He went on to add "Self confidence is paramount for a successful criminal lawyer. You must not only convince yourself but also the judge and jury."

After five years with the office, a public defender was given her first murder trial. Perceptibly nervous during her opening statement, she settled down during the remainder of the trial. Throughout the five days there was a continual flow of public defenders into the courtroom, providing her with moral support. The case grew out of an argument and altercation outside of a crowded bar. The defendant was charged with shooting the victim in front of over fifty people. The defendant's family came forward to place the blame for the shooting on the defendant's cousin, who had admitted his guilt to several witnesses but had never been apprehended by the police. The defendant had been identified by the sole prosecution witness who was on the outskirts of the crowd. The grandmother of both cousins came forward to identify the missing cousin as the shooter (he confessed to her and several other relatives). She went to the prosecutor's office several times to speak with someone about the case but was turned away. The police and prosecution had their man, so even a grandmother's critical testimony was to be ignored. The jury, however, did not dismiss her and her family so readily. They acquitted the defendant after less than two hours of deliberation. The triumphant public defender returned to her office where her victory was celebrated loudly during a raucous lunch.

Case Disposition and Sentencing

The Essex County criminal courts, following national trends for urban, high-crime jurisdictions, dispose of the overwhelming majority of their cases through guilty pleas, with a very small percentage (less then 5%) being settled by trial. The New Jersey Office of the Public Defender and its regional agencies do not maintain annual statistical records of case dispositions; however, since the Essex County public defenders presently handle over 90% of indictable cases, their office's disposition rates closely parallel the overall county statistics maintained by the AOC's trial court administrator. (Interviews with defenders, prosecutors, and case managers substantiated this assumption.) Thus, the disposition rates presented in Table 5.1 provide an accurate picture of the current trends in processing for the Essex public defenders. The table includes figures gathered by the Essex criminal case manager for 1999 and 2000.

As noted throughout this chapter, the criminal proceedings are divided between the pre- and post-indictment stages. The pre-indictment period begins with an arrest and can last for several months until the prosecutor is ready to present the case before the grand jury. Throughout this three or four month period the prosecutor maintains control over the case. The prosecutor's office recommends to the court which defendants will have their cases dismissed, plea bargained, or admitted into a PTI program or placed in the drug court. Their recommendations are almost always followed. Table 5.1 shows that these various pre-indictment decisions resolve over 60% of the cases entering the Essex County criminal courts. Public defenders working in these busy courtrooms operate as two-person teams in an assembly-line system of justice.

Table 5.1 Pre- and Post-indictment Case Disposition, 1999–2000

	1999	2000
Total Cases Disposed	16,823	15,239
Pre-indictment Cases	10,103 (56%)	9,883 (61%)
Downgrades	8,297 (46%)	8,260 (51%)
Dismissals	1,384 (8%)	1,278 (8%)
No bill	309 (2%)	262 (2%)
PTI	113 (1%)	79 (0.8%)
Post-indictment Cases	7,969 (44%)	6,441 (39%)
Dismissals	1,633 (9%)	1,238 (8%)
PTI	123 (2.7%)	192 (1.6%)
Guilty pleas	5,757 (32%)	4,558 (28%)
Trials	356 (2%)	378 (2%)
Acquittals	150 (1%)	142 (1%)
Convictions	206 (1%)	236 (1%)

Statistics tabulated by Office of Trial Court Administrator, Essex Vicinage

Once the superior court has handed down an indictment, the judge, rather than the prosecutor, controls the process as the case moves from arraignment through pretrial conferences and finally to trial. The public defenders are busiest with their client's case during the time from arraignment through the status conferences (also referred to as pretrial hearings in most jurisdictions) since a large percentage of their caseload is settled through plea negotiations (75%) or dismissals (20%). The remaining post-indictment cases are resolved by trial. Of the 370 trials conducted during 2000, public defenders were able to gain acquittals in approximately 40% of the cases. (Private attorneys were victorious in only a third of their cases.) It is startling to discover that out of the 15,239 defendants arrested in Essex County for an indictable offense in 2000, only 2% ultimately had their fates decided by trial. Public defenders estimated that they were involved in approximately ten trials each year. There was some confusion over whether the number of trials had increased or decreased in recent years. Most thought it had been relatively stable in the past decade, a trend substantiated by recent AOC trial court administrator statistics.

Once a defendant has pled guilty or is convicted following trial, the court must then decide on the sentence. Sentencing laws in New Jersey, following national trends, have become more severe and less discretionary. The judge has little leeway in the length of a sentence, which is largely determined by the defendant's crime and past criminal record. There are also several crimes in New Jersey where the sentence's length is specifically stipulated by law, such a crime involving the use of a gun or a crime against the elderly. Drug cases, including drug sales near a school or public building, are another large category of offenses that leave little room for the judge's discretion during the sentencing process. All of these crimes require the defendant to serve at least 85% of the sentence.

Obviously, these new sentencing laws have reduced the role of defense attorneys in the process. Previously, public defenders would spend a great deal of time composing pre-sentence reports. Their reports argued for their defendants to receive a minimum sentence under law or receive probation instead of incarceration. Several defenders noted that they presently write a pre-sentencing brief in only 10% of their cases, although they try to have the defendant's family in court to humanize their client before the judge.

The defenders were not upset by their decreasing role in the sentencing process but were uniformly disturbed over the severity in new sentencing laws, which several attorneys described as "draconian." They all believed it was a bad policy to have mandatory sentences that were "criminalizing a whole generation of youth." The state's war on drugs is responsible for penalties that send first-time offenders to prison for two years for selling miniscule amounts.

Several of the defenders observed that the younger defendants–those under twenty-five years of age–do not seem to grasp the reality of the harsh sentences they are about to serve. After observing numerous sentencing hearings, I agree with their conclusions. It is shocking to see a nineteen- or twenty-year-old defendant casually receive a five- or ten-year sentence, standing alone in a courtroom, friends or family nowhere to be seen. Little remorse is shown, as most defendants decline to address the court, relying instead on their lawyer to offer a few words on their behalf. They are quickly led out of the courtroom, handcuffed, striding defiantly. A number of public defenders conjectured that given a defendant's often-deplorable home conditions as well as his or her family history, having so many acquaintances already experience incarceration, a defendant views the imminent loss of freedom without fear or even visible concern. It is a last opportunity to exhibit defiance and contempt for the justice system.

The Work Week: A Range of Responsibilities

The public defender office is divided into two distinct groups: those working in the pre-indictment courts, and the much larger group assigned to specific defendants and operating primarily in post-indictment proceedings. The eight defenders assigned in pairs to the four pre-indictment courts remain within their specific courtrooms nearly every day from 9 A.M. until 4 P.M. They rarely appear at the Clinton Street office except to pick up their checks or attend a staff meeting. This group has a specific range of responsibilities related to their coverage of a specific courtroom rather than a particular defendant. In contrast, the post-indictment attorneys are assigned to specific defendants although their cases will all be before the same judge. These public defenders have wide-ranging schedules, varying greatly from day to day. On Mondays, nearly all of the defenders must appear in their assigned courtrooms to hear the week's calendar call. They learn which cases are going to trial and may even begin a trial later that afternoon. Monday also offers the chance for putting pleas on the record or an emergency status conference. Fridays are a second day when the defenders must trudge up the hill to the courthouse. This day is devoted primarily to sentencing and related motions. Mondays and Fridays are very busy for most defenders, given their heavy caseloads.

Tuesdays through Thursdays appear less hectic unless a defender has a trial. Otherwise, the lawyers spend their time prepping for trial, visiting clients in jail, talking to bailed clients on the phone, drafting motions for status conferences, and addressing a depressing amount of administrative trivia falling within the general rubric of paperwork. A few attorneys will personally investigate cases by traveling to the crime scene or attempting to talk with witnesses in the neighborhood.

Most defenders prefer to work in their offices when they were not required to be at the courthouse. The doors to their individual offices were almost always open, inviting their colleagues to drop in for a chat. Likely conversations were omnipresent, most commonly in the larger corner offices of first assistants or senior attorneys. Topics ranged from office gossip to serious discussions of trial techniques. Younger defenders were consistent in their praise of this open-door policy that served useful educational and socializing purposes, contributing to the office's prevalent sense of camaraderie. Lunchtime in the library provided another opportunity for knowledge to be spread and friendships to be strengthened. These periods of conviviality were noted by most of the defenders as one of the most attractive features of the Essex regional office, compensating for the drearier aspects of their job, especially their interaction with unpleasant clients, prosecutors, and judges.

There are a handful of senior defenders who avoid the office almost entirely, spending all of their time at the courthouse or working from home. One attorney explained his long hours working at home by stating that the secretaries know where to reach him in case of an emergency. The Essex deputy director established a policy of allowing his staff maximum freedom as long as they performed their job competently. All of the staff appreciate being treated as mature professionals, viewing it as one of the job's attractive features.

This relaxed policy clashed sharply with the harsh leadership constraints found in most private law firms where every fifteen minutes must be accounted for. Even the absence of a dress code, allowing the Essex defenders to work in their offices in casual attire, contributed to the welcoming comfort level appreciated by everyone. After a year of interviews and observations, I did not hear of more than one or two isolated examples of any of the defenders abusing his or her freedom by practicing law on the side or attending to personal business to the detriment of his or her client.

CHAPTER SIX

The Work Environment and Courtroom Relationships

The Essex County courthouse in Newark is located on a gently rising hill a half mile from the public defender office. The courthouse is a fairly modern twelve-story nondescript structure built in 1968, sandwiched between the Hall of Records and the county jail. The Essex regional public defenders spend the majority of their professional lives within the confines of this building.

The Courthouse: Physical Description

Entrance to the county courthouse is through a single door leading to a metal detector and an x-ray machine manned by two or three members of the sheriff's department. The building houses all of the criminal court judges as well as a third of the civil judges, the remainder located next door in the Hall of Records. The first floor serves primarily as the province of the trial court administrator and the criminal case manager. Their extensive offices house all of the criminal case data processed on massive computers. There is also a bail office to assist friends and family gain the pretrial release of defendants. The sheriff's department occupies the second floor. It is responsible for maintaining security throughout the building, with special responsibility for the courtrooms, as well as transporting defendants from the adjacent county jail to the required courtroom. The county prosecutor and his or her large staff occupy the third floor. Courtrooms and judges' chambers begin on the fifth floor and continue through the remaining six floors of the courthouse. The fifth floor is also the location of two special pre-indictment courts, the Central Judicial Processing Unit and the remand court, both presided over by municipal court judges. Entrance into these busy courtrooms is through a non-functioning metal detector. The sixth floor houses the county's judicial leadership, an administrative judge in charge of the county's judiciary, and the presiding judge of the criminal division. Four courtrooms are located on each floor. Behind each courtroom is a judge's chambers along with a large room for his or her support staff.

Each courtroom is organized in traditional fashion with the judge's elevated position on the far wall across from the entranceway. The calendar clerk and stenographer are located just below the bench. The prosecution and defense are found at separate tables about ten feet away, directly in front of the judge. Behind these tables is a low railing dividing the courtroom participants from the general public who are relegated to several rows of wooden benches. The first row is reserved for police officers and attorneys. Defendants who have obtained pretrial freedom through raising the required bail or being released on their own recognizance sit in the audience until their case is called. Those unfortunate defendants who did not obtain their pretrial freedom are detained in the county jail next door or in the Caldwell Annex; they are brought into the courtroom from the "lock-up" area by the court bailiffs from the sheriff's department. The bailiffs escort the defendant to his or her chair at the defense table. They remain directly behind the defendant, preventing contact with anyone seated beyond the wooden railing in the audience.

In an earlier book entitled *Chaos in the Courthouse: The Inner Workings of the Urban Criminal Courts*, I compared the criminal courts to a traditional village. The Essex County courthouse clearly falls within this description. It operates with the same "high level of intimacy and frequency of interaction between nearly all members of the courtroom workgroup."[1] Defendants are often upset when they observe their public defender joking with the prosecutor. Their gregarious interaction feeds the defendant's cynical view of his or her attorney, who should be more hostile toward his or her supposed adversary. Another village characteristic present in the Essex courthouse is the reflexive paranoia toward outsiders who attempt to penetrate the inner sanctum. This type of siege mentality was not unexpected in the Essex courthouse given recent negative media coverage of the county's faltering criminal justice system. All visitors were viewed suspiciously, usually questioned by a bailiff as to their reason for being in the courtroom. Anyone visiting a courtroom is easily frustrated by the judge and attorneys holding frequent sidebar conferences out of earshot of the audience. For more protracted discussions, the trio will leave the courtroom entirely, meeting in the judge's chambers. The use of legal jargon unfamiliar to most laymen is another tactic designed to further obfuscate the proceedings. A third and final point of comparison is the nearly total control that the judge maintains over the courtroom. The judge resembles the patriarchal head of the village whose word is not to be challenged. Spectators in the courtroom who chew gum, whisper to a friend, or forget to remove a hat will be quickly notified of the proper courtroom behavior either directly by the judge or indirectly through one of the bailiffs. Lawyers who fail to show proper deference or persist in a pattern of behavior found disrespectful will be threatened with contempt. On rare occasions the attorney might be removed from the court-room.

Despite the large number of cases processed by the Essex County superior courts, only two courtrooms reflect the heavy caseload. These are the two pre-indictment courts located on the fifth floor, which are responsible for the initial screening of all indictable offenses. Each court handles fifty to seventy-five cases a day. Both courtrooms are usually jammed with defendants and their relatives and friends. It is common for this group to spill out into the hallways, which are lined with benches that are crowded with grandmothers, girlfriends, and wives caring for a large number of small children trying to entertain themselves. They move continuously in and out of the courtroom, the duration of their stay determined by the children's unwillingness to observe the courtrooms' rigid rules of proper behavior. Out in the hallway, the children amuse themselves by playing inside the telephone booths making imaginary calls, racing up and down the hall, or roughhousing under the benches. On most days the fifth floor resembles a nursery school playground as the impatient toddlers are forced to endure the boring, protracted court proceedings that last several hours. Once inside the courtroom the children are usually confined to the last row where their guardians try to control them but rarely last a half hour before a bailiff asks them to leave.

The post-indictment proceedings, including trials, are conducted in the relative calm of the courtrooms located on floors seven through twelve. These courtrooms are only crowded when a highly publicized case is being tried. Normally the courtrooms are fairly busy in the morning with calendar scheduling, sentencing hearings, and status conferences. However, in the afternoon the majority are empty. The judges are probably back in their chambers working with their law clerks, secretaries, and calendar clerks resolving scheduling problems, responding to motions, or meeting with attorneys. Unless they are trying a case, most public defenders return to their offices following the morning recess. Given the high volume of crime in Newark and adjacent municipalities, it is surprising to most laymen wandering through the courthouse in the afternoon to discover so many courtrooms vacant. All members of the courtroom workgroup are busy, retreating into their private offices located either in the labyrinth of rooms behind the courtroom or offices outside of the courthouse.

Judicial Relations

As noted earlier, public defenders and prosecutors are assigned to a particular judge and his or her courtroom for approximately a year. Prosecutors and public defenders combined with judges, clerks, case managers, stenographers, and bailiffs form the courtroom workgroup. This modest-sized group develops a unique behavior pattern that can directly affect criminal case dispositions. The speed with which decisions are made as well as the specific case outcomes reached either through plea agreements or trial are all influenced by the interaction of this collection of courtroom officials. In the Essex County criminal courts, as in most jurisdictions, the judge appears to be the dominating member of the workgroup. Nevertheless, prosecutors and defense attorneys possess sufficient power to prevent the judge from controlling the cases in a tyrannical fashion. The reality of the courtroom situation is a three cornered power struggle with the judge in the most advantageous position. The judge's power is enhanced because of his or her proclivity toward being sympathetic to the prosecutor's position. This results in the public defender often being the odd person out in legal struggles over such issues as pretrial release, entrance into intervention programs, and resolution of critical pretrial motions. The alliance between judge and prosecutor may also be apparent during trials, although not in so blatant a manner. The explanation for the cooperative relationship between judge and prosecutor is probably derived from a shared concern with the public's perception of their crime-fighting responsibilities. They are political figures, appointed by the state legislature, whose performance is measured by crime rates, conviction rates, and the prison population. The public defender/defense attorney must oppose the power of the state and ensure that before a defendant is found guilty, the state has proven its case beyond a reasonable doubt.

The overall assessment of the Essex County criminal court judges by the public defenders was not overly positive. Their critical evaluations are likely affected by their perception of the judiciary's tendency to favor the prosecution. The Essex defenders thought that most judges shared the prosecution's belief in protecting society and ensuring public safety. They cited numerous instances where judge and prosecutor appeared to be acting in tandem to the detriment of a client's best interests. Most of the public defenders recognized the variation in quality and style of the Essex judges as they performed their numerous tasks. There was a difference of opinion over whether the judges were improving or declining in their overall level of performance. The majority of defenders detected a perceptible decline in the past decade. They thought too many "political hacks" were reaching the bench, in addition to an abundance of new judges who lacked any previous litigation experience coming to the bench from a corporate law firm that engaged in virtually no criminal work. Many defenders stated that the judges were not stupid but did not seem to care. Nearly all of the Essex defenders chafed at those judges who enjoyed using their "manipulative powers." A number of defenders found dealing with judges to be one of the major frustrations of the job, especially when the attorneys thought they had to entertain or baby-sit certain judges. These same defenders also noted that several of the better criminal judges (in their opinion) had retired or were transferred to the civil side of the courthouse. A few of the defenders theorized that those leaving were disproportionately sympathetic to the defense or neutral at the very least, implying a conspiratorial theory of pro-defense judges not being permitted to enjoy the same length of assignment in the criminal division as pro-prosecution judges. The county has had a tradition of its administrative judges and the presiding criminal division judge being former county prosecutors. A few of the more senior public defenders who had been with the office for more than twenty years dissented from these criticisms, believing that the most recent appointments to the criminal bench appeared less tyrannical and more reasonable than the older judges they remembered from the beginning of their careers.

The public defenders were well aware of the judiciary's declining powers, particularly with regard to their discretion in the sentencing process. Recent state legislation established specific sentencing guidelines that judges must follow or else write an explanation of why they chose to go outside of the prescribed limits, detailing the mitigating or aggravating factors justifying their decision.

Given the rarity of trials in the Essex criminal courts, the judges spend a great amount of time dealing with the plea bargaining process. Judges vary significantly, according to the public defenders, in their degree of involvement in the plea negotiations although the majority of defenders have served in courtrooms where judges play an active role in encouraging the settlement of a case through a guilty plea. Every defender interviewed recalled being coerced into returning to his client and convincing him or her of the judge's strong desire to resolve the case quickly with a plea. An aggressive judge could often work to the defender's advantage when a reluctant prosecutor is hesitant about accepting a plea advantageous to the defendant. Judges in Essex County are under a great deal of pressure from the Administrative Office of the Courts (AOC) in Trenton to reduce the backlog and resolve cases as quickly as possible. The AOC has also complained that lawyer readiness is an important contributor to court delay. Their criticism has been primarily directed toward the defense attorneys but the Essex defenders noted that they are not overly responsive to the AOC demands because there is little that can actually be done to them by the state organizations. Protecting the rights of their clients is their paramount concern (not to mention their constitutional obligation), and will not be sacrificed simply to accommodate the AOC's statistical imperatives to reduce court delay. In fact, all of the public defenders candidly admitted that delay is often a tactic helpful to a client's defense. A drawn out case can result in prosecution witnesses disappearing or moving away; evidence can also be lost or become tainted. When prosecutors refuse to plea bargain or merely drag their heels because of heavy caseloads, the Essex defenders stated they are frequently able to enlist the support of a judge in pressuring their adversaries into a plea bargain beneficial to their client. Inexperienced judges who are nervous about conducting a trial and exposing their ignorance are especially prone to utilizing coercive techniques in order to pressure both defense and prosecution into settling cases through plea bargaining.

Public defenders caution their colleagues not to get on the wrong side of a judge because he or she can influence a defender's next courtroom assignment. Most members of the Essex County courthouse workgroup are aware of certain judges having bad reputations for intemperate dispositions, inappropriate behavior, or sloppy job performance. Public defenders understand that inevitably they will have to spend a year in one of these unpleasant courtrooms, but no one wants to stretch that to two or three bad situations in a row.

Because public defenders are assigned to a judge for at least a year, it is critical for them to develop a survival strategy. Not only is the defender's psychological well being at stake but, even more important, the welfare of his or her client is dependent upon the defender forging of a satisfactory working relationship with the judge. All of the Essex defenders stressed the need to be sensitive to the judge's moods and behavioral practices. They recommended avoiding confrontations whenever possible because the client will likely feel the ramifications. The defenders also noted that an intelligent, experienced judge is willing to work with the defense, recognizing that this ultimately is in everyone's best interests. Although defense attorneys must never compromise a client's position, defenders acknowledge that in some instances it is advantageous to assist the judge in moving cases along expeditiously. This may force a defender to walk a fine line between his or her obligations to the client and his or her responsibilities as an officer of the court. Whenever these two positions clash irrevocably, public defenders agree unanimously that they must remain loyal to the client, regardless of whatever displeasure it may cause the judge.

The judges are one of the primary sources of frustration for public defenders, although not as persistent or egregious as the problems raised by prosecutors and clients. The first frustration grows out of the public defenders' belief that most judges are inexperienced in criminal law. Several defenders stated that some of their most difficult cases are the product of a judge trying to cover up his or her ignorance of criminal law and procedure. Rather than admit unfamiliarity with a point of law, a judge would resort to a heavy-handed, somewhat dictatorial style of decision making designed to intimidate anyone questioning his or her ruling. A second complaint echoed by most Essex defenders is the judges' attitude that public defenders work for them; in reality, they are all public officials working for the common good of the state and county criminal justice systems. Several of the Essex public defenders commented that this attitude was especially difficult for younger, less experienced public defenders who were more susceptible to being bullied and fearful of appearing overly aggressive. Closely related to this problem is the commonly held belief among defenders that most judges did not even realize how disrespectfully they talk to public defenders. Sometimes, several defenders noted, they are made to feel part of the court's entourage, on equal footing with the judge's law clerks, calendar clerks, and other support staff. (This was especially true for younger defenders whom the judges did not know previously).

Many defenders were puzzled by the judges' markedly divergent behavior in and out of the courtroom. While in chambers, a judge could be gregarious, exchanging jokes and courthouse gossip. In open court, however, a Jekyll/Hyde transformation occurred as the judge became acerbic or mean-spirited. The judge's demeanor could quickly shift whenever a problem developed which impacted the speedy movement of cases on the docket, causing a backlog. Usually both adversaries shared responsibility for the slow-down, but because of the perception of most judges that the defense always benefits from delays, the defenders were more likely to be the target of the court's wrath.

The Essex defenders believed strongly that most of the county's judges favored the prosecution, but not in a consistent or obvious manner. Most defenders admitted that despite their pro-prosecution proclivities, the Essex judges did make an effort to control any excessive or blatant favoritism. There existed several judges, a few of whom were former prosecutors, who a number of Essex defenders characterized as actually favoring the defense. This surprising finding was explained by one defense attorney as the result of the judges remembering the underhanded tricks and questionable tactics they observed among their fellow prosecutors, and, upon reaching the bench, vowing to protect defendants from such unethical and illegal practices. Several public defenders thought that most of the judges favored private attorneys over public defenders. This was apparent when granting continuances or trying to resolve scheduling conflicts. The rationalization for this preferential treatment was that the public defender was going to be stuck in the courthouse anyway. Additionally, the public defender would be guaranteed his or her salary regardless of a case outcome, but for the private attorney, "time was money"–economic survival was dependent upon developing a satisfied clientele. Time wasted in the courtroom meant the loss of critical billable hours. Since most of the judges had been in private practices before reaching the bench, they were exceedingly empathetic to these economic realities.

In conclusion, the Essex defenders found the county's superior court judges to be unsympathetic to their clients' plight. These sentiments were not blatantly apparent but persistently lurked below the surface in their continuous efforts to move cases along as quickly as possible. As a whole, the Essex criminal court bench was described as a young group of jurists, not particularly knowledgeable or interested in the criminal law, most lacking enthusiasm for their current assignment. The defenders noted that there are several exceptions to this uninspiring depiction, but based on my observations I believe it is a fairly accurate one. The major problem for an Essex public defender arises when he or she is assigned for twelve months to the courtroom of one of the less competent judges who may also favor the prosecution. This is a very long period of time to be confined to a courtroom with a judge who will likely be making your professional life over the next 365 days very unpleasant.

Police

The Essex public defenders were surprisingly sympathetic toward the police, understanding the pressure and difficulty of patrolling the dangerous neighborhoods of Newark and surrounding towns. The amount of random violence and number of wasted lives the officers observe on a daily basis inevitably takes its toll on whatever humanitarian instincts they may have possessed when they first joined the force. Most defenders thought that the police department had been improving in recent years, becoming more professional and less corrupt. There were fewer occasions when they were behaving like "Keystone Cops," although the number of police characterized as lazy or racist remained too high. The narcotics officers were the worst offenders, frequently planting evidence or lying on the witness stand. Several defenders added that the police seem to target the poorest black areas for their most aggressive patrolling. Some police officers also have a tendency to arrest on very little evidence, not bothering to check out the facts, which could have quickly resolved the problem. Instead suspects are brought to a local or county jail and detained for long periods of time while the police attempt to verify their stories. One public defender noted "it seems that the weaker the case, the slower the police move." Most public defenders believed that the police were under pressure from their supervisors to maintain a high number of arrests. This resulted in a large number of "nickel and dime" arrests that are mainly drug related. The defenders describe these police tactics as simply driving up to any busy street corner in the evening hours where they are able to "shake everyone down and make a number of drug and weapons arrests." This practice may displease the judiciary by clogging their dockets but the police believe it is an effective technique for controlling the streets.

The two most common instances of police-public defender interaction are in the procurement of discovery material and testimony on the witness stand for the prosecution. All of the public defenders interviewed had had bad experiences with police officers who falsified arrest reports or lied on the witness stand. Narcotic officers often stated that they had had the suspects under surveillance for a long period of time before they moved in to make the arrests. Defenders knew that it was more common for the police to drive through a neighborhood and observe a suspicious late-night cluster of individuals acting furtively. The police would frisk everyone in the immediate area, usually discovering drugs and weapons. The defenders also thought that many officers tried too hard to make a case, distorting or falsifying evidence. Because of the police department's history of unlawful behavior, the public defenders had an easy time convincing the streetwise Newark juries to be suspicious of police testimony.

The Essex public defenders were frequently frustrated by the snail-like pace with which the police complied with their requests for discovery. The initial arrest report would usually be available to the defenders as part of the case folder shortly after the defendant's initial appearance at the Central Judicial Processing Unit (CJP). Unfortunately, subsequent investigations by the police that uncovered new incriminating evidence as well as prosecution witnesses could be lost in the system for months. The defenders were not certain if the desultory tactics were caused by the police officers' incompetence or done purposefully. There was also confusion as to whether the police or the prosecutor—or both—were responsible for the large amount of lost information, most of which would eventually reappear at an inopportune time for the defense.

Although police officers shading the truth on the witness stand or even lying outright presented difficulties for public defenders, most agreed that a policeman who told the truth was the greatest obstacle to courtroom success. Honest police officers were difficult to shake, presenting the defense little opportunity to challenge their credibility. However, when a police officer was perceived as "playing loosely with the facts," public defenders agreed they had a much easier time poking holes in the officer's testimony and creating a reasonable doubt in the minds of the jury. Prosecutors also evaluate the strength of their cases on the perceived credibility of the testifying police officers. They are usually much more amenable to plea bargains in cases relying upon the testimony a police officer whose performance on the witness stand casts doubt upon the veracity of his or her statements.

Relations between the police and public defenders are commonly strained because of their opposite positions in the adversarial struggle. Nevertheless, there seemed to be a shared understanding that both the defenders and the police were simply doing their jobs. Once a case was completed, any acrimonious feelings rarely continued outside the courtroom. Both parties were so overwhelmed with cases they rarely had time to harbor long-term feelings of bitterness.

Prosecutors

Public defenders interact much more frequently with prosecutors than either the police or judiciary. As in most American courthouses, the prosecutor in Essex County is the most important actor in the local criminal justice system. The prosecutor plays a pivotal role in monitoring police practices, determining which cases can go forward as well as designating the specific charges. The Essex public defenders were uniformly upset over the willingness of the county prosecutors to allow so many weak cases to go forward to the grand jury. The dilemma is worsened because of the prosecutor's control over the superior court grand jury, which rarely rejects a case lacking probable cause.

The Essex regional defenders characterize their adversaries in the prosecutor's office as a group of young, underpaid, not-too-bright individuals laboring in a politicized work environment where they are constantly looking over their shoulders for their supervisor's approval. The camaraderie so obvious in the public defender's office is noticeably lacking with the prosecution. In contrast to the defenders who exhibit strong support for one another, especially during trials, prosecutors are described as being under intense pressure not to lose a case. The defenders relish their role as legal underdogs, battling the imposing prosecutorial strength of the state. The public defenders stated that the Essex prosecutor's office did contain a small group of career prosecutors who were responsible for handling the most serious cases, particularly those designated for trial. Several members of this group of experienced lawyers were overly zealous in their prosecutorial fervor. These true believers were the most frustrating of opponents, often embittered and unreasonable. The majority of prosecutors were described as inexperienced and underpaid, planning to leave the office after a few years, to be replaced by a new contingent of political appointees, recently graduated from law school. The Essex prosecutor's office has been extremely volatile in the past fifteen years, with the leadership changing every few years, causing a massive turnover in personnel. A cynical, somewhat irreverent public defender described the typical prosecutor as "a grown-up version of the high school nerd who was always picked on and now has the chance to get back at his tormentors."

Despite the major differences between the two offices (public defender and prosecutor), many judges view both adversaries as members of the courtroom team working together to assist the judiciary in moving cases and reducing the backlog. Judges often become frustrated with the prosecutors because of their inability to make an instant decision without first getting their supervisor's approval. The public defender who has been granted much greater autonomy is able to gain the judge's favor by being able to resolve problems instantaneously. A somewhat related problem caused by the paucity of career prosecutors is the necessity of having inexperienced prosecutors assigned to the pre-indictment courts (CJP, remand, and PDC) where a large number of critical decisions concerning the downgrading, dismissal, and diversion of thousands of cases are made. The public defender office, in sharp contrast, staffs these courts with senior veterans who easily dominate their youthful adversaries from the prosecutor's office.

The Essex public defenders are most critical of a small group of prosecutors who are aggressive and relentless in their efforts to convict. They refuse to be cordial or professional, failing to grasp the humanity of the defendants. Even more annoying than these intractable opponents are a smaller group of prosecutors with reputations for occasionally using under-handed tactics. This group holds back on discovery material, sometimes "misplacing" documents that may prove advantageous to the defense. One defender explained this unprofessional behavior as a likely outgrowth from their frequent reliance on informants or "snitches" in order to build a case. Under pressure to win as many cases as possible, believing they are working under the public's mandate to do whatever is necessary to keep the streets safe, prosecutors have an easy time justifying their questionable behavior.

In evaluating the prosecution's plea bargaining capabilities, many public defenders characterized them as somewhat ineffective because of the great pressure placed on their office to dispose of cases as quickly as possible. Most public defenders believed that they had the upper hand in plea negotiations. In addition to their concern over moving cases, prosecutors also realized that if a case goes to trial they are likely to face both a hostile jury and a group of senior public defenders with an impressive record of courtroom victories. Once a prosecutor is defeated at trial, he or she is often hesitant to return to the courtroom and therefore more amenable to a negotiated settlement, even one that is clearly advantageous to the defendant.

Even though the defenders viewed prosecutors as relatively weak adversaries, they were often frustrated by the prosecution's control over the discovery process, stating that the prosecution often failed to disclose important information until the last possible minute when it would be of minimal value. A few prosecutors were found to believe that they had a right to keep certain discovery materials from defense attorneys. Others were described by defenders as maliciously enjoying playing games with their adversaries. Experienced defenders advised that the best strategy was to go out independently and acquire as much information as they could with the assistance of their investigators, not relying on the erratic cooperation of the prosecutor.

Because prosecutors and public defenders are required to work together in the same courtroom for at least a year, all of the lawyers interviewed stressed the importance of developing a reasonable working relationship, hopefully based on mutual respect. After working together for several months, the possibility exists, however, that defenders and prosecutors can become too cordial and relaxed. Several defenders warned that when there is a decline in adversariness, the client can become very upset. Most defendants are already dubious of their public defender's commitment to their case, so when they view the supposed adversaries socializing, the trust between client and attorney may be completely destroyed. Several experienced public defenders advised their colleagues to modify their relationship and level of trust to a particular prosecutor. Because there was significant variation in the attitudes and professional behavior among the numerous prosecutors, it was critical for their clients that defenders be able to recognize these differences.

Comparing the current crop of prosecutors with their predecessors from twenty years earlier, senior public defenders thought there had been a perceptible decline in competence. Several of these experienced defenders remembered fearing prosecutors who consistently had the upper hand in plea negotiations as well as during trials. It is difficult to discern whether this perceived decline is a product of reduced financial resources in the county or the change in attitude of the current leadership. County prosecutors recently have been discredited and enmeshed in embarrassing political setbacks. This has resulted in an unsettling pattern of short tenures, which appear to have created something of a leadership void. The older public defenders remember a period fifteen to twenty years ago when they would occasionally socialize with the assistant prosecutors, inviting them to office parties, but present relations have become less cordial, especially with the newer members of the staff.

In summary, the public defenders found the Essex prosecutors to be a dispirited, directionless organization plagued by internal politics. The office maintains performance statistics, which only intensifies the apprehension of younger prosecutors who are terrified of losing a trial. This results in a beneficial situation for a public defender, who can adroitly coerce a young prosecutor into a plea bargain advantageous to the defender's client. Operating on a short leash and feeling the pressure from supervisors, it is no wonder that morale is low in the prosecutor's. The public defenders, describing the problems they see in the prosecutor's office, usually utter a sigh of relief that their benevolent leadership has treated them as responsible professionals whose judgment is trusted.

Courthouse Personnel: Clerks and Case Managers

Tension exists between Essex public defenders and the case managers, who are also referred to as calendar coordinators. The criminal case managers operate under the county trial court administrator, whose file-filled, computer-driven offices are located on the first floor of the courthouse. The entire county case management structure is controlled by the AOC located in Trenton. The office was created to assist the state supreme court (particularly the chief justice) in supervising the statewide justice system. The appointment of county trial court administrators is made by the administrative director of the courts housed in the state's judicial complex in Trenton. Most public defenders view the AOC as an "ivory tower" institution with little hands-on experience and, therefore, an idealized view of the realities of the criminal justice system. The Essex County judiciary is much more responsive to the demands of the AOC and their local case managers for expeditious movement of cases. Public defenders, however, because of their constitutional obligation to provide competent representation for their clients, cannot always assist in the AOC's quest for reduced backlogs and diminished delay statistics. The failure of case managers to appreciate the public defenders' professional responsibility toward their clients is probably the main source of tension between these two groups.

The case managers presently serve as gatekeepers for determining which defendants qualify for a public defender because of their indigency. Just prior to making the initial court appearance, a defendant fills out Form 5A, which affirms the defendant's request for a public defender and provides background information validating his or her financial status as an indigent. From numerous interviews with Essex County criminal justice officials, it seems that all requests for a public defender are granted with virtually no effort being made to verify the background information. The absence of a viable screening procedure is acceptable to all members of the courtroom workgroup. The unstated assumption is if a defendant wishes to choose a public defender, then the court need not complicate matters by probing into his or her personal finances. It is highly unlikely that a defendant will select a public defender just to save a few dollars if he or she is actually able to afford a private criminal lawyer. When one's freedom is at stake, it is not a sensible time to shop for a bargain.

The Essex County deputy public defender has the most contact with the case manager. He meets on a weekly basis at the courthouse with the criminal case manager's office, where he is given current statistical information on case dispositions, backlogs, and court delay. He does not find these statistics that important and rarely shares them with his staff. As noted, the public defender's responsibilities are to his or her clients' best interests, not the expeditious movement of cases through the court system.

Witnesses

The Essex public defenders all agreed that defense witnesses are a difficult group to effectively utilize. Frequently coming from inner city neighborhoods, the typical witness lacks communication skills. In most instances, the witnesses, victims, and defendants share a common social bond and value system in sharp contrast to the judges, jurors, and attorneys. Simply trying to locate a witness can be an extremely frustrating experience. Confusion as to a witness's name due to aliases or nicknames, as well as missing addresses or reliable phone numbers are all factors which confound a defender or investigator. Even when a witness does show up, he or she cannot be relied upon to accurately recount the original version of the events, especially when facing an intimidating prosecutor during cross-examination. Impressing the jury by remembering crucial dates and events is rarely achieved. An additional problem is the inability of most witnesses to communicate effectively and clearly articulate their responses. I was continually surprised by how incapable witnesses for both sides were of expressing themselves. Their nervousness, discomfort, and sparse vocabulary combined with poor memories made their impact upon the jury fairly negligible in most trials. Juries strained to hear the testimony as witnesses mumbled their responses in a barely audible tone. Judges continuously had to ask witnesses to speak up, repeat their answers, and raise their heads.

Public defenders warned that they had a brief window of opportunity to effectively utilize witnesses who were reluctant to appear or were on the verge of falling apart just before the trial. Many useful witnesses refused to come to a defendant's assistance out of fear of angering the police or prosecution. Many witnesses had been in the system recently themselves or were presently on probation. Overall, all defenders agreed that witnesses should be used as little as possible. The major thrust of one's defense should be attacking the prosecution's witnesses; this was the safest way to create reasonable doubt in the minds of the jurors.

Clients: An Overall Assessment

A major reason why the Essex County public defenders are able to provide their clients with an effective, personalized defense is because their office employs a verticalized system of representation. A public defender is assigned to a defendant a few days after the initial court appearance. The defender will remain with this client until the case is closed. Although there is minimal contact with the defendant during the quiescent pre-indictment period, once the grand jury has indicted the client, the public defender will begin to interact with the client more regularly. Most public defender programs operate horizontal systems of representation rather than vertical, where a series of different public defenders represent the client at each stage of the proceedings–initial appearance, preliminary hearing, grand jury, arraignment, and trial.

Even though most Essex public defenders characterize their clients as distrustful and unappreciative, they are nevertheless dedicated to providing them with the best representation they can offer. The defenders are continually frustrated by their inability to gain the trust of their clients. Equally troubling is the unwillingness of their clients to follow their advice. Clients are described as being angry at the entire criminal justice system, including their public defender. Public defenders are tainted in the defendant's eyes because their salaries are paid by the same New Jersey state treasury that also funds the judiciary and prosecution. Adding to the client's suspicion of his or her attorney's trustworthiness and loyalty is the cordial, even congenial relationship observed by the defendant between judges, prosecutors, and defense attorneys. Sidebar conferences conducted in hushed tones out of earshot of the defendant and jury arouse further suspicion, deepening the distrust. Defendants are unappreciative of their attorneys primarily because of the likelihood of their impending punishment. Their public defenders are usually viewed as ineffective losers because of the defenders' inability to extricate their clients miraculously from their current legal problems. Most clients fail to appreciate the efforts and accomplishments of their public defender, who is often able to convince the prosecutor to reduce charges significantly in exchange for a guilty plea. Since nearly all indicted defendants eventually plead guilty, with only 2% to 3% obtaining acquittals after trial, the overwhelming majority of public defender clients are disappointed by the outcome of their case. The public defender may believe that he or she has been very successful by gaining a two-year sentence in a case where the defendant could have easily been sentenced to twenty-five years after a trial, but the frustrated client still has to serve the two-year term in a dangerous state prison.

A few defenders appeared to have a morbid fascination with some of their clients, describing relationships as both the best and worst part of their job. One experienced public defender enjoyed the interesting personalities he met, occasionally establishing a positive long-term relationship extending beyond the case's conclusion. He showed me several letters mailed to him from prison and elsewhere from former clients updating him on their current situations. His office was littered with artwork and other mementos that had been mailed to him by grateful clients.

Most of the Essex public defenders were not enamored with their clients, past or present. They did, however, maintain a dispassionate empathy for their clients, who were often described as individuals who had led lives full of bad choices. As one defender stated, "My clients are usually decent people who do stupid things." Several of her colleagues spoke about their clients as pathetic individuals, living difficult lives that were in perpetual chaos. The degree of compassion shown toward clients varied significantly. The deputy defender noted that they draw their clients from a difficult population, with many suffering from drug and alcohol addiction, as well as a large percentage being mentally unstable and emotionally immature.

An experienced public defender described his clients' typical behavior pattern as following a basic paradigm. "The defendants are like infants who cannot face immediate unpleasantness which is better in the long-run." He compares their inability to defer gratification as being analogous to babies being forced to take bitter medicine. He and several other defenders noted the added complication of having so many defendants who are continually high, irrational, and in serious denial. This combination of negative character traits undermines the ability of public defenders to communicate with their clients in a rational, productive manner.

Their clients' anger, immaturity, emotional instability, and lack of intelligence undermined the lawyer-client relationship, but most public defenders persevered to work diligently on their clients' behalf. It was reassuring to hear so many public defenders acknowledge that despite frustrating interactions with clients, they nevertheless strive to demonstrate to their clients that the attorneys do care. As one female defender with fifteen years experience explained, "Clients teach me to listen and remain honest. Regardless of the outcome, maybe I can have a positive impact on their future. . . . Their humanity is important but they also must learn to assume responsibility for their acts." Several defenders noted that on many occasions, they go even further beyond their professional responsibilities and help a client find a place to live, locate a job, or gain placement in a rehabilitation program.

Nearly all of the public defenders who had been with the Essex office for at least fifteen to twenty years observed that clients have noticeably changed. Drugs are credited with being the major cause of a perceptible decline in client intelligence and rational thought. One of the senior public defenders stated, "My clients used to at least be street smart. They could communicate effectively, making a positive impression upon white jurors. Now, they have no respect for you or the justice system." He believes the problem began in the mid-1980s when Newark was engulfed in a crack epidemic. Today's young clients are the babies born in the midst of this drug crisis. Another senior defender describes them as "harder, showing little remorse or compassion, refusing to take responsibility for their actions. They demand their attorneys come up with miracles."

A few of the more sophisticated and street-smart defendants appreciate the varying abilities of Essex public defenders. They request specific attorneys. Word on the street quickly spreads when one of the public defenders has performed a "legal miracle." Unfortunately, office policy cannot accommodate a client's specific request because attorneys are assigned randomly. Without such a policy, some attorneys would be overrun with clients while others, particularly the less experienced lawyers, would have almost no one to defend. Defendants often demand a change in attorneys, which is also almost never granted. Requests are most commonly based in frustration from not being able to extricate themselves from a disastrous predicament. Defendants may try to blame their problems on an ineffective attorney, but the Essex office rarely acquiesces.

Defendants in Denial: Veracity and Confusion

The inability to effectively communicate with their clients was a persistent frustration for all of the public defenders. Interviews revealed a wide range of inhibiting factors. A number of public defenders thought that most of their clients lacked intelligence and continually exercised poor judgment in deciding what information to share with the defenders. One defender explained her strategy was "to carefully lay out all the dots of the case but they continually had trouble connecting them." They were repeatedly forced to remember how unsophisticated their clients were, weakened further by depleted vocabularies. Their sense of powerlessness, intensified by being under great stress, further weakened their capabilities. As one defendant stated, "Everything was happening too fast."

The public defenders had a difficult time making their clients (who were overwhelmingly lower class, or working class at best) appreciate the middle-class values underlying the legal system and all of its critical actors, including the judge and jury. The defendants could not comprehend how their lives were in conflict with these middle-class institutions that control society. Relying on their peers, defendants frequently exhibited a false bravado, maintaining a blind, irrational optimism in the face of a desperate reality. They constantly demeaned their attorneys' efforts, charging that they knew more and could probably do a better job defending themselves. It was unfortunate that so many of the defendants lacked family support or knowledgeable friends to give reasonable advice, assist the public defender, and compensate for their own ignorance and emotionality.

Given the difficulties in communication, the public defenders were forced to devise various strategies to break through the client's resistance and distrust. Most defenders tried to enlist the support of whatever family members they could locate. Defenders also found that numerous visits to see their clients in jail also seemed to improve their attentiveness and cooperation. Not only were detained clients a captive audience, but they also had a greater degree of urgency in resolving their legal problems. These clients were most amenable to applying to a diversion program or negotiating a plea bargain. Conversely, defendants released on bail or on their own recognizance were rarely interested in coming downtown to the public defender offices. Each hoped that some mystical force would cause the case to disappear or somehow fall between the cracks of the Essex County court system. Unfortunately, the day of reckoning would eventually arrive.

A large part of a public defender's efforts go into explaining the consequences and seriousness of a client's case. One lawyer tried to have his client imagine the case from the viewpoint of a skeptical or open-minded juror. Sometimes the client could be jarred into a realization that his or her fantasized defense would not be very convincing to a rational juror. Utilizing discovery, most defenders presented the uncontested facts in the prosecution's case, hoping that eyewitness identification, physical evidence, and, most damning of all, testimony from co-defendants would shock their clients into understanding the seriousness of their positions. Several black public defenders thought they had an advantage in working with clients of the same race, but there was not universal agreement on the issue. A few public defenders stated that their clients asked them if they were Jewish, believing in a stereotypical impression of shrewdness and courtroom success. One young defender candidly admitted that one needed a great deal of patience when conversing with clients, and he lacked both the desire and ability to penetrate his clients' psyches. Public defenders also indicated they had great difficulty in communicating with their clients' families, friends, and witnesses from the neighborhood.

Public defenders described a large percentage of their clients as being in denial, a psychological term indicating a person's refusal to accept unpleasant facts, replacing them with a more amenable, albeit fantasized reality. Inexperienced public defenders are often duped by clients utilizing this defense mechanism, but quickly learn to adopt a cynical, more realistic attitude toward a client's version of the events in question. Discovery and further investigation will usually provide a more reliable version of the incident. The most common reason for defendants to enter denial is because they are embarrassed by what they have done. Family and friends trying to be supportive also contribute to denial by offering distorted explanations for what occurred, typically trying to reduce the defendant's blameworthiness. Public defenders admitted they sometimes are unable to snap a client out of it. Many of their clients are emotionally unstable and often paranoid, which further exacerbates the attorneys' inability to save their clients from themselves.

Public defenders insist on their clients telling them the truth so they will not be surprised during the trial. Essex defenders do not care if a client is guilty. This information will have no impact on the effort of any defense attorney. Defendants often have a difficult time accepting this reality. They stubbornly cling to their sanitized, often fictitious version of the facts, fearing their lawyers will not like them or do their best, although ironically they are only making the attorney's job more difficult. Clients occasionally insist on testifying in their own defense, presenting their distorted version of the facts. Lawyers aware that their clients are about to commit perjury when testifying are placed in a difficult ethical position. Professor Monroe Freedman, in his respected book on the subject, argues that a defense attorney can allow a client to tell his or her story but the attorney should not ask questions or in any way make it more palatable to the jury.[2] It is a slippery ethical slope that defense lawyers try to avoid by convincing their clients that the prosecution's cross-examination will severely weaken their testimony. (Additionally, when a defendant takes the stand, the prosecution is able to introduce the client's past criminal record—as related to the issue of credibility—which can have a profound impact upon the jury). In closing, the client is not only a frustrating individual to deal with, but is often his or her own worst enemy. The client's low intelligence, social isolation, paranoia, and overall instability are significant obstacles to the public defender's chances for a successful effort.

Meeting with Clients

Even though clients released on bail can visit their public defenders in the comfort of the Clinton Street offices, they rarely avail themselves of the opportunity. In fact, as one public defender stated, "They avoid us like the plague once they've gained their pretrial freedom." Seeing the lawyer reminds the defendant of his or her impending doom. Once out on bail, however, most defendants prefer not to be reminded of their legal problems. Even defense witnesses who might be crucial to the case also fail to appear. Clients can meet with their public defenders in one of the interview rooms on the fifth floor of the Clinton Street offices or in the attorney's private office on the sixth floor, but in the year spent researching this book, I observed less than a half-dozen defendants meeting with their lawyer. Once a case has progressed into the post-indictment period, especially after arraignment, most public defenders conduct harried meetings with their clients in the courthouse hallways or in the stairwells. Defendants prefer phoning their public defender at his or her office, although this is often not very successful.

Most of the defenders do not enjoy visiting their clients in jail but realize they have little choice. Jail visits, particularly out to the Caldwell Annex, take time that could be spent more profitably. Clients in jail spend a great deal of time complaining about the conditions, as well as their overall predicament. Most defenders agree that very little is accomplished by these jail-house visits, which frequently only serve to make the defendant even more upset. One experienced public defender, clearly in the minority, endorsed jailhouse visits as a way of showing a defendant that he or she has not been forgotten. The defender also tries to give his client a rough outline of what is going to happen at the forthcoming court appearance. He solicits the client's assistance in locating witnesses. The primary objective for both jail and office visits is the same according to all of the Essex public defenders: to educate their clients as to the seriousness of the charges they are facing and encourage them to make a realistic decision about whether to plead guilty or go to trial.

Difficult Clients

Every public defender indicated an experience with an especially difficult client. These defendants, according to one public defender, "are such a pain in the ass you silently root for the prosecutor." Defenders become especially upset with disgruntled clients who berate them, accusing them of being in collusion with the prosecutor. Equally annoying are combative clients who are distrustful and reject advice and criticize tactics. Most defenders find it extremely difficult dealing with a client who is informing on co-defendants in order to obtain a lighter sentence. (It is also problematic when one's client is the one being "ratted out.") It is the accepted wisdom that public defend-ers cannot escape these frustrating clients because as a senior defender noted, "Simply stated, some of our clients are really bad guys."

What can be done when confronting an undesirable client? An experi-enced public defender noted that clients do become more manageable as you move closer to trial. She also advised not to pressure them. She found a low key, upbeat demeanor occasionally works. Most defenders were unable to offer positive suggestions other than trying to "dump the client," which is rarely successful. Interestingly, many of these unpleasant clients take the ini-tiative and try to dump their attorney. This also is almost never granted. The deputy director handles all requests from defendants demanding a new attorney. The director's initial response is always negative, urging the client and defender to try to work out their differences, but if problems continue the director will yield. The general principle remains, however, that clients cannot choose their attorney or shop around for a more desirable one.

Most public defenders understand the client's frustrations but continued complaints about the quality of representation can anger even the most empathetic attorney. As one defender stated, "If a client begins to bitch about me and threatens to get a private attorney, I open my door and encourage him to get one." For defenders who are successful in dropping a client, a team leader (supervisor) advised, "You should always know the new defender you are dropping the client on and try to assist them in any way you can to bring them up to speed." The Essex defender office realizes that a client's demand to switch attorneys is usually really a delaying tactic, but sometimes the lawyer-client relationship deteriorates to the point where it is counterproductive, and a change is warranted.

How far can an attorney go in coercing a client to plead guilty? Several defenders indicated great frustration over being forced to go to trial when the defendant should have pled guilty. This usually occurs in the most serious cases where the stakes are the highest—in other words, in cases where even the plea will result in a lengthy prison sentence. One senior public defender, whose patience has worn thin over the years, commented, "I am not bothered if the client becomes angry. I give it to them straight. I am no longer willing to coddle them." Another experienced Essex defender is careful to always inform the judge, being sure it is on the record, when he has strongly recommended a plea to his client but his advice was rejected.

Lack of Appreciation Over Time

In contrast to the experience of many attorneys in private practice, the Essex county public defenders rarely feel appreciated by their clients. This would not be of much concern in most public defender offices because attorneys rarely stay more than two or three years, but in the Essex Regional defender office a very large percentage of the staff remain for over ten years, several until retirement. Essex County public defenders, therefore, have the added burden of not only being unappreciated, but also having endured working in a thankless job for ten or more years. How are the Essex public defenders able to sustain their combative edge and maintain compassion over an extended period of time? The most consistent answer was they do it for the enjoyment of successfully litigating a case. Nearly all the Essex defenders acknowledge that it is a thankless job, some going so far as to define the client as a necessary evil. The defenders admit they are largely driven by their own egos. Their competitive juices drive them to win the case, rather than deep feelings about the defendant or their constitutional obligations to provide competent representation.

All of the Essex public defenders thought their clients almost uniformly failed to appreciate their efforts, especially in plea negotiations where even a "great deal" was not recognized as a significant accomplishment. One defender commented that he initially tried to impress his clients "by kicking the prosecutor's ass" in the courtroom, but agreed that his clients were not impressed. The longer one is with the office, the less impact the defendant's attitude has upon the defender. A veteran Essex defender summarized this evolutionary process by stating "The fact that we [Essex public defenders] aren't considered real lawyers bothers you in the beginning, and feeds on your self-respect, but when you've been successful in a few trials you gain self-confidence. You don't really need the blessing of your client anymore."

Many of the senior public defenders offered advice to the younger attorneys who were still troubled by the lack of positive feedback from their clients. The gist of their comments was to toughen up and realize that there was no time for hand-holding or becoming distraught over a series of losing cases. They also warned that one could not avoid becoming cynical and hardened after being lied to so frequently by clients. One philosophical defender described his job "as taking lemons and turning them into lemonade. The creative part of this job is to think of a way to manipulate your client." Another attorney found the best way to survive a career as a public defender was "to not get caught up in each case and emotional tragedy because it would drive you nuts." He added that this attitude does not mean he is any less of an advocate for his clients' legal rights, but his involvement in their problems ends at 4:30 P.M. when he heads home to his family. He adamantly refuses to discuss his work outside of the office.

Several senior public defenders warned that one must get past the squeamish aspects of the job, such as viewing grisly crime scene photos and witnessing an autopsy. One defender admitted that he has actually grown to enjoy the grittier aspects of his job. Several Essex defenders mentioned the necessity for allowing a lot of the more unpleasant aspects of the job to simply "slide off your back." A corollary to this point of view was to be able to see the humor in even the darkest side of life. Many defenders found the gallows humor that permeates the office not only a necessary emotional release valve but also a positive force joining the defenders together. This ability to maintain role distance–a sociological concept allowing an individual to function in an extremely difficult situation by emotionally distancing himself or herself–was first observed in MASH units during the Korean War when surgeons joked around while performing life-saving operations. It is not surprising that several public defenders described their office as a "legal MASH unit" performing triage on an unending flow of emotionally damaged defendants facing imminent loss of their freedom.

Special Client Problems

In this chapter clients have been described as being the most unpleasant aspect of the public defender's job, but certain categories of defendants can make the job even more troublesome. The most frequently mentioned category of difficult clients was the mentally ill. Their cases were described by Essex defenders as being bounced around the justice system for extended periods of time until they became administratively buried or fell between the cracks. Psychiatric problems are compounded by the high percentage of defendants suffering from severe alcohol or drug addiction. The problem has intensified dramatically since the mid-1980s when crack cocaine first appeared in Newark. Several defenders noted that it has become increasingly difficult to prove incompetence to stand trial or use the insanity defense. Without a prior history of psychiatric problems, the defenders found the threshold for establishing insanity nearly impossible to surmount. Competence to stand trial and use of the diminished capacity defense are also difficult, requiring an inordinate amount of work. The public defenders are fortunate to have a group of available psychiatrists to assist them, but they are rarely successful and this defense is utilized in only the most serious cases. A number of defenders added pessimistically that there are no really good results in cases with mentally ill clients. It was pointed out that even if a defender is successful in making an insanity plea, the client's status is uncertain for ten years so it is often better to take a plea if the defendant can tolerate a prison setting.

A second category of difficult client is the occasional sociopath or especially violent defendant. Every Essex defender related an incident involving one of these scary sociopaths but no one had been physically harmed, or so traumatized as to be unable to effectively represent the individual. The last category of problem defendant is that statistical rarity, a client who the public defender believes is innocent. All defense attorneys, public as well as private, prefer defending a guilty client. In most instances, defense attorneys admit they usually do not want to know one way or the other; their narrow focus is on providing a competent defense, forcing the prosecution to prove his or her case beyond a reasonable doubt. The defense is under no obligation to explain a client's innocence or come up with an alternative explanation for who actually committed the crime. The burden of proof rests squarely on the prosecutor. One defender clarified his professional position by explaining his job is not to judge but to defend. The judge and jury must decide whether or not his client is guilty. The added pressure of representing a client who the defender believes is innocent creates an emotional nightmare. Several Essex defenders in this difficult dilemma complained of sleepless nights, nervous stomachs, and anxiety attacks. Fortunately, as most defenders agreed, this kind of problem defendant does not come along very often.

The Client Relationship: Some Final Thoughts

Despite the continual frustrations in dealing with unappreciative and distrustful clients, nearly all of the Essex public defenders admitted a deep concern over their clients' predicaments. An experienced defender cautioned that a defender must "step back and realize that your clients are in great pain and real stress. They are powerless. Many are manipulative and continually complain but what else can they do?" Another attorney, who had been with the office for fifteen years, explained the client's dilemma in terms of his or her immaturity and inability to know whom to trust. She explained, "the [criminal justice] system is insensitive to the defendant's reality and humanity. The system makes no effort to accommodate the difficult growing up process the defendant is going through and the courts really need a little patience." This analysis sounds more like that of a social worker than a defense attorney, and several of the Essex defenders (most of whom were female) admitted viewing their job as being in large part mental health counselor, educator, social worker, negotiator, and only occasionally lawyer. The majority of the Essex defenders, however, rejected the social worker role and defined their job more narrowly in legal terms. As one defender stated, "I'm just making sure I am giving my client a good defense, trying to make certain the system is not screwing him too badly."

Most of the Essex defenders were sensitive to the difficult environment in which their clients had grown up and its impact upon their current legal troubles. Several defenders admitted that if they had grown up on the violent streets of Newark or Irvington instead of in middle class suburban communities, they also might be involved in drugs, violence, and gangs, eventually winding up in the criminal justice system. Most defenders recognized their clients' immaturity and inability to defer gratification as they live for the moment, unconcerned with the future consequences of their actions. A senior public defender was disturbed by the "Adult Babies Syndrome," a term he used to describe a situation in which he was representing young defendants who were the children of earlier clients he had defended fifteen to twenty years ago.

Public defenders relaxing in their relatively peaceful offices can calmly comprehend their client's hostility toward the world. They realize that defendants often transfer this anger to their attorney, who appears to be part of the same system that is trying to take away their freedom. Yet the Essex defenders cannot forget their professional obligation to provide a competent defense for these troubled, frustrated clients. As will be seen in the next chapter, it takes a very unique individual to be able to maintain one's professional obligation under such difficult working conditions.

CHAPTER SEVEN

Personal and Professional Issues

This chapter will focus on the positive and negative aspects of a public defender's job as well as the salience of office politics, the problem of burn-out, the necessity for redefining success, and the process of developing a professional reputation. At many points, a comparison will be made between Essex public defenders and private criminal defense attorneys.

Positive Aspects of the Job

Despite the depressing work conditions, unappreciative clients, and modest wages, the majority of Essex County public defenders had been with the office for over ten years. Interviews with these long-term employees disclosed a number of positive aspects of the job, which affected their decision to remain with the Essex regional office. The most common reason given for staying was the camaraderie among the legal staff. Nearly every attorney commented positively about his or her colleagues in the office. Not only did the esprit de corps create an attractive workplace, it also provided a wealth of experience that was readily shared. It contributed to the professional development of everyone, especially the younger attorneys, with one exclaiming that "I love waking up each day knowing I am coming to work. It keeps me feeling alive. It is like having a lot of big brothers." Another new attorney, echoing similar sentiments, added "There is always someone to assist you. Even if you have to come in on the weekend there will always be someone to patiently work with you."

In addition to providing encouragement and knowledge, the interaction between colleagues was distinguished by a surprising amount of humor, candor, and informality. The ambience of the Essex defender office was in sharp contrast to the formal competitiveness typical of private law firms, especially among associates trying to make partner. The friendly environment of the public defender office was most apparent during a dinner for three departing attorneys. The dinner was held at a popular Portuguese restaurant in Newark's Iron-Bound section. Away from the depressing confines of the Essex County courthouse, the public defenders easily progressed into carefree conviviality. The open bar at the far end of the cavernous reception hall was packed with thirsty public defenders. In addition to a few wives in attendance, the Essex defenders were joined by a smattering of prosecutors, law clerks, and private criminal lawyers in the celebration honoring two former defenders leaving the office for private practice and a third who was transferring to a rural regional office closer to his home. Both lawyers moving into private practice were enticed by lucrative offers. One had been with the office for only a few years, but he was recently married and his wife was expecting twins in a few months. He would be joining a prestigious local firm in its litigation section. The other attorney, who had been with the office for a decade, had what he described as a once-in-a-lifetime opportunity. He would be joining a long-time friend who was a successful record producer. He would be providing a wide range of legal services within the newly developing field of entertainment law.

Following an hour or two of drinking and nibbling on appetizers, an impressive buffet was presented. The highlight of the evening followed dessert when each honoree was toasted and roasted in a series of humorous testimonial speeches. The three departing attorneys then had their chance to thank everyone and say goodbye in an eloquent and emotional manner. The formal ceremonies concluded with a short speech by Judge Len Ronco, better known as the Duke of Essex. Judge Ronco, a special surprise guest, was a legendary figure not only because he was the first public defender appointed to direct the Essex regional office when it was created in 1967, but also as a result of his prominence for several decades as an Essex County prosecutor, judge, and county commissioner. With an easygoing manner and a lacerating sense of humor, he had the captive audience laughing with each anecdote.

With the conclusion of formal ceremonies, the crowd dispersed into small groups. The conversations grew louder as the emotional farewells and heartfelt good wishes grew in intensity, fueled by the final round of drinks. The genuineness of the warm bond between the attorneys was palpable as they delayed their departure. It was obvious that the defenders were conflicted between their sincere happiness in seeing one of their colleagues move on to a promising new opportunity and the equally strong sense of melancholy caused by the loss of a good friend.

The collegial atmosphere of the office allows for the development of a family-like atmosphere where friendships are formed that for several attorneys continue outside the office. It is not unusual for a group of especially close defenders to vacation together, while another cluster live in close proximity to each other, socializing on the weekends. The most obvious manifestation of this collegiality is seen during lunchtime when large numbers of attorneys gather in the library around a large table. The candor, humor, and compassion exhibited during their midday meal break offered tangible proof of the mutual support society frequently mentioned during interviews. There was an easy interplay between the leadership, the senior attorneys, and their junior counterparts as they joked, gossiped, and griped good-naturedly, though loudly. Conversations continued throughout the afternoon as the defenders consulted one another for assistance in personal as well as legal matters. Nearly everyone maintained an open-door policy, which facilitated the continuous interaction. Credit for the friendly, supportive atmosphere, according to everyone, goes directly to the regional director, whose easygoing managerial style as well as widely-respected intelligence sets the tone for everyone.

Another important positive attribute of defender work was the opportunity to engage in litigation. Nearly all of the defenders enthusiastically proclaimed their intense enjoyment of courtroom battles, turned on by both the intellectual and competitive aspects of litigation. Several mentioned the euphoria of winning a trial. One defender explained that sometimes during a trial "you get into a zone where you actually feel like you are controlling a jury." One experienced lawyer explained that even though there were only a handful of trials each year (he had been averaging approximately ten), that was sufficient to retain his enthusiasm. He enjoyed the continuous effort to improve his trial techniques, which provided both intellectual and professional satisfaction. Another senior defender succinctly stated the importance of the litigation opportunities. "If you love being a trial attorney this place is heaven." A handful of defenders who had briefly experienced working in a corporate law firm returned to the defender office, despite taking a major cut in salary, because they missed the excitement of trying a case.

A third positive aspect of the job mentioned by most public defenders was the degree of autonomy and personal freedom granted by the office leadership. Everyone was deeply appreciative of the independence. It was refreshing being treated as an adult and a legitimate professional in a quasi-bureaucratic organization like a public defender office. The Essex regional director sets an unmistakable tone for freedom and trust granted to each of the defenders. Their freedom is in sharp contrast to the prosecutors who are on a short leash having to clear almost every decision with a superior, as well as most law firms where beginning associates and junior partners are closely monitored.

The defenders also noted that the director does not concern himself with how you spend your time as long as there are no complaints from either the client or judge. During midweek (Tuesday through Thursday) when an attorney does not have a trial or any other business before the court, he or she can work at home or any other preferred locale. As long as the secretaries know where to reach you, one can roam at will.

Several of the Essex public defenders who had either worked briefly in a private law firm or had a spouse or friends presently employed in the private sector believe that the flexibility, informality, and avoidance of financial concerns (i.e., finding clients, creating sufficient billable hours, meeting office expenses, etc.) combine to make the defender office an attractive place to work. Obviously, there is a self-selection process at work influencing the type of young lawyers who want to become public defenders, but the Essex office provides an even greater degree of personal freedom, which even extends to the absence of a prescribed style of dress. One defender praised the opportunity to dress informally because it allowed him to save money on dry cleaning and spend less on new suits. He also enjoyed the opportunity to dress in comfortable, relaxed clothing.

Many public defenders, particularly single parents and women with younger children, were extremely grateful for the flexibility in their hours. Rarely having to work past four-thirty in the afternoon, the defenders were able to maintain a reasonable relationship with their families. Each attorney was guaranteed vacations and did not feel they were at the mercy of their clients twenty-four hours a day. Most defenders commented that they were able to leave their work behind when they left the office at the end of the day. In summary, working for the Essex defender office was completely compatible with raising a family.

Although there was some grumbling about the inadequacy of their salaries, it was generally viewed as not of major significance. Most defenders were not fixated on financial rewards and found it advantageous to be unconcerned with fiscal problems related to the practice of law, such as finding clients, collecting fees, and paying each month's office expenses. They appreciated the fact that their salaries were guaranteed regardless of the number of clients or the outcome of cases. For a number of defenders, this absence of having to worry about the "bottom line" was a major reason why they were attracted to the office and chose to remain.

Nearly all of the public defenders agreed that dealing with distrustful and unappreciative clients was one of the most distasteful aspects of the job, yet a sizable minority commented that individual defendants could also provide a very positive experience at both the professional and personal level. One respected, middle-aged defender who primarily handled serious felonies was moved by the relationship he could occasionally build with "someone when you are fighting for their life. A powerful connection can be formed." Part of the close relationship, explained another defender with similar experiences, is caused by "you and the client taking on the State. Having everyone against you." Several other attorneys also mentioned the gratification derived from assuming the underdog role. Most defenders found a smattering of clients who were interesting, colorful personalities. Their unusual life experiences, struggling against the difficult economic and social circumstances plaguing their inner city neighborhoods, gained the admiration of several defenders. They often wondered aloud if they could have survived in such a hostile setting. These defenders relished the rare opportunity to help a deserving client.

Negative Aspects of the Job

The job of a public defender in Essex County is not without its frustrations, several of which are seemingly intractable. The local legal culture examined in Chapter Six described several key actors who can make a defender's professional life very unpleasant. Clients, prosecutors, judges, case managers, and their supervisors in Trenton at the AOC combine to form a number of daily irritants for every public defender. Clients continually confound and anger the public defenders for a variety of reasons. The clients' distrust and lack of appreciation are the most common irritants, although their failure to communicate or listen is also annoying. Most defenders noted that their clients could be "real assholes" who believe they know more than the attorneys. They frequently undermine or sabotage the defender's best efforts by their ignorant, selfish, and irrational behavior. Prosecutors can also be an irritant, particularly those whose behavior undermines a mutually beneficial working relationship. Judges who view defenders as if they work for them are also difficult members of the courtroom workgroup. The Essex defenders are especially upset by judges who are either lazy, ignorant, or biased in favor of the prosecution. The final problematic group are the criminal case managers whose administrative priorities are opposed to the public defender's professional responsibilities. The case manager's rigid belief in the critical importance of moving cases and reducing backlogs clashes directly with the defender's obligations to his or her client's best interests (which may, in fact, require calculated, strategic delays). An additional source of tension is the case manager's parent organization, the AOC, which can be even more adamant in their relentless drive for statistics, paperwork, and what several defenders refer to as administrative trivia and "mindless crap."

The public defenders are equally frustrated by problems growing out of systemic weaknesses of the county's chaotic criminal court process. Beginning with the pre-indictment period, defenders complained about the overabundance of cases, most of which wind up being downgraded to disorderly offenses ultimately resolved in the municipal court. Sloppy police work is primarily responsible for this problem although more effective prosecutorial control over the charging process as well as closer judicial scrutiny could also improve the situation. Defenders explained that by improving the front-end resources during intake processing, they would be able to reduce the alarming amount of inaccurate information presently being passed along to them. Defenders often are unable to correct the problem for several months since prosecutors are not required to share discovery until after arraignment. Even more troubling to the defense are the consequences of New Jersey's increasingly severe sentencing laws, particularly with regard to drug cases.

Clients are reluctant to risk trial when the penalty, if convicted, often means a lengthy prison term. The lack of trial options and "loser cases" deprives Essex defenders of their most cherished professional activity–litigation. For most defenders there is little satisfaction to be derived from plea negotiations, even though they may save their clients significant amounts of prison time. The Essex defenders are upset over the impact of the harsh sentencing laws upon their clients.

Professor David Lynch's study of 217 New York State public defenders identified a number of the most aggravating and stressful aspects of their job. These irritating factors included not knowing when a case might be called into trial; having no defense if a case was called (Essex public defenders referred to these as "paper bag cases"); satisfying conflicted parties; dealing with upset clients and families; arguing with prosecutors; and having no trial options because of harsh sentences.[1] Although these complaints may be worded slightly differently, in essence they were repeated by the Essex defenders interviewed for this book. The similarities in findings indicate that these defender frustrations may not be linked to a specific criminal court system's idiosyncratic malfunctions but are probably systemic problems found throughout the country.

Supervising and Accountability

One of the most surprising aspects of the Essex County public defender office was its relaxed work atmosphere, with almost none of the restrictive features usually associated with bureaucratic organizations. As part of the state public defender program with combined legal and support staff totaling almost ninety employees, on paper the office appears to resemble a typical bureaucratic organization. Nevertheless, the staff lawyers operate with a remarkable degree of freedom. The office's leadership (the regional director and his four team leaders), in contrast to the more tightly supervised attorneys in civil law firms, grants a remarkable amount of independence to the individual attorneys. Where private law firms utilize office managers and senior partners to monitor and direct the professional behavior of junior partners and associates, the public defenders are granted near total freedom. Working in pairs within each courtroom, junior and senior defenders coordinate their professional efforts. All of the defenders were in agreement over their independence and lack of supervision, but as one senior attorney noted "if you screw up, you get called in and get nailed to the wall. However, if judges or clients don't call or complain, [deputy director] Mike doesn't care where you are or what you're doing."

The regional deputy director and his team of first assistants have all been in place for over five years, creating a stable work environment. Even though defenders operate with broad discretionary authority, they also know that the director can be counted upon for support and guidance. The director is a calming influence in an organization that functions within an often-chaotic Essex County criminal justice system. Interaction with clients, prosecutors, and judges is frequently stressful. All of the Essex defenders described the director as an empathetic, reasonable person whose friendship and guidance are critical ingredients in the successful operation of the office.

All defenders were conscious of their serious responsibilities, requiring them to provide competent representation for Essex County indigents charged with indictable offenses. Most of the defenders agreed that attorneys whose performance was below average and who were unhappy in the office usually left on their own after a year or two rather than being fired by the director. It did not take novice public defenders very long to realize that they were not suited for the position. There were also occasional problems with senior defenders who suffered from serious medical concerns such as heart conditions or the more common malaise of burnout, produced by too many years on the job. In most instances, these older defenders who were unable to carry out their job were transferred to one of the pre-indictment courts where the work demands were less arduous and more routine, with less serious consequences for ineffective representation.

Redefining Success

The Essex County public defenders have a difficult time distinguishing themselves from their colleagues on any number of criteria that are usually helpful in determining one's rank within an organization. The most common variable available for measuring professional success is one's salary, but the defenders' salaries are determined through union negotiations, calculated primarily on the basis of years of service. There are few opportunities for promotion with only a director and four first assistants. Everyone else is paired off in one of the courtrooms with his or her designated judge. Their small offices are sparsely furnished, with larger corner rooms for the director and his first assistants. Cases are distributed among the defenders randomly with the exception of homicides and capital offenses, which are given to seasoned veterans. Egalitarian principles govern nearly all aspects of the Essex public defender's professional life. Their relative success rates in obtaining dismissals, downgrades, acquittals, entrance into diversion programs, or an advantageous plea bargain are neither discussed nor publicized in office documents. With so few cases going to trial, each defender has only five to ten opportunities a year to achieve an acquittal. Most defenders agree that success at trial is often a function of the unique facts of the case rather than the superlative lawyering skills of the attorney. Every defender complained about being forced to defend an insistent client in a "paper bag case" that was impossible to win.

Important pre-indictment decisions to dismiss, downgrade to a lesser charge, or allow entrance into a diversion program are almost entirely prosecutorial decisions with minimal input from the defense attorney. Nearly all of the defendants indicted negotiate a plea bargain rather than go to trial.

(Less than 5% of all indictments went to trial, 317 out of 6,400 in the year 2000.) A lawyer's skill as a plea negotiator is very difficult to determine because it is based on many extraneous factors such as the defendant's past criminal history and willingness to testify against a co-defendant. The timing of a plea can also be critical. The earlier in the proceeding, the better the deal from the prosecutor. In conclusion, it is very difficult for a public defender to develop a reputation based upon the outcome of his or her clients' cases. The handful of defenders who were most respected in the office were appreciated for their willingness to assist younger lawyers and offer emotional support rather than for compiling an impressive list of courtroom victories.

Private attorneys by contrast have a fairly easy time defining success either personally or relative to other lawyers. The most obvious measure is financial success, easily quantified by salary; additionally, the prestige of the law firm, the size of the office, and the clout of the clients are only slightly less tangible indications of status. Within the firm, position in the office hierarchy—associate, junior partner, senior partner, or managing partner—reinforces the financial success, giving the firm's top partners power to make decisions affecting the entire office. It is also easier to evaluate courtroom success for one's clients in civil cases because most victories or defeats can be defined by the amount of money won or lost.[2] The pressure to succeed is usually greater in private law firms, especially with prestigious corporate firms where the rewards may be greater but the defeats can be catastrophic to one's career. For attorneys in smaller firms or in solo practice, success through legal victories is crucial not only for ego satisfaction but even more important for economic survival. Office rent, secretarial salaries, home mortgages, and college tuitions are all dependent upon the private attorney's legal success.[3]

Essex County public defenders are swamped with loser cases that no one expects them to win. Additionally, the defenders are reconciled to their economic compromise with the State of New Jersey whereby they receive a guaranteed salary, albeit of modest proportions, with a decent benefits package. Their obligation to work in the chaotic environment of the criminal courts in addition to their unimpressive offices on Clinton Street is balanced by a reasonable nine to five workday from Monday through Friday, which permits a reasonable family or social life. As noted earlier, there is likely a self-selection process at work steering young law school graduates seeking money, power, and prestige toward the large corporate law firms while those not so interested in a six-figure salary who have an interest in public service are attracted to legal institutions like the public defender office (especially if the young lawyer has a keen interest in litigation).

Because public defenders are driven by a dual commitment to both the client's best interests as well as their own professional self-esteem, they are forced to redefine success so it can accommodate the unusual realities of their professional position. Complicating the problem further for the Essex defenders is their unusually long tenure with the office. With so many of the staff attorneys having been with the office for over ten years (many of whom are contemplating spending their legal careers in Newark), their egos demand an acceptable, credible formula for measuring success. Although the Essex defenders have similar salaries and offices, especially if they have been with the office a similar amount of time, they nevertheless still feel the need to develop a positive reputation vis-à-vis the other attorneys in the office. All of the Essex lawyers have self-generated images of their own lawyering skills. Interviews with the Essex defenders disclosed near unanimous agreement in identifying a select group of five or six experienced attorneys as being the best lawyers in the office, and an even smaller group (three to four) designated as the office "fuck-ups." Between these two small groups, there was little consensus among the Essex defenders as to where they ranked in this theoretical hierarchy of competence. There was also almost no comparison between defenders regarding specific legal skills such as negotiating pleas, cross-examining witnesses, or drafting effective pretrial motions. The most logical explanation for the absence of evaluations is that so many of these skills are performed behind closed doors, in isolation. Also, there is scarce opportunity for the public defenders to observe each other since they are practicing in separate courtrooms. With heavy caseloads of seventy to eighty cases at any time, defenders are unable to casually wander through the courthouse observing their colleagues in action.

Most defenders admitted that they were forced to construct their own conception of a successful defense attorney, which they would then hold up to the self-evaluation of their professional performance. They would receive an occasional pat on the back from a supervisor or colleague. Clients on rare occasions would also commend them for their lawyering skills. The Essex defenders agreed that they measured their own success relative to what they believed their fellow attorneys were accomplishing. The defenders stated a need to maintain personal standards of performance in order to motivate themselves and then validate their efforts.

During interviews, most public defenders boasted of a courtroom triumph but given the paucity of trials, these isolated victories failed to provide a complete picture of a defender's overall ability. Defenders acknowledged the decisive role played by prosecutors in the dismissal or downgrading of a client's case. The significance of effective plea bargaining was an even more complex question. The Essex public defenders were sharply divided over the relationship between competence as a plea negotiator and professional reputation. Most defenders believed they were successful in a case if they prevented their client from "being screwed." Given the difficult cases handled by the office, this seemingly modest definition of success is probably justified. The prosecution, equally besieged by growing caseloads, rarely brings a case before the grand jury that is not backed up with an impressive amount of evidence, indicating they are fairly confident of victory. Thus, given a client whose conviction appears almost certain, most public defenders pride themselves on their negotiating skills, reducing a client's sentence from a lengthy amount of time in prison to a much shorter sentence or even probation. These Essex defenders believe that it is a victory any time a client's initial exposure is reduced. With so many Essex defendants being charged under New Jersey's harsh drug laws—where first offenders commonly receive two- to five-year prison terms for possession of drugs with intent to sell—any avoidance of state prison is a "major accomplishment," according to one defender. A few Essex defenders thought any plea bargain was not a satisfactory disposition if their client wound up in prison. They could not therefore include supposed "plea bargain victories" into their calculation of a successful performance.

A few Essex defenders refused to take credit for courtroom victories. Their skepticism grew out of a belief that anyone could win with a good set of facts. Since the cases were distributed randomly, a defender simply had to play the hand dealt to the best of his or her ability. If the defender was fortunate enough to have a case where the client was innocent or the set of facts favored the defense, the job was essentially to try to not lose the case. Conversely, a defender did not have to feel bad about losing cases where the prosecution had the advantage. These defenders refused to define the success of their performance in light of the overwhelming significance of the facts. Taking neither blame nor credit also meant a constricted view of the job.

The majority of Essex public defenders refused to evaluate their performance in what they termed the overly simplistic idea of winning or losing, basing their assessment instead on whether they had done a good job. With so many difficult or "loser cases," a public defender cannot gauge his performance by its outcome but rather by the quality of the effort. A defender's self-esteem is therefore primarily the product of a prudent self-evaluation tempered by the comments of colleagues and supervisors. Even though trials may be infrequent, they nevertheless do provide the defining moments in most defenders' legal careers. A few defenders, nearly all women, added an additional criterion for success: improving the social welfare of the client. One defender explained this as "being able to reduce the social malaise engulfing my client." Having a client placed in the drug court or a credible rehabilitation program as well as receive critical psychiatric counseling are all examples of this broader, more humane perspective.

I did not observe the public defenders boasting to one another of courtroom triumphs, although many felt comfortable relating successful moments to me during the interview. They are more likely to tell one another amusing incidents or relate the bizarre behavior of judges and prosecutors. As litigators, they are keenly aware of their adversarial objectives and professional standards of performance. They maintain, albeit rarely voiced, a clear sense of their own competence, particularly relative to the other Essex County defense attorneys, both public and private.

Perceptions of Professional Status

The Essex County public defenders are nearly unanimous in their very positive opinion of the overall high quality of representation by the regional office. The general consensus was that the office had fifteen to twenty very good criminal lawyers with the top five or six being equal to the finest defense attorneys in the northern half of the state. Essex defenders also thought their office was among the best within the statewide system of regional offices. They all believed that they had been improving in recent years with the addition of several excellent young attorneys.

Interviews disclosed, however, that most Essex defenders were aware of their diminished reputation in the minds of the members of the bar (primarily civil practitioners in law firms) as well as the general public. Several defenders commented that they overheard private criminal lawyers on a few occasions speak disparagingly of the Essex office to prospective clients in an effort to gain another client. These had to be isolated incidents since so few defendants are able to afford private counsel (over 90% of Essex defendants are indigent and utilize the public defender office).

After observing the interaction between private criminal lawyers and Essex County public defenders in the courthouse, and after conducting brief interviews with several members of the defense bar, it was clear that private defense attorneys respected the public defenders, especially the fifteen experienced defenders who comprise the top echelon of the Essex Regional office. These sentiments are consistent with the findings from my 1978 research on private criminal lawyers. This eleven-city study in which nearly two hundred private criminal lawyers were interviewed discovered "very little animosity between the public and private criminal defense bar. In several cities, most notably Denver and Washington, D.C., the public defender office went out of its way to help the private bar whenever possible. This usually took the form of conducting seminars on recent decisions as well as mailing out newsletters. . . . Several offices also opened their law libraries to any private practitioner wishing to utilize their facilities." The national sample of private criminal lawyers was consistently irritated by losing potential clients to public defender programs that made little effort to determine the financial capabilities of defendants.

In Essex County, where nearly all of the defendants opt for a public defender leaving only a handful of possible clients for the private defense attorneys, the screening issue has the potential to create serious tensions between the two groups of lawyers. Fortunately, this has not occurred. The reason for the amicable relationship between the private and public defense bar is most likely related to the care and even-handedness with which the Essex defender office distributes multiple-defendant cases to the private attorneys on the pool list. It is also related to an attorney's realistic assessment of the overwhelming percentage of obviously impoverished defendants passing through the intake procedures at the Central Judicial

Processing Unit. Several judges and defense attorneys acknowledged the perceptible decline in the private defense bar during the past thirty years. The small group of private criminal lawyers still practicing defend white-collar criminals and drug dealers, admitting that they are becoming increasingly dependant upon negligence and matrimonial cases.

Local lawyers, working in larger law firms and less conversant with the criminal courts, had a less favorable opinion of the public defenders. They shared the general public's frustration with a group of committed professionals devoted to defending clients accused of serious crimes who were most likely guilty. It was even more upsetting to have these defense lawyers being paid with state monies provided by their tax dollars. The Essex defenders explained this lowly status as a logical by-product of "guilt by association" with their despised clients. The public defenders disclosed that even family and friends had difficulty comprehending how they could waste their legal careers defending criminals. What kind of possible job satisfaction could one achieve by turning these sociopaths back on the streets? Most laymen cannot comprehend the honorable aspect of a public defender's professional responsibility, ensuring that every defendant, regardless of personal wealth, has his or her constitutional right to receive a competent defense upheld. The public defenders also justified their position by explaining that it is actually the prosecutor's failure to prove his or her case beyond a reasonable doubt rather than the ability of the defense attorney that decides a case. One defender repeated the classic rationale offered by the great criminal lawyer Clarence Darrow, who said "if a client of mine tells me a story which is hard to believe, I nonetheless take the story and do the best I can with it to convince the court and jury. If after the conclusion of the trial, after the jury has heard the prosecution's story and my client's story and finally after all twelve have agreed with my client then I am willing to concede that I was wrong in the first place."

Most defenders noted that one positive aspect of the job is its ability to provide countless anecdotes and amusing stories, which prove very entertaining at social gatherings. On a more serious note, nearly all of the senior Essex defenders thought criminal lawyers must operate as lone wolves because of their unpopular clients. They should not be concerned with status or reputation with the general public or legal community. The Essex defenders were in agreement that the only group they wished to impress with their legal skills were their adversaries in the prosecutor's office. As potential opponents, it was useful to develop a reputation as a skilled adversary that might intimidate an inexperienced prosecutor, coercing him or her into offering a favorable plea bargain rather than being humiliated during a trial in open court for all to view. Several senior defenders thought there had been a decline in trials during the past decade due to the improved reputation of their office.

Defendants awaiting trial in the county jail quickly learn the names of the most respected public defenders, but office policy requires random appointments with no chance to choose a more popular alternate. Occasionally a repeat offender's request for the same attorney will be honored, especially if the client is on probation and his or her file has not been officially closed. Several Essex defenders confessed that after a while the drive to win becomes more fueled by one's ego rather than compassion for one's client. When burnout occurs after lengthy service as a public defender, even this ego-driven intensity becomes depleted.

In conclusion, it appears that concern over status and reputation did not trouble most of the public defenders interviewed. Instead they valued the opportunity to litigate challenging cases and work with a group of similarly motivated colleagues.

Office Politics

Given the unique demands of the public defenders' professional environment and the notable strengths of the Essex regional office with its excellent leadership and palpable sense of camaraderie, it is not surprising to find a minimal amount of tension among the staff. Interviews with the defenders disclosed little awareness of office politics or personality conflicts. With union bargaining establishing decent wages (determined primarily by length of service) and few opportunities for promotion, two of the major causes of office bickering had been eliminated. Nevertheless, with a staff of nearly fifty attorneys of widely varying backgrounds and personalities, some conflicts were unavoidable. The analysis of this issue is based primarily upon personal observations over a twelve-month period, although several defenders contributed candid comments. Discussing the tension and divisiveness within an office that prides itself on collegiality and cohesion was a difficult proposition, but fortunately in most instances the defenders spoke honestly and thoughtfully.

Compared to many organizations of similar size, particularly private law firms, the Essex defender office is remarkably diverse. Thirty percent of the attorneys are black, which is three times the national average for public defender programs, and women attorneys make up 30% of the office, which is double the national average. Turning to the socio-economic status of the Essex defenders' parents, the office is divided equally among working class/blue collar, middle class (non-professional), and professional. In contrast to national statistics that show most public defender offices badly over-represented by attorneys with less than five years experience (approximately three-fourth of the typical defender program), the Essex office is divided into four fairly equal groups: 23% with less than ten years experience, 32% with eleven to fifteen years, 21% with sixteen to twenty years and 24% with over twenty years of service. In her book on the Chicago (Cook County) public defender program, Lisa McIntyre described the abbreviated tenure of defenders as a "transit station on the road to a career."[4] McIntyre found that 55% of the city's defenders left the program before completing five years of service.[5] This figure grew to 83% by the end of ten years. In sharp contrast to the nationally renowned Cook County program, the Essex office lost only 23% of its staff by the tenth year, and nearly half of the lawyers had been with the program for over fifteen years.

What, if any, are the consequences of the notable diversity found within the Essex regional office legal staff? First examining the sensitive issue of race, there did not appear to be any perceptible tensions affecting social interaction or professional performance caused by the color of an attorney's skin. One middle-aged black woman defender agreed that "racism doesn't seem to cloud the professional behavior," but cautioned that "once it comes up black lawyers will not let it go underground." She also emphasized that race was an important issue because of their client base (nearly all the defendants are black) and all attorneys needed to be sensitized to their problems. Another black woman attorney observed that "issues of race are present wherever you go and people will rarely be honest about it so it is very difficult to get an accurate understanding of the problem." An experienced white woman attorney endorsed these comments, adding her own awareness of racial cleavages within the office although there was no actual hostility between the groups, just social distance. The more experienced female black defenders were the most outspoken on racial issues, while black men and younger black women were more assimilated into the mainstream and expressed less concern over the question. A number of the older black women decorated their offices with African paintings and artifacts exhibiting pride in their ancestry.

For white attorneys, race had little salience. It was an accepted fact of office life that even though there was no memory of race-based incidents, there was a natural clustering of social groups by race—but these may have been more influenced by the lawyer's age than skin color. The omnipresent collegiality, each attorney's demanding work schedule, and the director's effective, relaxed style of leadership combined to create a color-blind work environment. It is also unlikely that a racially biased lawyer would consider coming to the Essex County defender program given the overwhelming percentage of black defendants he or she would have to represent.

Gender issues also do not have much significance within the Essex office. A few women did note that most of the senior male defenders remained with the office because of their love of litigation. Their competitive drive was fueled by the intellectual and emotional excitement derived from trying a case before a jury. By contrast, many of the women said their reasons for staying with the office were related to gaining satisfaction from working with their clients and trying to assist them in getting their chaotic lives back into some sort of livable order. These women also enjoyed trying cases, but the social satisfaction derived from helping their clients was even more rewarding.

One obvious split within the Essex office is a generational divide, although its boundaries are easily crossed. The chasm is partially created by the more senior attorneys having their offices on the seventh floor of the Clinton Street offices while most of the younger attorneys are located on the floor below.

The senior attorneys are divided into two distinct groups. One group includes the most senior defenders in the office, all with over twenty years of service. Nearly all of them work long hours in one of the pre-indictment courts, rarely venturing down the hill from the courthouse (except possibly to pick up a paycheck). Several members of this group suffer from physical ailments such as a heart condition. A few appear to be burned-out emotionally, unable to satisfy the demanding responsibilities of going to trial.

A second group of experienced attorneys has between ten to twenty years of service. This group is predominantly white and male. They are found on the seventh floor down the hall from the director's office. They include many of the top litigators in the office and are respected both inside and outside the office for their lawyering skills. Most are on the edge of having to decide whether or not to remain with the office for the rest of their careers or take a last chance on leaving the office for a more lucrative position in the private sector. This group is the most social and convivial of any in the office. They can be heard regularly during the lunch hour laughing and gossiping in the library, as well as in afternoon "schmooze" sessions in smaller groups clustering around one another's offices. Their animated conversations are open to everyone, frequently attracting younger attorneys who depend upon this group's collective wisdom. I believe the oft-mentioned *esprit de corps* of the Essex defender office emanates directly from this group of talented, personable attorneys who thrive on both the social and intellectual challenges of their position.

Two additional divisions within the Essex defenders office were noted by a sufficient number of staff attorneys to merit discussion. First is an inevitable tension created by noticeable differences in the abilities of certain attorneys. Several defenders identified a small group of lawyers who "did not pull their weight" or were characterized as barely competent. Since it is difficult to fire staff members, the slack must be picked up by the more competent lawyers who, occasionally voiced their resentment over "being penalized for doing a good job." With union-negotiated wages failing to sufficiently reward exemplary performance, most of the defenders deal with office inequities by trying not to be over-concerned with them. They commit themselves to continued excellence out of personal pride. Despite efforts to get past this annoying problem, there is an undercurrent of griping about "office slackers."

A second mildly divisive factor mentioned by a few of the Essex defenders is the existence of a small group of attorneys who are somewhat to the political left of most of the office, which is overall fairly liberal. The small fringe group is jokingly referred to by a few as the "pinkoes" or the "lefty do-gooders." It is mainly composed of women who tend to view their clients in a larger social context, beyond the specific criminal charges a client is facing. They are likely to recognize the defendant's humanity and identify social, economic, and emotional factors that contributed to his or her criminal behavior. They also express greater concern over the defendant's future survival after the conclusion of his or her pending legal matter. The abundance of young clients with serious drug and alcohol addictions who come from dysfunctional families and are facing serious charges only heightens these defenders' social and political position on any ideological spectrum.

Fortunately, the leadership abilities of the regional director along with several of his first assistants prevents any potentially divisive factors from interfering with the office's superior professional performance, nor does it appear to undermine the overall collegiality of the office. The director plays no favorites, maintaining an open-door policy for all attorneys regardless of seniority. He rarely meddles in the quiet grumbling that is inevitable in any bureaucratic organization made up of more than a hundred individuals. The overall impact of the various divisive factors seems negligible, especially with regard to the quality of representation achieved by the office. A large measure of the credit for maintaining such a positive, professional work environment goes to the regional director but nearly all of the defenders were equally committed to this goal. Those attorneys who did not buy into this perspective were allowed to go off and "do their own thing," as long as their professional responsibilities were satisfied.

There was a general consensus among Essex defenders that although office politics was of minor importance in the regional office, it was a very different situation at the Statewide Defender Headquarters in Trenton. The recent unexpected death of State Defender Ivy Torres, a Republic appointee (during Governor Christine Whitman's administration), elevated one of her top assistants, Robert Garcia, to the top spot of interim director. Upon assuming this position, Garcia immediately began reorganizing the appellate division, forcing out three of the most experienced attorneys. Within a year, a new Democratic governor, James McGreevy, was elected, so it is likely that Garcia's time in office will be brief. The top leadership position of state defender has been given to a qualified Hispanic attorney in recent years, although the Trenton office presently seems to be in a state of flux. There has also been a long-standing rivalry between public defenders from the northern and southern halves of the Garden State, which further complicates the struggle for control of the agency. Essex defenders calmly analyzed the forthcoming battle in Trenton but were confident that it was unlikely to have meaningful consequences for their regional office.

A new state director was hired in 2003. As predicted by several, Garcia's replacement came from one of the northern counties and was in fact Yvonne Segars, a first assistant with strong credentials from the Essex County regional office.

Burnout and the Problems of an Aging Office

There are many positive aspects to having an office filled with experienced attorneys, but sometimes this can reach the point of diminishing returns. In a stressful job with a highly repetitive, depressing series of unappreciative clients, it is no wonder that problems of burnout are a serious concern. One-fourth of Essex County's public defenders have been with the office for over twenty years. Nearly all of the most senior attorneys candidly admit that they have grown increasingly cynical. As one twenty-year veteran explained, "After you've been around too long you become jaded, don't listen to your clients, and rationalize as to why defendants should all plead." A difficult job market has forced some defenders to remain with the office longer than they intended, further exacerbating the burnout problem.

Little can be done to alleviate the problem, so most accept burnout as a hazard of the profession. It is generally acknowledged that almost no one is fired so the director must rotate positions or assign the burned-out defender to one of the less demanding pre-indictment courts. Estimates of the number of senior defenders suffering from burnout were consistently placed at around four or five attorneys. This means that more than half of the most experienced attorneys are doing acceptable work as they move within five years of retirement. One senior defender who admits to being burned out and "hanging around too long," describes his work in one of the pre-indictment courts as a "mindless, legal purgatory." The Essex director was frustrated because he had little flexibility in dealing with personnel problems, but he tries to remain sensitive to the problems of long-term defenders. A related problem caused by having an entrenched staff that has been with the office for a lengthy period of time is the inevitable occurrence of numerous health and disability emergencies. Nearly half of the lawyers working in the pre-indictment courts are either suffering or recovering from a serious medical condition such as a heart problem or hypertension. Twenty years of stressful defense work with frustrating clients is blamed for the various health problems, especially with the defenders who have a family history of high blood pressure, heart disease, and intestinal disorders. The director and several other public defenders noted that another factor contributing to burnout was the lack of positive incentives available for superior performance, compounded by the absence of approval or appreciation from judges, clients, or other members of the bar outside the office. This forces each defender to become self-motivated, driven by personal standards and goals. It is often difficult to sustain inner-directed achievements for an entire career without some tangible rewards.

A few of the younger attorneys who have between five and ten years service voiced concern over the burnout problem because the office has become so top-heavy with a growing number of dispirited public defenders who do not appear to be pulling their weight. They were mildly critical of the leadership's inability to correct what they viewed as a serious problem. These younger attorneys are quickly approaching a critical time in their professional careers when they must decide whether or not to remain with the office until retirement. They are troubled by the crowded job market and the recurring economic downturns that are likely to continue to diminish their future employment opportunities. They fear being trapped in a job that can wear them down both physically and emotionally. They are already considering how they can afford a larger home for their growing family, as well as being able to pay for their children's college education.

Comparisons with Private Criminal Lawyers

Essex public defenders are keenly aware of their private counterparts, holding firm opinions about the relative strengths and weaknesses of each group. The defenders were unanimous in declaring their guaranteed salaries and reasonable hours to be major advantages over the majority of private criminal lawyers who were continually struggling to survive economically. The defenders thought the job provided the flexibility necessary to raise children and enjoy their family. In contrast to private attorneys in solo practice, the defenders always had a dependable colleague to rely on if an emergency required their absence from the office. Essex defenders were especially pleased to avoid going out "hustling for clients," and then doggedly harassing them to collect a fee. Even though their salaries were described as modest or adequate, it was worth it not to have to be concerned with the bottom line. The congenial office atmosphere allowed the defenders to relax away from the courthouse in the company of friends. Unfortunately, private criminal lawyers work largely in isolation with only their strong egos to sustain them in difficult times.

Most public defenders believed that they were better-qualified criminal lawyers than most of the private attorneys on the pool list. The defenders recognized four or five excellent private criminal lawyers who they found very impressive, but beyond this elite group they were confident of their superiority in the criminal law field. Several defenders were annoyed by private lawyers on the pool list who always requested assistance. It reinforced their opinion that the local bar was both disinterested and ignorant of the criminal law, especially its more complex points. The defenders were frustrated when observing the pool attorneys making numerous mistakes in the courtroom. It was acknowledged by nearly all of the Essex defenders that some private criminal lawyers had distinct advantages, particularly in their relationship with judges and prosecutors. Examining the judiciary first, the defenders agreed that private attorneys received preferential treatment in terms of scheduling cases. Judges, especially those who had practiced privately before coming to the bench, tried to accommodate the private lawyers in most situations. Public defenders thought judges treated them as if they were courtroom functionaries while private attorneys were placed on a more elevated professional plane. Private attorneys were given greater latitude in the courtroom and permitted a degree of zealous advocacy that the defenders felt was rarely granted to them. The defenders thought this discrepancy was a function of their continuous presence in front of the same judge for a year, while a private attorney would travel from courtroom to courtroom, facing a wide array of judges. A private attorney's isolated appearance before any judge broke the monotony of the public defenders' monopolization of the court's caseload.

The Essex defenders also believed private attorneys had numerous advantages in dealing with prosecutors. Many of the private criminal lawyers are former prosecutors who continue to have friends in the office. Private lawyers were charged with using these past and present associations in order to obtain beneficial plea bargains for their clients. Younger prosecutors were often in awe of successful private attorneys, intimidated by their stature, and fearful of opposing them in a trial. One experienced public defender summarized the situation by stating that the prosecutors "see us [defenders] all the time as we share the same courtroom for a year at a time. It is a clear case of familiarity breeding contempt." Another public defender thought private attorneys often had an easier time controlling their clients than public defenders. He reasoned "because the defendants are paying a lot of money for their attorney, they are more likely to show up for appointments and assist in their defense." Defendants who can afford a private attorney are viewed by their contemporaries as having achieved an impressive status, whereas those unfortunate defendants forced to rely on a public defender are to be pitied. Private attorneys also benefit because most of their clients are able to raise the required bail and obtain pretrial freedom. These defendants can assist their attorneys more easily than indigent defendants represented by public defendants, who must remain in the county jail because of the inability to make bail. Several public defenders added that private attorneys seem to have an easier time disposing of cases during pre-indictment. They have a perceptively better record of getting their clients in pretrial diversion programs, drug court, and other rehabilitation programs, which can lead to suspended sentences without incarceration. They also appear more effective in obtaining downgrades and dismissals during the first month or two following arrest. Public defenders complained that their effectiveness during the pre-indictment period is limited because of a heavy caseload that often includes forty to fifty pre-indictment cases, which languish while the defenders spend most of their time on post-indictment cases approaching trial or plea settlements.

Few Essex public defenders choose to become private criminal lawyers when they leave the office. They are all too aware of the drawbacks and difficulties of practicing criminal law. They prefer to apply their litigation skills to the more lucrative practice of civil law with a successful law firm.

Despite some subtle advantages just noted, the Essex defenders did not believe that there were significant differences in the outcomes achieved by either public or private criminal lawyers. If Essex County follows national trends reported by the U.S. Justice Department's Bureau of Justice Statistics in November 2000, both types of counsel have nearly identical conviction rates. The study by Caroline Harlow discovered that 71% of private counsel cases were settled by guilty pleas, compared to 72% for public counsel. Private attorneys were able to obtain acquittals in 1.3% of cases, while public counsel acquittals were 1.6%. Both groups had 4% of their cases end in conviction after trial.[6] The report also found that clients of both private and public counsel received about the same sentences in cases involving violent crime or property crime, although private-counsel defendants sentenced in drug cases fared slightly better, receiving lighter sentences.[7] Statistics from the AOC and the Essex County criminal case manager do show that the regional public defenders are far more successful in trials, gaining acquittals nearly 50% of the time.

CHAPTER EIGHT

Lessons Learned: An Agenda for Public Defender Reform

The preceding five chapters have presented a comprehensive examination of a relatively effective public defender reform program operating in Essex County (Newark), New Jersey. Although the Essex experience may prove useful to other jurisdictions attempting to implement a public defender reform program, many public defender agencies during the past twenty-five to thirty years have developed their own reform models. These defender agencies have sought to escape from the inhibiting institutional and operational problems undermining traditional defender programs (similar to the New York and Chicago programs discussed in Chapter Two). A reform program generally attempts to gain adequate funding in order to become a more viable adversary to the prosecutor. Several jurisdictions have created state-run agencies to guarantee adequate funding. Additionally, many reform programs have implemented merit-based hiring and promotion policies designed to minimize the amount of political interference and hopefully guarantee the necessary independence from outside political pressure. The reform goal has been to create working conditions that will encourage staff attorneys to remain with the defender agencies for a longer period of service, creating a stable, professional environment. Along these same lines, many reform defender agencies have also tried representing the client with a vertical, or man-to-man, coverage, with the same attorney remaining with the defendant through the entire dispositional process. This contrasts with most traditional systems still utilizing the horizontal or zone coverage, which allows for a continual shifting of attorneys at nearly every stage of the dispositional process.

The first section of this concluding chapter will analyze one of the more successful reform defender agencies, located in Washington, D.C. It is an

interesting and somewhat unique alternative model of a reform defender
agency. The subsequent sections of the chapter will offer a series of conclusions based primarily upon the extensive analysis of the Essex regional
office and its capability as a successful paradigm for other jurisdictions
attempting to reform the local public defender agency.

A Unique Reform Alternative: The Washington, D.C. Defender Service

The District of Columbia's Public Defender Service, blessed with ample
financial support from the federal government, has been a model program
since its inception in 1960. Initially named the Legal Aid Agency, in 1970 it
was renamed the Public Defender Service and given broader responsibilities
beyond simply defending indigent defendants. It is an independent agency of
the District, governed by an eleven-member board of trustees. It presently
employs approximately one hundred attorneys, with a support staff of another
hundred individuals including twenty-eight investigators. In contrast with the
Essex County defender office and most other public defender programs
across the country, the District's Public Defender Service (PDS) operates not
only a trial division but also several additional divisions responsible for juvenile clients, appeals, offender rehabilitation, drug court, mental health cases,
parole violations (Special Litigations Division), and civil legal services.

Beyond its far-ranging programs and the absence of financial problems,
the D.C. defender agency is distinguished by its hiring and training programs. The training program begins each October, lasting nearly eight
weeks. It combines teaching trial practice techniques with substantive lec-
tures on criminal law. The beginning staff attorneys also learn how to conduct field investigations. The training session ends with a mock trial
competition before a panel of D.C. superior court judges. The defenders
continue their legal education during their tenure with the PDS with informal mentoring twice-monthly sessions organized into trial practice groups.
The novice attorneys are assigned to a trial practice group under the leadership of a senior colleague. They receive instruction in recent changes in the
criminal law, discuss case strategy, and celebrate the courtroom victories of
their fellow attorneys. A final educational program is PDS's Criminal Practice Institute, a two-day annual conference where prominent defense attorneys present seminars on courtroom advocacy, constitutional law, and
various topics related to indigent defense services. The conference produces
a two-volume treatise entitled *Criminal Practice Institute Manual*, a bible for
Washington-area criminal lawyers. Although the Essex public defenders
engage in a useful informal educational process relying on the mentoring of
young attorneys by senior colleagues, it pales in comparison to the Washington defender services' excellent training programs.

Because of the excellent reputation of the PDS the agency is able to
choose new attorneys from hundreds of applicants. In recent years, PDS has

averaged five hundred applicants for about ten vacancies. The standardized hiring procedures bring each year's class together in October for the training session. In 2002, the pay scale extended from an annual salary of $40,000 for recent law school graduates who had not yet passed the D.C. bar to a sliding scale between $47,000 to $63,000 depending on the number of years of legal experience. Every new attorney hired is required to make a three-year commitment to the office. Applicants came from a broad national sample, with representatives from many of the finest law schools.

Despite the attractive program and the three-year commitment, the PDS does not retain many lawyers beyond five years of service. The Washington defender agency maintains a fairly small group of senior attorneys in contrast to the Essex regional office, which has a majority of its attorney staff with more than ten years of experience. The Washington defender program also differs from Essex County in the speed with which beginning attorneys are thrown into the courtroom defending clients accused of serious crimes. The District's PDS carefully prepares the young lawyers by having them spend the first year working in the juvenile courts. In the next few years they are allowed to represent adult defendants in misdemeanor bench trials and less serious felony cases. During the first few years PDS staff attorneys are monitored by a designated supervisor. They are also given the opportunity to serve as co-counsel in felony cases involving senior citizens.

Since 1970 when Congress enacted the Criminal Justice Act (CJA) for the District, the PDS has had to share the indigent defendants caseload with the city's private criminal lawyers. The 1970 law mandates that the private bar be responsible for the less serious cases (including traffic offenses) as well as multiple-defendant cases raising conflict-of-interest issues. The act also requires the Washington defender agency to operate a CJA office to assist the court in the selection and assignment of private attorneys to these cases. The PDS maintains a panel list that presently includes over three hundred private attorneys wishing to defend indigent defendants. The city's public defender office interviews all defendants to determine if they qualify for the office's services. Following a determination of indigency, the office facilitates the appointment of a CJA private attorney to the proper case. The PDS justifies its decision to keep the more serious cases for itself because of the office's superior resources. To assist in the continuing legal education of the CJA attorneys, the PDS offers a summer training program in June and July that covers a wide range of criminal law issues including a new series of seminars on juvenile delinquency practice.

The trial division of the D.C. defender agency maintains a "duty day" staff attorney available every business day to answer questions from the general public, make referrals to outside agencies, answer legal questions for members of the D.C. bar, and provide "boiler plate" sample pleading to CJA. lawyers. On occasion they also receive requests from judges to provide substitute legal counsel in difficult cases. The District's Public Defender Service is divided into five major divisions that exemplify the breadth of operations.

The trial division employs sixty-three attorneys to represent indigent adults charged with felonies and serious misdemeanors. They also defend juveniles charged with serious acts of delinquency. Once an attorney has been assigned a case by a panel of superior court judges, the defender will remain with the client through all stages of proceedings until final disposition. Since 1970 the PDS has maintained an appellate division manned by twelve attorneys. They not only file numerous briefs for their PDS clients but also handle requests from the D.C. court of appeals for *amicus cutiae* briefs involving unusual or complex legal issues. The division also conducts a monthly lunchtime training series on various topics related to current appellate issues.

The mental health division (MHD) utilizes seven lawyers and two social workers to assist D.C. residents who need legal assistance because they have been involuntarily committed for treatment of mental illness. The division works out of the city's mental hospital, St. Elizabeth's. The MHD lawyers have recently developed a community-based, comprehensive treatment alternative for mentally ill people in the criminal justice system who are charged with less serious offenses. A fourth section is the special litigation division, which is responsible for post-conviction litigation on behalf of inmates and parolees. The main job of the ten attorneys assigned to this division is to represent clients before the U.S. Parole Commission who are facing revocation because they have been arrested on a new criminal charge or a technical violation of community supervision requirements. The legal staff also spends increasing amounts of time writing *habeas corpus* petitions for clients who are being detained for long periods of time while the Parole Commission slowly moves through its heavy backlog. The most recently created division is the Civil Legal Services Unit, which employs its eight attorneys to address issues defendants face in the difficult effort to re-integrate back into the community. This unit deals with a wide range of complex corollary issues such as civil forfeiture, eviction, denial of public benefits, and deportation.

The Washington public defenders are assisted by an excellent group of investigators who are aided by an innovative intern program. The program has been in existence for twenty-five years. Each semester fifty to eighty college students are chosen for the program, which begins with an intensive training component. The qualified students are then assigned in pairs to attorneys in the trial division. The interns usually work on less serious cases, assisting junior staff attorneys while full time investigators work on the more serious cases.

Washington's public defender program is endowed with abundant funding and political independence, two factors distinguishing it from the New York and Chicago programs. The District's program differs from Essex County in its breadth of specialized programs. It takes an unusual holistic approach to the problems of the indigent clients, encompassing their mental health, their addiction problems, and a variety of parolee issues related to re-entry into society. The best example of the District's broad approach to client problems is PDS's newly developed Division of Offender Rehabilitation. Staff attorneys work with social workers in an effort to assist the client as he or she deals with mental, educational, and economic difficulties. The Essex County defenders' involvement in their local drug court is a commendable multi-faceted attack upon their clients' problems but falls far short in comparison to the District's well-funded program intelligently designed to break the dysfunctional lifestyle strangling so many of their clients. Beyond the wide range of programs offered by the District's PDS, the adult trial divisions of Essex County and Washington are quite similar. They both provide continuous vertical representation of clients, operate in a non-politicized environment, and are assisted by excellent support services. It would be interesting to see how the Essex defender office might expand client services to more closely approximate the Washington, D.C. model if the office had the benefit of federal budgetary assistance.

A Comparison of Four Cities

It might be expected that four large, post-industrial cities with high crime rates would operate their public defender programs in a similar fashion. It is therefore somewhat surprising to learn of the significant differences among the New York, Chicago, Washington, and Newark (Essex County) defender programs. The primary similarity shared by all four programs is the high percentage of cases disposed of by guilty pleas, with only a handful of cases going to trial.

Despite the similarities in clients and disposition rates, the four cities operate markedly different defender programs. There is wide variation in the degree of politicization, adequacy of funding, stability of personnel, and quality of leadership. The differences in institutional and procedural variables have caused each program to develop a unique work environment. The attorneys working as defenders in each city develop contrasting professional relationships with other actors in the justice system (i.e., judges, prosecutors, and case managers) as well as the rest of the local bar.

The independence of a public defender program from political influence is a critical variable affecting the ability of a defender to be a viable adversary. Most clients believe that public defenders are inherently flawed by their financial dependence on the same public treasury that also funds judges and prosecutors. This book, however, has described public defender programs with perceptible differences in their political environments. The defender programs in New York City and to a lesser degree in Cook County are directly affected by political pressure. New York City's Legal Aid Society has been the most pervasively entangled in politics as a result of its continued confrontations with Mayors Giuliani and Koch. Since the threatened strike in 1994 the society has lost a third of its caseload. After publicly chastising the society, the mayor forced it to compete for new contracts in each borough on an annual basis. In Chicago, the Democratic Party controls most city agencies in terms of personnel and policy decisions, and the public defender program also falls under that influence. Undermining professional independence even further, the city's chief defender is selected by a Committee of the Judiciary that also has an influence on the appointment of all new staff attorneys.

The Washington, D.C. Public Defender Service and the Essex County regional defender office are equally free of political pressure. Washington's PDS is federally funded while the Essex defender program is part of a statewide system with headquarters in Trenton. Both defender agencies are significantly better funded than their Chicago and New York counterparts. With better salaries and a respectable benefits package, the District and Essex defenders are encouraged to remain with the office for long periods of time. Their fiscal advantages also produce better support services, such as investigative staff, regular access to expert witnesses, and the development of special programs for addicted clients.

By providing decent salaries and a professional work environment, the District and Essex defender programs are able to attract high-quality recent law school graduates and retain them for many years. The stable Essex defender office has more than half of its legal staff remaining with the program for more than a decade. By comparison, the Cook County and New York City defenders rarely stay for more than three to four years, most viewing the time as a "transit stop" in their legal careers as they move toward a high-paying position in a prestigious law firm.

A major factor contributing to the quality of professional life of a public defender program is the effectiveness of the office's leadership. Essex County's success is directly related to its excellent regional deputy director who has earned the loyal support of his entire office. They appear deeply appreciative of his even-handed, intelligent style of leadership. Washington D.C.'s public defenders have also benefited from a tradition of competent leaders. The Chicago and New York leadership, by contrast, has been in an embattled position in recent years, subject to the shifting political current that has been especially tempestuous in New York. It is true that most staff attorneys battling within an entrenched criminal justice system and representing recalcitrant clients are too busy to ponder the political games played by their office's leadership. Nevertheless, these supervising officials can set a tone if they are persistently threatened from above, which can ultimately affect the entire office. The Legal Aid Society in New York has the additional problem of being challenged by competing contract law firms and private defense attorneys working as 18-B lawyers. The Public Defenders Service in Washington peacefully co-exists with the three hundred CJA-panel private defense attorneys, although the assigned counsel are usually relegated to the less serious cases.

Although the Essex defender office participates in the excellent county drug court, the Washington defender office is noteworthy for its development and operation of a wide range of special programs including a drug court and offender rehabilitation unit, as well as special civil litigation and parole violation units. It is an impressive and unique effort to attack their clients' broader socioeconomic problems, which no other city's defender agency is presently attempting.

This chapter has shown that the Essex and Washington, D.C. public defender offices are distinguished by stable, adequately funded, apolitical, independent programs. The result is a system of indigent defense in which the staff attorneys operate within a supportive, professional work environment. In contrast, the New York and Cook County defender agencies are overwhelmed and, especially in New York City, in constant flux. All four programs appear to have been operating in their unique styles for a fairly long period of time, which raises serious concern over the ease and likelihood of improving the quality of their services. Nevertheless, the impressive work environments found within the Washington and Essex County defender programs certainly offer guidelines for improving the quality of indigent defense.

Early Expectations Revisited

Public defender programs, especially those operating in large cities, are usually described as bureaucratic organizations. I was expecting to find the Essex County defender office, which has a forty-seven person legal staff and an additional fifty support personnel, to closely correspond to these bureaucratic norms of structure and behavior. Standard features of bureaucratic organizations as described by sociologists such as Max Weber and others depict a clearly defined hierarchical structure, with power passing down the line of command.[1] The required regimen for each office or sub-division is clarified through a rather rigid list of operating procedures. Individuals within the organization are discouraged from using personal discretion. Instead, they are to follow the unambiguous rules of behavior, which are applied equally without consideration of individual idiosyncrasies. The members of an idealized bureaucracy are like cogs in a well-oiled machine; no member of the organization is irreplaceable so when someone fails to satisfy the requisite standards of performance he or she will be removed and replaced by a new "cog." The blueprint or organizational plan of an archetypal bureaucratic institution permits one at a glance to comprehend its flow of power between units of the organization, as well as delineate their prescribed responsibilities.

A second expectation, related to the bureaucratic ethos of most public defender programs, involves the type of lawyers attracted to these legal bureaucracies, especially their anticipated length of service and ultimate career aspirations. Young lawyers are thought to select work in a public defender office (or even with a prosecutor's office) as a "way station" in their legal career, providing useful litigation experience that will be beneficial in moving on to their first "real" job as a lawyer with a law firm. This explains why most lawyers spend less than three years with a public defender office. Another group of beginning attorneys join a public defender office with more idealized goals, wishing to defend wrongly accused defendants. They often initially view clients as victims of an insensitive criminal justice system as well as broader socioeconomic forces that trap them in a cycle of poverty. These "bleeding hearts" according to many accounts soon become disillusioned, frustrated because of hostile, unappreciative clients. These lawyers also rarely last more than three years, defeated by the disappointing futility of their professional efforts.

Public defender agencies are also thought to attract those recent law school graduates who because of low grades or lack of professional contacts are unable to join a preferred private law firm. The social preferences of some of these firms may also explain why large numbers of women and minorities choose public service agencies such as a defender program.

Regardless of what motivated a young lawyer to choose to begin his or her professional career with a public defender program, nearly all of them begin looking for a new job after about two years with the agency. Unfortunately, not all of these beginning attorneys are successful in making the jump into private practice or some other type of more desirable professional opportunity. If a move is not made by the fifth year, it is likely that the defender may be stuck in the office for a long time, because the longer one stays, the more difficult it is to find new employment. These attorneys who are unable to leave inevitably become frustrated and after a few years are burned out, a term that describes attorneys who have lost the competitive edge as well as the requisite concern over their clients' best interests. They are simply riding out the time until they can retire. Fortunately, given the high percentage of public defenders leaving within three years, the number of burnouts is kept to a minimum, but even a small number of dispirited attorneys can undermine the enthusiasm of an entire office. In her study of Chicago's public defender office, Lisa McIntyre discovered that three-fourths of the staff had been there for less than five years and only 10% of the defenders had been there for over ten years.[2]

In comparison to prosecutors, it is generally assumed that public defenders are generally at a disadvantage and the weaker adversary. The prosecutor's office offers the same opportunity for trial experience as the defender's but it is usually able to pay higher salaries and is considered a much more respected public agency, protecting the local citizens by punishing criminals who threaten the safety of society. Additionally, the prosecution usually employs a significantly larger number of investigators to assist the young staff attorneys. Not surprisingly, prosecutors can usually depend on the assistance of the police in the gathering of evidence and in many instances they can also receive support from the judiciary in terms of favorable rulings. Both groups combine to give the prosecutor an adversarial advantage in most cases. All three appear bound by their professional obligation to protect society. The police and prosecutor often work closely together, controlling access to information that might prove useful to the defense. It is little wonder that the public defender and his or her client are rather pessimistic in overcoming the prosecutor's numerous advantages, which can on occasion be reinforced by the judiciary.

Beyond the legal difficulties facing public defenders in the courtroom is the equally frustrating problem of lack of respect from clients and the general public. This attitude is reflected in the oft-quoted article by Jonathon Casper entitled "Did You Have a Lawyer When You Went to Court? No, I Had a Public Defender," which appeared in the *Yale Review of Law and Social Action*.[3] Most defendants' view their public defender as merely another agent of the state, whose allegiance is closer to the prosecutor and judge than to the client. Already upset by an inability to pay for an attorney of their own choice, indigent defendants are skeptical about the quality and commitment of their public defender. They believe in the widely accepted adage that "you get what you pay for," and since they are not paying anything they must not be receiving a legal defense worth anything. Adding to their cynicism is a belief that if the public defender was any good the defender would be out in private practice. The youth and inexperience of many public defenders further compounds the problem.

Most private practitioners, particularly those working in civil law firms with little exposure to the local criminal justice system, are also thought to be rather critical of public defenders, placing them near the bottom of the legal profession's pecking order. The private practitioners reason, in a rather self-serving way, that if the public defenders were better lawyers they would be employed in private firms, members of the private practitioners' own elite bar associations. The basis for the low opinion of the general public toward public defenders is largely based on "guilt by association," as well as an ignorance of the due process guarantees of the U.S. Constitution. Most laymen cannot grasp how a defender is willing to make a career out of representing so many obviously guilty clients. What kind of personal reward can a public defender gain from returning these "criminals" to the streets where it will only be a matter of time before they commit a new crime? Even friends and family members have a difficult time comprehending why a trained attorney would join a public defender office, rejecting the status and income offered by private law firms to become a "legal pariah."

When I was about to begin my empirical study of the Essex County office, I reviewed in my mind the rather depressing expectations of a public defender's professional life. I envisioned a group of beleaguered, frustrated, and minimally competent young attorneys. They were cogs in the criminal justice assembly line, unable to do more than stand alongside their clients as they traveled on an inexorable path toward probation or prison. The only way for these young defenders to extricate themselves from this professional morass was to find a new position as quickly as possible. Those unable to make an early escape would soon burnout and disappear quietly from view.

After more than a year of interviewing and observing the Essex County regional defender office, it was both surprising and gratifying to learn that nearly all of my previously held expectations were not valid characterizations of the Newark-based defender program. The most striking finding was the low turnover rate in the Essex regional office where over three-fourths of the lawyers had been with the office over ten years. A positive by-product of this stable office was the obvious camaraderie that infused the office. The staff attorneys were initially attracted to the defender office because of the opportunity it offered to gain trial experience. The staff's love of litigation continued to be an important factor in the decision to stay with the office, although the excellent leadership and supportive work environment were also important. Despite the Essex regional office's structural similarity to most other public defender organizations, the individual staff attorneys were granted broad discretionary powers. The director trusted his staff to perform at a high level of professionalism, and they responded positively to being "treated like adults." Another important feature of the office was its vertical system of defense, with an attorney remaining with his or her client from the initial assignment until final disposition of the case. The entire post-indictment representation would occur before a single judge to which the defender was assigned for approximately one year.

My expectations regarding the efficacy of the prosecutors, especially with regard to their expected dominance over the public defender also failed to materialize. It was discovered that as part of a statewide defender program, the Essex County regional office was able to offer salaries and provide support staff that were clearly superior to the county prosecutor's office. In New Jersey the prosecutors are dependent primarily on county rather than state funding. This causes significant variation in prosecutorial salaries around the state. Essex County not only suffers from high poverty and crime rates in several large blighted areas in Newark and surrounding communities but also has a weakened tax base as many of its wealthier citizens move farther west beyond the county's boundaries.

The county's financial woes have directly affected the capacity of the prosecutor's office to offer salaries that are equal to those of the defender office. Additionally, funds for support services such as expert witnesses and forensic scientists as well as for professional development also fail to match those available to Essex County defenders through the state defender agency. Compounding the fiscal deficiencies is the persistent influence of politics, most apparent in the key leadership positions but with ramifications felt throughout the entire organization. These financial and political problems have caused a high turnover rate, losing experienced, competent prosecutors who were replaced by large numbers of recent law school graduates. The youthful prosecutors are constantly looking over their shoulders for direction and support. It is not surprising to find the Essex regional defenders both confident and relatively successful in their professional dealings with their prosecutorial adversaries.

Although public defenders can be expected to represent 70% to 80% of the criminal cases according to national studies conducted by the National Institute of Justice, it is surprising to learn that the Essex public defenders handle over 90% of all adult felony cases in the county. (Misdemeanors are handled by municipal public defenders and assigned counsel depending on the magnitude of the case load). At the initial court appearance before the Central Judicial Processing Unit, two representatives from the Essex defenders office are available to assist all defendants. As a result of their near monopoly on the county's criminal caseload, each public defender labors under sizable caseloads that range from seventy to one hundred cases at any time, although more than half of these clients are languishing in the moribund pre-indictment period. Their greatest concern is with the thirty to forty clients who have been indicted and are moving through the arraignment and pre-trial conferences toward the occasional trial. Most public defenders estimated their involvement in only eight to twelve trials a year, but these are the high points of their professional career. Experienced Essex defenders explained their ability to manage such large caseloads through performing effective legal triage early in the proceedings. Legal triage, similar to its medical equivalent used in emergency rooms and MASH units, is a system of prioritizing the seriousness of each case, taking into consideration the strength of the prosecution's case as well as the merits of the defense position.

The Essex defenders were a realistic group of attorneys who were not overly troubled by their clients' lack of trust and respect. Their effort grew out of the strong sense of professionalism that defined the Essex defender office. The intelligent, compassionate leadership of the regional director set a tone for the entire office. Equally important to the office's success was the lengthy tenure of so many of its staff attorneys. This created a large cadre of experienced defense attorneys to serve as excellent mentors for newly hired lawyers, as well as worthy adversaries for the Essex prosecutors.

In contrast to most attorneys who are able to define professional success in quantifiable terms of either number of victories or six-figure annual salaries, Essex public defenders must be more creative, utilizing less obvious measures. Defending indigent clients who have in most instances committed criminal acts does not provide many opportunities for clear-cut victories, nor do indigent clients offer any possibility of lucrative fees. The prosecutor has many advantages in the adversarial struggle with the defense despite the formidable burden of proof. The prosecutor can select which cases to pursue, eliminating the weaker ones where the defense might have had a chance for a courtroom victory. Prosecutors also control the flow of critical information from their office to the defense. Cases brought before the grand jury nearly always result in indictments, a carefully chosen group of "sure winners" for the prosecution. The public defender's objective in most cases is simply to minimize the damage to his or her client by negotiating a plea bargain so the defendant will receive probation and no prison time, or a much shorter sentence than he or she was initially facing. I have heard public defenders proudly proclaim a victory after a jury awarded life imprisonment to their client (instead of the possible death penalty). Unlike the prosecutor who can discard difficult or problematic cases, the public defender is constitutionally bound to the client no matter how hopeless the situation may be.

Given this grim reality, it is amazing to observe so many Essex defenders maintain an upbeat, positive disposition after fifteen or twenty years on the job. Tempered by reality, they have developed their own creative definition of courtroom success, which stretches from a successful plea bargain to an outright acquittal. For defenders, the process is as significant as the outcome of the cases. The always-supportive encouragement of fellow defenders is a major reason for the lengthy tenure of the staff. Similar to a military unit fighting against overwhelming odds in a pivotal battle, the Essex public defenders band together, inspired to feats of selfless bravery, rather than let down their fellow soldiers. Returning to their Clinton Street offices after a frustrating day in court, the defenders take comfort in knowing that they will be rejuvenated by the empathy and encouragement of their colleagues—and able to face another round of difficult cases the next day.

Mired in a Creaky System: Public Defenders vs. Bureaucratic Malaise

It is very fortunate that the Essex regional office has been able to formulate an environment that sustains the staff attorneys because once they venture off to the courthouse or jail, the stark reality of the depressing job soon encapsulates them. They are mired in a creaky justice system, located in a city whose crime and related social and economic malaise are among the worst in the nation. It is a setting that fails to inspire hope or optimism. For those defenders who are able to maintain a modicum of altruism and concern for the broader issues of social justice, motivation comes less from the rare courtroom victory than from the opportunity to improve the quality of a client's life. To place a client into a decent drug rehab program or anger management program, to gain re-admittance into a housing project or locate an employment opportunity are all examples of the wider variety of positive actions by which Essex defenders recognize their true contribution to their clients' best interests. These are their most significant accomplishments.

The occasional social or legal highlight is overwhelmed by the daily frustrations of the public defender's professional life. The continuous flow of clients, many facing serious criminal charges that can easily place them behind bars for ten or more years, keeps the defenders extremely busy. The Essex County courts and justice system typifies the failing urban social and economic systems at the beginning of the twenty-first century. The response of New Jersey, like most states concerned with escalating crime and social problems, has been to enact increasingly severe laws that not only clog the courts but fill the state prisons to capacity. Since the passage of an especially punitive group of drug laws in the mid-1980s, New Jersey's state's prison population has tripled.

Compounding the professional problems of Essex County public defenders are their difficult and contentious relationships with other members of the courtroom workgroup. These range from the expected obstacles raised by the county prosecutors and police officers to the less obvious problems created by their own clients and the supposedly neutral judges and case managers. The police and prosecutors are characterized as exceeding their prescribed adversarial responsibilities. The Essex defenders accused police officers of frequently misplacing or losing critical reports that are required by state discovery rules to be turned over to the defense. The defenders were even more critical of police officers who shaded the truth or outright lied on the witness stand. Prosecutors also contributed to the delay in turning over important documents to the public defenders. In open court, most prosecutors appeared to behave cordially or exhibit professional indifference toward the public defenders. A minority of prosecutors was openly antagonistic toward the Essex defenders, procrastinating on even the most the most innocuous request.

Public defenders recognized the variation in the behavior of judges toward them. The defenders thought that the most frustrating judicial decisions were the product of inexperience or ignorance of the law rather than blatant hostility. The most universal criticism of Essex County judges by the public defenders was the commonly held belief that public defenders were working for them instead of the defendants. These judges lumped prosecutors and defense attorneys together as members of a courtroom workgroup responsible to judicial direction. The judges believed that the primary job of case managers and both legal adversaries was to assist the judiciary in moving cases along as expeditiously as possible. Reducing the backlog and shortening the length of time from arrest to disposition would permit the judges to win the appreciation of the AOC in Trenton, which supervised their performance. Most judges failed to appreciate the responsibilities of a public defender to his or her client, which occasionally required delaying a case as much as possible, a strategy which exacerbated the tensions between the defenders and the superior court judges as well as the case managers.

Clients rarely provided much satisfaction to the public defenders. The relationship was often plagued by suspicion and lack of respect. Many clients could not comprehend how lawyers who were being paid by the same state that was trying to convict them could be expected to be really trying their best to gain an acquittal. Additionally, the defendants observed the public defenders acting cordially toward the prosecutors, being especially friendly once formal proceedings were recessed. Angered by an inability to pay for a "real lawyer," many indigent clients continually complained about their attorney's competence and commitment. The defendants' most nagging concern was how good a lawyer could they possibly have when the state was willing to provide the lawyer for free? One public defender, acknowledging the plausibility of his clients' concerns, commented "Yeah there is an adversary system at work here but it isn't exactly the way it is supposed to be aligned. It's the judge and all the lawyers against the defendants and victims, a true class struggle." Most defenders identified the often-strained relationship with the client as the worst part of the job.

One positive feature of the job noted by several Essex defenders was the absence of any serious consequences if they were less than successful in their lawyering efforts. Their work rarely captured the interest of the local television, radio, or press. It appeared to the defenders that no one was watching and hardly anyone outside of the criminal justice community seemed to care. The absence of media attention to even the most serious cases handled by the Essex defenders, including hundreds of murders, rapes, and carjackings, may be puzzling to someone from small town middle America, but these frequently-recurring catastrophes were urban scars that most local residents would like to forget. The only two criminal cases that captured the public's attention during the year of court observation were both extremely violent and involved white victims. The first case involved an irate passenger attacking an airline employee while impatiently waiting to board his plane. His rage boiled over when he thought he observed the attendant mistreat his wife. He lifted the attendant up into the air, dropping him on his head and causing spinal injuries. The second incident was a knife attack and robbery of a church handyman inside a rectory while services were being conducted a few feet away.

Public defenders realistically understand that nearly all of their clients are guilty of something (although not necessarily what they have been charged with) and the prosecutors are able to develop a strong case so that going to trial is rarely a feasible option. Weak cases and innocent defendants are usually removed from the system by the police and prosecution well before the grand jury is convened to indict for probable cause. This results in the overwhelming number of defendants being forced into plea bargains, pleading guilty in exchange for a reduced sentence. Public defenders justify these repeated outcomes by explaining that they are not really "losing a case" if they have been able to negotiate a successful plea bargain, gaining a sentence for the client that is much less severe than the one he or she was initially facing.

The leadership of the Essex County defender office understands the difficult working conditions and unappealing clients undermining the staff attorneys' performance. They grant the defenders a large measure of autonomy and discretion, subjecting them to minimal supervision or evaluation. Their recent unionization further insulates the Essex regional public defenders from bothersome performance reviews or annual salary disputes. Despite being subjected to very little pressure or exposure, the Essex defenders perform at a high level of professional competence, frustrating their adversaries and surprising their clients.

The downside of these unappreciated legal efforts, hidden from public view, is the lack of professional or public recognition. As noted in the McIntyre study of Chicago, public defenders practice in obscurity, ensuring that even the occasional courtroom victory, which is likely to raise the public's ire, will rarely be noticed. The defenders can therefore continue to enjoy a personal sense of accomplishment without alerting taxpayers that their taxes are funding a group of attorneys that is instrumental in letting criminals back into society. Obviously, the "laboring in obscurity" is not for everyone, particularly the ego-driven attorneys that are plentiful among litigators. The absence of publicity does not bother the Essex County public defenders, who appear to be an egalitarian organization, led by a benevolent leader, the regional deputy director, who reinforces the equal treatment philosophy. Differences in pay are controlled by the annual union agreement and are largely based on seniority rather than subtle gradations in level of performance. The office is structured horizontally, with only five supervisory positions (director and five first assistants) and few opportunities for promotion.

Given the generally negative attitude of indigent clients toward their attorney, public defenders soon grow accustomed to not expecting any show of gratitude regardless of the outcome. Their colleagues provide the only acknowledgment of a courtroom victory or a difficult-to-achieve plea bargain. Returning to the Clinton Street office after a successful disposition, riding an emotional high, an Essex defender can count on a warm reception. Word of a colleague's good fortune spreads quickly through the office. Fellow attorneys, including investigators, drop by to offer congratulations. Everyone knows this accomplishment will not make the evening news, nor is it likely to prompt the defendant to come forward and offer his or her thanks. Such happy moments may be infrequent occurrences, yet the genuine warmth and collective happiness of the office toward an individual's success plays an important part in developing the esprit de corps that has made the Essex office such a stable organization.

The Essex County public defenders practice law in a chaotic criminal justice system that is often on the verge of grinding to a halt. They receive little recognition and rarely experience clear-cut courtroom victories. On the positive side, most of the professional pressure is self-imposed with rare consequences for a lost case. If one's ego and lifestyle do not demand a lofty salary, working as an Essex County public defender allows an attorney to escape the unpleasant financial aspects of finding clients and collecting fees. When personal or family expenses escalated because of pressure for a larger home or a child's tuition, the defender would reluctantly leave the Essex office.

Explaining Essex County's Success

In contrast to the traditional public defender programs such as the Chicago and New York agencies, the Essex regional office is a relatively successful operation. Its performance and professional reputation also compare favorably to the somewhat negative stereotypes of public defenders generally. The primary feature of the Essex regional office, and likely the major reason for its success, is its ability to maintain a stable professional staff of competent defense attorneys. They work in what most of the defenders describe as a nurturing environment. There are several possible explanations for the staff being able to maintain such a supportive workplace, but the intelligent, humane leadership style of the current director is probably the most plausible. By giving each attorney a significant amount of autonomy, yet offering advice and guidance when necessary, the director has maintained the delicate balance critical for the program's success. Pairing experienced attorneys with their younger counterparts has created a mentoring system that is unobtrusive yet effective.

The apolitical nature of the Essex office also contributes to its success. Its institutional independence is particularly helpful for the younger defenders who do not have to worry about constantly second-guessing themselves or being overly sensitive to shifting political currents. Important personnel decisions (hiring, firing, and promotions) are made on the basis of merit without a hint of patronage or nepotism. Because they are part of a statewide system, the Essex public defenders are able to escape from the shifting, complex local political scene. Recent unionization has also contributed to a contented staff by providing modest salaries enhanced by regular increases and an attractive group of benefits including pension benefits. Being part of a statewide system that has consistently ranked among the highest paid in the nation is a critical ingredient in the Essex success story. In 1986 a national survey conducted by Steven Schlesinger for the Bureau of Criminal Statistics of the U.S. Justice Department discovered that the New Jersey defender system spent more money per case than any other state system. The Garden State spent $431 per case while Arkansas, which was at the bottom of the states surveyed, spent only $63 per case.

A final factor influencing the professionalism of the office is the vertical system of case management. By having defenders remain with their initially assigned clients all the way to the final disposition, defenders feel more like actual attorneys and less like bureaucrats taking a position along the criminal justice assembly line. Adequate support staff and competent colleagues as well as opportunities for professional growth all reinforce the Essex defenders' professional self-esteem. Working for an organization that tries to protect its employees from the harsher aspects of an often-thankless job is greatly appreciated by the Essex County public defenders. They only have to glance across the courtroom at the struggling prosecutors to realize the numerous advantages offered by the Essex defender office.

The Exportability Factor

Is the Essex regional public defender office a useful model for other jurisdictions struggling with the problem of providing effective legal representation for indigent defendants? Or are there too many idiosyncratic features in the Essex County criminal justice terrain that negate the usefulness of such a comparison? Obviously, Essex County and the Newark metropolitan area are not going to be a perfect match for all locales, but it does conform to the most basic demographic and crime statistics found in most contemporary urban areas, especially the large number of cities experiencing high rates of both crime and poverty.

Demographically, Essex County, with Newark at its center, conforms to a pattern all too prevalent in our older urban/metropolitan areas located in the Northeast and Midwest. Newark is located in the center of the county, with 270,000 people jammed into a densely populated inner city. Its population is dominated by minority groups with blacks and Hispanics accounting for 60% and 30%, respectively, of the city's population. Traveling away from Newark's central core toward the north and west, the county's remaining 470,000 residents grow whiter and more affluent the farther one travels. Most of the county's serious crime is found within Newark and its contingent communities of Irvington, Hillside, and East Orange. All of these cities were filled with working-class to middle-class white neighborhoods prior to the 1967 riots, but the areas are presently black and Hispanic, dominated by large pockets of poverty. The western and northern suburbs include such affluent towns as Montclair, West Orange, Millburn, and Short Hills. They suffer primarily from non-violent property crimes such as burglaries and auto theft, as well as occasional drug cases. The defendants in these cases are primarily middle class and rarely require the service of a public defender.

The Essex County criminal courts dispose of their heavy caseloads in a manner similar to most jurisdictions plagued by excessive poverty and crime. Although the county's courts are facing serious delay problems, ranking among the worst in the nation, its disposition rates for dismissals, plea bargains, and trials approximates national trends. Of the 16,000 defendants indicted in 2000, nearly half had their charges reduced to a lesser crime in exchange for a guilty plea, while another third plead guilty to a felony. Only 2% of the defendants went to trial with two-thirds being convicted. Nearly 20% of the defendants were able to have their cases dismissed.

The courtroom workgroup, including judges, lawyers, and court clerks, resembled nearly every other urban justice system that I have observed during the past thirty years. My research during this period took me to fifteen cities across the country (New York, Philadelphia, Baltimore, Washington D.C., Miami, Atlanta, New Orleans, Houston, St. Louis, Chicago, Detroit, Denver, Los Angeles, San Francisco, and Oakland), where I interviewed over five hundred judges, prosecutors, and defense attorneys. The operation of the local justice system in all of these cities, including Essex County, was quite similar. Judges battled steadily increasing caseloads while prosecutors controlled the plea bargaining process. The private defense bar had nearly vanished, leaving the overwhelming majority of defendants in the hands of assigned counsel or public defenders.

Despite the overall similarity between Essex County and other urban justice systems, there are also several distinctive features that should be noted.
These unique characteristics may limit the exportability of the Essex County
regional public defender program to other jurisdictions. I believe, however,
that these unique features are not significant enough to undermine the value
of the lessons learned from the Essex public defender operations. It is also
feasible for other jurisdictions to incorporate these features into their own
indigent defense systems. The first distinctive feature of the Essex public
defender program is that it is limited by a statewide system that provides
representation only to indigent defenders charged with indictable offenses.
These offenses are referred to in most other jurisdictions as felonies and
expose the defendant to a year or more possible incarceration in a state
prison if convicted. Less serious cases, usually designated as misdemeanors,
have maximum penalties of less than a year, which is to be served in a
county jail. These cases fall within the jurisdiction of the municipal courts. In
New Jersey these crimes are referred to as disorderly persons offenses. The
most obvious benefit derived from the state regional defender program's
narrow focus on only the more serious criminal cases is to spare them
involvement in a great mass of cases, thereby allowing them to work with a
reduced, manageable caseload, concentrating their efforts on the most serious cases. This does not infer that the Essex defenders are blessed with
"light" caseloads. The defenders interviewed estimated that at any given
time they are handling between 75 to 90 cases. Their office figures for 2000
show the defenders averaging approximately 430 cases per lawyer. These
figures are comparable to the maximum acceptable level of cases recommended by the National Legal Aid and Defender Association, which is 400
cases per attorney.

A second unique feature of the Essex defender office is its position within
a statewide program that controls nearly all personnel decisions. The state
defender agency also negotiates with the defender's union and lobbies the
state legislature for adequate funding. Nearly one-fourth of the states operate
similar statewide programs. Overall, these statewide systems appear to operate more effectively and experience fewer financial problems than local or
county administered public defender agencies. State systems in Florida and
Colorado are often characterized as model programs, with New Jersey's program also receiving a positive evaluation. These statewide systems are generally apolitical with adequate funding. In states like New Jersey that have
significant disparities in wealth and poverty among the various counties, it
allows for all public defenders to receive uniform salaries regardless of local
economic problems. By contrast, prosecutors are dependant on county
funding. Thus in Essex County with its fiscal problems and urban poverty,
the prosecutors have below average salaries, not even equal to the public
defenders.

A third distinctive feature is the unusually large percentage of defendants
in the Essex County criminal courts requiring the service of public defend-

ers. Although national figures for indigent defendants run quite high, estimated between 70% and 80%, in Essex County over 90% of the defendants charged with indictable offenses are indigent and require the services of a county public defender. These statistics guarantee the Essex regional office a large caseload as well as nearly excluding private defense attorneys from practicing in the county's criminal courts. Estimates by local attorneys indicated that only 10% to 15% of private attorneys still practice criminal law on a regular basis, while a slightly larger group (25% to 30%) are members of the pool list offering their services in multiple-defender cases.

It is very difficult to compare the Essex County regional office with other kinds of indigent defense systems. Assigned counsel systems are found primarily in less populous jurisdictions with significantly lower caseloads. Comparing Essex with the recently developed contract law firms is also difficult. They have not been in operation for a sufficient period of time to permit reliable and valid empirical analysis. Another difficulty is caused by the variety of contract firms operating within a city. In New York City, for example, there are numerous associations of lawyers negotiating with the city for a set percentage of the criminal caseload. Depending on the size of the firm and the percentage of cases contracted for, these offices are likely to develop markedly different delivery systems. Most are still in the experimental stages, establishing standards of proficiency that can still satisfy their bottom-line expectations.

Lessons Learned: A Final Assessment

When the Essex County regional defender office was selected for study, it was thought that this office would be representative of urban defender programs. It was expected that the Essex regional office would be plagued by the same problems affecting defender programs nationally, such as sizable caseloads, insufficient funding, high turnover in personnel, low professional esteem, and only a handful of courtroom victories. Although many of my preconceived notions about the difficulties of being a public defender were confirmed during my study of the Essex County office, there were many important positive discoveries. My ultimate conclusions are favorable, particularly when one considers the many problems lurking within the county's criminal justice system. Even though most indigent defendants do not appreciate the efforts, the Essex regional defenders provide competent representation. Compared to most defender agencies across the country, the Essex public defenders are an experienced group, with two-thirds of the staff having been with the office for over ten years. Burnout may be a negative consequence of extended service in so demanding a work environment, but most of the veteran defenders provided the mentoring guidance and support that has made the Essex office such a unique and hospitable workplace.

There are several additional factors that contribute to the supportive nature of the Essex regional office. There is a conscious effort by the leadership to minimize the negative bureaucratic features so common in similar organizations. The office enhances an egalitarian spirit that encourages interaction between all levels of attorneys regardless of length of service. This extends to the courthouse where defenders on trial commonly have colleagues drop by to offer encouragement. The pressure from superiors that is likely to upset, even unravel, younger defenders is minimized by granting all of the staff attorneys a large degree of autonomy. They quickly learn how to make critical case decisions without running to a supervisor for approval. Defenders are able to make important plea-bargaining decisions and other strategic judgments on their own or in consultation with their courtroom partner. Young prosecutors by contrast appear to be always on the verge of running out of the courtroom in order to obtain approval from a superior.

The monetary advantages of unionization and a statewide defender agency committed to quality indigent defense have also aided in the development of a stable Essex defender office. Essex defenders frequently stated in interviews how important it was for them to have the meaningful assistance of the state agency in their professional development as criminal defense lawyers. Although there is some initial training, the state funds defender participation at educational conferences and seminars. Experienced Essex defenders expressed their commitment to educating the younger attorneys. Many Essex defenders were also appreciative of the availability of competent investigators and persuasive expert witnesses.

In selecting a young lawyer from the pool of numerous applicants, which has grown as the economy worsens, the defender leadership would be wise to choose a mature attorney who is confident and has a genuine interest in litigation. Ideological commitment to the defense appears less important than a thirst for courtroom experience. A strong ego may also prove beneficial given the absence of positive feedback from one's client—and the rest of the legal profession as well. Although Essex defenders receive decent salaries, the money will never be more than modest. Any attorney whose self-esteem is based upon the size of the salary or attractiveness of the office will find very little satisfaction defending Essex County's indigent defendants. It is interesting and possibly instructive to note how many of the Essex defenders had parents with working class roots, many with union backgrounds. Even though altruism is not necessary to become a successful public defender, a high percentage of the staff, especially the female and black attorneys, were active in civil rights or related social reform organizations prior to joining the defender office.

Beyond the background characteristics of potential public defenders, there is a self-selection process at work. Most defenders interviewed understood the realities of working in a bureaucratic organization representing indigent clients. The Essex regional office loses most of its young attorneys within two years after appointment. They leave the office on their own accord rather than being fired. The office and the young lawyer are in mutual agreement that a mistake has been made. Resignations in subsequent years are typically triggered by unexpected financial pressures or once-in-a-lifetime job opportunities. Given the high cost of living in the New York metropolitan area, it is remarkable how few attorneys have departed.

Coming to grips with the reality of a public defender's professional life is a veritable necessity if one wishes to make a career of defending indigent clients. The most critical mental adjustment is to realize that job satisfaction cannot be based upon the gratitude of one's clients or the compilation of courtroom victories. Instead, a public defender must redefine personal success in terms of advantageous plea bargains saving one's client years of possible incarceration. Having a case dismissed or downgraded to a lesser offense or being able to place a client in a diversion program or a drug rehab program are often notable achievements even if the client refuses to acknowledge it. These results may not appear significant to the larger society outside the courthouse, but they are recognized by a defender's colleagues as significant accomplishments that form one's professional reputation with the people who best understand and appreciate its worth—one's colleagues within the public defenders office.

Beyond the internal psychological struggles and self-doubts haunting public defenders, they must also overcome equally daunting external obstacles each day at the courthouse. These troublesome frustrations include not only their professional adversaries, the prosecutors, but a host of additional annoyances, from bullying judges, prevaricating police officers, incompetent clerks, and disrespectful clients. The most surprising aspect of this study is that so many Essex County public defenders are willing to confront all of these internal and external problems for the better part of their professional life. Even understanding their strong attraction to litigating criminal cases and the importance of working with such a fine group of colleagues, I remain in awe of their professional commitment to guaranteeing the Sixth Amendment's right to a competent legal representation for all defendants regardless of financial status.

The Future

Although the Essex regional defender office presents a positive model for providing quality defense for indigents in serious criminal cases, it may nevertheless be difficult for other jurisdictions to adopt and implement their procedural innovations. The main reason for my pessimism is based on the economic woes plaguing nearly all state and local governments since the 9/11 tragedy. Even before this cataclysmic event, the public defense of indigents in criminal cases was badly under funded, remaining an incredibly low priority in public financing for all levels of government. This is not surprising given that the group that is to benefit from such funding for improved legal defense is the thousands of indigent defendants accused of criminal acts against society. It is naive to expect this same society, particularly its law-abiding, tax-paying members, to enthusiastically support spending their tax dollars for improved legal defense of indigent defendants, most of whom will eventually be found guilty of some crime. The electorate can logically argue against granting accused defendants a better chance of escaping conviction, thereby allowing them to return to the streets, posing a continued threat to the community's safety.

Despite the logical basis of objections to improving the quality of public defense provided to indigents accused of crimes, our legal system and the constitutional premise upon which it is based demands equal treatment under law regardless of one's financial resources. Especially given our nation's reliance upon an adversarial system of justice premised on fairness and the assumption of innocence with a strong burden of proof placed upon the prosecution, *all* defendants require competent legal defense as guaranteed in the Sixth Amendment to the Constitution. Additionally, the Fourteenth Amendment's requirement of equal protection under the law indicates our nation's commitment to a just legal system whose search for the truth should not be influence by the economic resources of either the defense or prosecution. Seventy-five years ago Winston Churchill succinctly stated the significance of this type of national commitment to equal protection when he wrote, "A calm dispassionate recognition of the rights of the accused . . . the unfailing faith that there is a treasure, if you can only find it in the heart of every man . . . are the symbols, which in the treatment of crime and the criminals mark and measure the stored up strength of a nation."[4]

If our nation can maintain its commitment to an equitable system of legal defense, public defenders are a critical element in ensuring constitutional guarantees. The Essex County regional defenders office offers a positive model for providing effective legal defense for indigent defendants. Adequate pay, inspired leadership and political independence should lead to a stable group of public defenders whose professional behavior guarantees that our constitutional imperatives are alive and well in our nation's criminal courts.

Notes

Preface

1. Roger Hanson, et al., *Indigent Defenders* (Williamsburg, Va.: National Center for State Courts, 1992), pp. 93–106.

2. Abraham Blumberg, "The Practice of Law as a Confidence Game," *Law and Society Review* 1: 15–39 (1967); Jonathan Cooper, *Criminal Courts: The Defendant's Perspective* (Englewood Cliffs, N.J.: Prentice Hall, 1978); James Kunen, *How Can You Defend Those People* (New York: Random House, 1983); Jerome Skolnick, "Social Control in the Adversary System," *Journal of Conflict Resolution* 11: 52–70 (1967); David Sudnow, "Normal Crimes: Sociological Features of the Penal Code in a Public Defender Office," *Social Problems* 12: 209–215 (1965).

Chapter 1. The Right to Counsel for Indigent Defendants: A National Perspective

1. 1. Walter Schaefer, "Federalism and State Criminal Procedure," *Harvard Law Review* 70: 1–8 (1956), p. 8.

2. Robert Herman, et. al, *Counsel for the Poor* (Lexington, Mass.: Lexington Books, 1977), p. 208.

3. *Powell v. Alabama,* 287 U.S. 69 at 71 (1932).

4. *Gideon v. Wainwright,* 372 U.S. 335 at 343–44 (1963).

5. Lee Silverstein, "The Continuing Impact of *Gideon v. Wainwright,*" *American Bar Association Journal* 51: 1023–1041 (November 1965), p. 1025.

6. *Strickland v. Washington,* 466 U.S. 668 at 694 (1984).

7. Ibid., p. 689.

8. *Faretta v. California,* 422 U.S. 806 at 832–33 (1965).

9. *Kirby v. Illinois,* 406 U.S. 682 at 689–90 (1972).

10. Lee Silverstein, *Defense of the Poor* (Chicago: American Bar Foundation, 1965), p. 1.

11. *Indigent Defense Services in Large Counties, 1999* (Washington, D.C.: Bureau of Justice Statistics, U.S. Department of Justice, November 2000), p. 1.

12. Ibid.

13. Silverstein, *Defense of the Poor*, p. 45.

14. Richard Klein and Robert Spangenberg, *The Indigent Defense Crisis* (Washington, D.C.: American Bar Association, 1993), p. 5.

15. Ibid., p. 6.

16. Norman Lefstein, *Criminal Defense Services for the Poor: Methods and Programs for Providing Legal Representation and the Need for Adequate Financing* (Washington, D.C.: American Bar Association Committee on Legal Aid and Indigent Defendants, August 1981), p. G-2.

17. Alissa Worden, "Privatizing Due Process," *Justice System Journal* 15: 390–418 (1991).

18. Ibid., p. 396.

19. Paul B. Wice, *Criminal Lawyers* (Beverly Hills, Calif.: Sage Publications, 1978); Paul B. Wice and Peter Suwak, "Current Realities of Public Defender Programs: A National Survey and Analysis," *Criminal Law Bulletin* 10: 161 (1974).

20. Wice, *Criminal Lawyers*, p. 205.

21. *Defense Counsel in Criminal Cases* (Washington, D.C.: Bureau of Justice Statistics, U.S. Department of Justice, 1999).

22. Wice, *Criminal Lawyers*, p. 203.

Chapter 2.   Public Defender Agencies:
The Traditional Approach

1. *Defense Counsel in Criminal Cases* (Washington, D.C.: Bureau of Justice Statistics, U.S. Department of Justice Statistics, 2000).

2. Ibid., p. 4.

3. Ibid., p. 6.

4. Carol Defranco and Marika Litras, *Indigent Defense Services in Larger Counties, 1992* (Washington, D.C.: Bureau of Justice Statistics, U.S. Department of Justice, 2000), p. 4.

5. Richard Klein and Robert Spangenberg, *The Indigent Defense Crisis* (Washington, D.C.: American Bar Association, 1993).

6. Jane Fritsch and David Rohde, "Two-Tier Justice: High Volume Law," *New York Times,* April 9, 2001, p. B5.

7. Defranco and Litras, *Indigent Defense Services*, p. 4.

8. Paul Wice and Peter Suwak, "Meeting the *Gideon* Mandate," *Judicature,* S: 8–400 (March 1967), p. 404.

9. Klein and Spangenberg, *Indigent Defense Crisis*, p. 1.

10. Defranco and Litras, *Indigent Defense Services*, p. 5.

11. David Sudnow, "Normal Crimes: Sociological Features of the Penal Code in a Public Defender Office," *Social Problems* 12 (3): 235–276, p. 260.

12. Paul B. Wice, *Criminal Lawyers* (Beverly Hills, Calif.: Sage Publications, 1978), p. 204.

13. Ibid., p. 172.

14. Lisa McIntyre, *The Chicago Public Defender* (Chicago: University of Chicago Press, 1987), p. 24.

15. Ibid., p. 39.

16. Ibid., p. 55.

17. Ibid., p. 61.

18. Ibid., p. 58.

19. Ibid., p. 120.

20. Ibid., p. 178.

21. Ibid., p. 181.

22. Michael McConville and Chester Mirsky, "Criminal Defense of the Poor in New York City," *NYU Review of Law and Social Change* 15 (4): 581–664 (1986–1987), p. 619.

23. Ibid., p. 648.

24. Ibid.

25. Ibid., p. 782.

26. Ibid., p. 774.

27. Ibid.

28. David Heilbroner, *Rough Justice: Days and Nights of a Young D.A.* (New York: Pantheon Books, 1990), p. 45.

29. Adele Bernhard, "Private Bar Monitors Public Defense," *Criminal Defense* 13: 1–27 (Spring 1998), p. 26.

30. Ibid., p. 30.

31. Jane Fritsch and David Rohde, "Two-Tier Justice: High Volume Law," *New York Times,* April 9, 2001, p. B1.

32. Susan Saulny, "Raise Ordered for Lawyers Aiding Poor," *New York Times,* May 7, 2002, p. B1.

33. Fritsch and Rohde, "Two-Tier Justice," p. B1.

34. Ibid., p. B5.

35. Ibid.

36. Fritsch and Rohde, "Legal Aid's Last Challenge from an Old Adversary," *New York Times,* September 9, 2001, p. 50.

Chapter 3.   The Essex County Regional Defender Office: The Evolution and Organization of a Reform Defender System

1. Lawrence Resnick, "New Public Defender Guaranteed a Practice," *Newark Star Ledger,* June 25, 1967, p. 16.

2. Joseph Rosenberg, "The Public Defender Admits Client Finances Not Probed," *Newark Evening News,* p. 12.

3. Ibid.

4. "Cahill Backs up Public Defender," *Asbury Park Evening News,* February 16, 1971, p. 4.

5. "A Work for the Defense," *Newark Star Ledger,* February 9, 1971, p. 42.

6. Michael Hayes, "Essex Public Defender Amused at Criticisms," *Newark Sunday News,* February 7, 1971, sec. 1, p. 25.

7. "Ronco Appointed as State Deputy Public Defender," *Newark Evening News,* September 6, 1967, p. 1.

8. Hayes, "Public Defender Amused," p. 25.

9. Ron Palumbo, *No Cause for Indictment* (New York: Holt, Rhinehart and Winston, 1971) p. 7.

10. Linda Ocasio, "The Underbelly of a City in Transition," *New York Times,* May 13, 2001, sec. 14, p. 1.

11. Ibid., sec. 14, p. 8.

12. Richard Ben Cramer, *Joe DiMaggio: The Hero's Life* (New York: Simon and Schuster, 2000) p. 141.

13. *State Police Annual Report* (Trenton, N.J.: State of New Jersey, 1997), p. 6.

14. Roger Hanson, et al., *Indigent Defenders* (Williamsburg, Va.: National Center for State Courts, 1992), pp. 93–106.

Chapter 4. The Staff Attorneys: Background and Career Patterns

1. Whenever possible, comparable data from national studies of public defenders and the entire legal profession will be offered. Unfortunately, there is not an abundance of such information, particularly in terms of the broad range of issues covered in this volume.

2. Lisa McIntyre, *The Chicago Public Defender* (Chicago: University of Chicago Press, 1987), p. 55.

3. John Heinz and Edward O. Laumann, *Chicago Lawyers: The Social Structures of the Bar* (New York: Russell Sage Foundation, 1982); Eve Spangler, *Lawyers for Hire* (New Haven, Conn.: Yale University Press, 1986).

4. Jerome Carlin, *Lawyers on Their Own* (New Brunswick, N.J.: Rutgers University Press, 1962); Paul B. Wice, *Criminal Lawyers* (Beverly Hills, Calif.: Sage Publications, 1978); Arthur Wood, *Criminal Lawyers* (New Haven, Conn.: Yale University Press, 1967).

5. Tom Moran, "Jeering Section Can't Stop Mrs. Dow," *Newark Star Ledger,* July 20, 2004, p. 13.

6. Paul B. Wice, *Criminal Lawyers*, p. 75.

Chapter 5. Procedural Issues: Processing and Litigating Cases

1. Estimate provided by First Assistant Public Defender Joel Harris during an interview with the author, April 8, 2000, Madison, N.J.

2. *Key Indicators of Calendar Status, Report No. 1* (Trenton, N.J.: Administrative Office of the Courts, July 1, 2000).

3. Ibid.

Chapter 6. The Work Environment and Courthouse Relationships

1. Paul B. Wice, *Chaos in the Courthouse* (New York: Praeger Publications, 1985), p. 48.

2. Monroe Freedman, *Lawyers Ethics in an Adversary System* (Indianapolis: Bobbs-Merrill, 1975).

Chapter 7. Personal and Professional Issues

1. David Lynch, "The Nature of Occupational Stress Among Public Defenders," *Justice System Journal* 19 (1): 17–35 (1997).

2. Paul B. Wice, *Criminal Lawyers* (Beverly Hills, Calif.: Sage Publications, 1978).

3. Ibid., p. 201.

4. Lisa McIntyre, *The Chicago Public Defender* (Chicago: University of Chicago Press, 1987), p. 79.

5. Ibid., p. 201.

6. Caroline Harlow, *Defense Counsel in Criminal Cases* (Washington, D.C.: Bureau of Justice Statistics, U.S. Department of Justice, 2000), p. 1.

7. Ibid.

Chapter 8.   Lessons Learned: An Agenda for Public Defender Reform

1. Max Weber, *The Theory of Social and Economic Organizations* (Glencoe, Ill.: Free Press, 1997); Amitai Etzioni, *Modern Organizations* (Englewood Cliffs, N.J.: Prentice Hall, 1964); Herbert Simon, *Administrative Behavior,* 2nd ed. (New York: Macmillan, 1976).

2. Lisa McIntyre, *The Chicago Public Defender* (Chicago: University of Chicago Press, 1987).

3. Jonathan Casper, "Did You Have an Attorney? No, I Had a Public Defender," *Yale Review of Law and Social Action* (Spring 1971), pp. 4–9.

4. Wayne La Fave, "Alternative to the Present System of Bail," *Illinois Law Forum* (Spring 1965), p. 19.

Bibliography

Alschuler, Albert. "The Defense Attorney's Role in Plea Bargaining." *Yale Law Review* 84 (1975): 1179.

Arcuri, Alan. "Lawyers, Judges, and Plea Bargaining: Some New Data on Inmates' Views." *International Journal of Crime and Penology* 4 (1976): 171.

Benjamin, A.E. et al. "The Prevalence of Depression, Alcohol Abuse Among U.S. Attorneys." *International Journal of Law and Psychiatry* 18 (1990): 233.

Bernard, Adele. "Private Bar Monitors Public Defense." *Criminal Justice* 13 (Spring 1998): 1.

Blumberg, Abraham. "The Practice of Law as a Confidence Game." *Law and Society Review* 1 (1967): 15–39.

Bright, S.B. "Counsel for the Poor." *Yale Law Journal* 103 (1994): 185.

Butcher, Allan K., and Michael Moore. "Meeting Gideon's Trumpet: The Crisis of Indigent Defense in Texas." Austin, TX.: State Bar of Texas, Committee on Legal Services to the Poor in Criminal Matters (September 22, 2000).

Casper, Jonathan. *Criminal Courts: The Defendant's Perspective.* Englewood Cliffs, N.J.: Prentice-Hall, 1978.

Champion, Dean. "Private Counsels and Public Defenders: A Look at Weak Cases, Prior Records, and Leniency in Plea Bargaining." *Journal of Criminal Justice* 17 (1989): 253–263.

Cramer, Richard Ben. *Joe DiMaggio: The Hero's Life.* New York: Simon and Schuster, 2000.

Cummings, Charles F, and John E. O'Connor. *Newark: An American City.* Newark, N.J.: Newark Bicentennial Commission, 1979.

Defense Counsel in Criminal Cases. Washington, D.C.: Bureau of Justice Statistics, U.S. Justice Department, November 2000.

Defranco, Carol J. *State Funded Indigent Defense Services, 1999.* Washington, D.C.: Bureau of Justice Statistics, U.S. Justice Department, 2001.

Deutsch, Paula. "Gideon v. Wainwright's Application in the Courts Today–Effects on a Legal Aid Attorney." *Pace Law Review* 10 (1990): 387.

"Effective Assistance of Counsel for the Indigent Criminal Defendant." *NYU Review of Law and Social Change* 14 (1986): 1.

Eisenstein, James, Roy Flemming, and Peter Nardulli. *The Contours of Justice.* Boston: Little, Brown, 1988.

Emmelman, Debra S. *Defending Indigents: A Study of Criminal Defense Work.* Doctoral dissertation, University of California, San Diego, 1990.

Etzioni, Amitai. *Modern Organizations.* Englewood Cliffs, N.J.: Prentice-Hall, 1964.

Feeney, Floyd. "Public Defenders, Assigned Counsel, and Retained Counsel: Does the Type of Counsel Matter?" *Rutgers Law Journal* 22 (1991): 361.

Flemming, Roy. "Client Games: Defense Attorney Perspectives on Their Relations with Criminal Clients" In *Criminal Justice: Law and Politics,* edited by George C. Cole. Wadsworth, Calif.: Brooks Cole, 1993, 228–253.

——. "If You Pay the Piper Do You Call the Tune? Public Defenders in America's Criminal Courts." *Law and Social Inquiry* 14 (1989): 393.

Fritsch, Jane, and David Rohde. "For Poor, Appeals Are Luck of the Draw." *New York Times,* April 10, 2001, p. 1, B6.

——. "Lawyers Often Fail New York's Poor." *New York Times,* April 8, 2001, p. 1, 38.

——. "Legal Aid's Last Challenge from and Old Adversary, Guiliani." *New York Times,* September 9, 2001, p. 1, 38.

——. "Two-Tier Justice: High-Volume Law." *New York Times,* April 9, 2001, p. 1, 38.

Getty, Gerald, and James Presley. *Public Defender.* New York: Grosset and Dunlap, 1974.

Gilboy, Janet, and John Schmidt. "Replacing Lawyers: A Case Study of the Sequential Representation of Criminal Defendants." *Journal of Criminal Law and Criminology* 70 (1979): 1.

Glovin, Bill. "Price of Progress." *Rutgers Magazine* (Spring 2001): 21.

Goodpaster, Gary. "The Adversary System, Advocacy, and Effective Assistance of Counsel in Criminal Cases." *NYU Review of Law and Social Change* 14 (1986): 90.

Hall, Donna. "Job Satisfaction Among Male and Female Public Defenders." *Justice System Journal* 18, 2 (1995): 121–136.

Hansen, Roger et al. *Indigent Defenders Get the Job Done and Well.* Williamsburg, Va.: National Center of State Courts, 1992.

Hansen, Roger, and Joy Chapper. *Indigent Defense Systems.* Williamsburg, Va.: National Center of State Courts, 1991.

Harlow, Caroline W. *Defense Counsel in Criminal Cases.* Washington: D.C.: Bureau of Justice Statistics, U.S. Justice Department, 2000.

Heilbroner, David. *Rough Justice: Days and Nights of a Young D.A.* New York: Pantheon Books, 1990.

Heinz, John, and Edward Laumann. *Chicago Lawyers: The Social Structure of the Bar.* New York: Pantheon Books, 1990.

Hoffman, Paul. *Courthouse.* New York: Hawthorne Books, 1979.

Holden, Pauline, and Steven Balkin. "Costs and Quality of Indigent Defense: Ad Hoc vs. Coordinated Assignments of the Private Bar Within a Mixed System." *Justice System Journal* 10 (1985): 159–172.

Holly, W.D. "Re-Thinking the 6th Amendment for the Indigent Criminal Defendant." *Brooklyn Law Review* 64 (Spring 1998): 181.

Indigent Defense Contracting Systems. Washington: D.C.: Bureau of Justice Statistics, U.S. Department of Justice, 2001.

Klein, Richard. "Legal Malpractice, Professional Discipline, and Representation of the Indigent Defendant." *Temple Law Review* 61 (1998): 1.

——. "The Relationship of the Court and Defense Counsel: The Impact on Competent Representation and Proposals for Reform." *Boston College Law Review* 29 (1988): 531.

——, and Robert Spangenberg. *The Indigent Defense Crisis.* Washington, D.C.: American Bar Association, 1993.

Krantz, Sheldon et al. *The Right to Counsel in Criminal Cases: The Mandate of Argensinger v. Hamilin.* Boston: Ballinger Company, 1976.

Kunen, James. *How Can You Defend Those People.* New York: Random House, 1983.

Lee, Monica. "Indigent Defense: Determination of Indigency in State Courts." *State Court Journal* (Spring 1992), 16–23.

"Lure of OPD Strong for Essex Region's Krakora." *The Defender* 2, 1 (Winter 2001): 2.

Lynch, David. "The Nature of Occupational Stress Among Public Defenders." *Justice System Journal* 19, 1 (1997): 17–35.

Margules, Joe. "Resource Deprivation and the Right to Counsel." *Journal of Criminal Law and Criminology* 80 (1989): 673–725.

McConville, Michael. "The Rise of Guilty Pleas in New York." *Journal of Law and Society* 22, 4 (1995): 443–474.

——. *Standing Accused.* New York: Oxford University Press, 1993.

——, and Chester Mirsky. "Criminal Defense of the Poor in New York City." *NYU Review of Law and Social Change* 15, 4(1986–1987): 581–664.

McDonald, William F. *The Defense Counsel.* Beverly Hills, Calif.: Sage Publications, 1983.

McIntyre, Lisa. *The Chicago Public Defender.* Chicago: University of Chicago Press, 1987.

McWilliams, Michael. "The Erosion of Indigent Rights." *ABA Journal* 79 (March 1993): 8.

Mirsky, Chester. "The Political Economy and Indigent Defense in New York City." *Annual Survey of American Law* 4 (1999): 89–107.

National Symposium on Indigent Defense 2000: Redefining Leadership for Equal Justice. Washington, D.C.: Office of Justice Programs, U.S. Department of Justice. June 29, 2000.

Neubauer, David. *Criminal Justice in Middle America.* Morristown, N.J.: General Learning Press, 1974.

Ocasio, Linda. "The Underbelly of a City in Transition." *New York Times,* May 13, 2001, sec. 14, p. 1.

Ogletree, C.J. "Beyond Justification: Seeking Motivators to Sustain Public Defenders." *Harvard Law Review* (1993): 1239.

Palumbo, Ron. *No Cause for Indictment.* New York: Holt, Rhinehart and Winston, 1971.

Platt, Anthony, and Randi Pollock. "Channeling Lawyers: The Careers of Public Defenders." In *The Potential for Reform of Criminal Justice* edited by Herbert Jacob. Beverly Hills, Calif: Sage Publications, 1974, 235–262.

Prager, Irene et al. "Job Analysis of Assistant Public Defenders." *Psychology, Crime and the Law* 31 (1996): 37.

Saulny, Susan. "Raise Ordered for Lawyers Aiding Poor." *New York Times,* May 7, 2002, B1.

Schaefer, Walter. "Federalism and State Criminal Procedure." *Harvard Law Review* 70 (1956): 1.

Silverstein, Lee. *Defense of the Poor.* Chicago: American Bar Foundation, 1965.

Simon, Herbert. *Administrative Behavior.* 2nd edition. New York: Macmillan, 1976.

Skolnick, Jerome. "Social Control in the Adversary System." *Journal of Conflict Resolution* 11 (1967): 52–70.

Smith, Christopher. *Courts and the Poor.* Chicago: Nelson-Hall, 1991.

Smith, Steven, and Caroline De Franco. *Indigent Defense.* Washington, D.C.: Bureau of Justice Statistics, U.S. Department of Justice, 1996.

Smolowe, Jill, and Julie Johnson. "The Trials of the Public Defender." *Time* 141, 13 (March 29, 1993): 48.

Spangenberg, Robert et al.. *Containing the Cost of Indigent Defense Programs.* Washington, D.C.: Bureau of Justice Assistance, U.S. Department of Justice, 1999.

—— et al. *Maximizing Public Defender Resources.* Cambridge, Mass.: Abt Associates, 1983.

—— et al. *National Criminal Defense Systems Study.* Cambridge, Mass.: Abt Associates, 1984.

Spangenberg, Robert, and M.L. Berman. "Indigent Defense Systems in the U.S." *Law and Contemporary Problems* 58 (1995): 31–49.

Sudnow, David. "Normal Crimes: Sociological Features of the Penal Code in a Public Defender Office." *Social Problems* 12 (1965): 209–215.

Taylor, Jean G. "An Analysis of Defense Counsel in the Processing of Felony Defendants in Denver, Colorado." *Denver Law Journal* 50 (1973): 9–44.

Taylor-Thompson, K. "Individual Action v. Institutional Player–Alternating Visions of the Public Defender." *Georgetown Law Review* 84 (July 1996): 2419.

Uphoff, R.J. "The Criminal Defense Lawyer: Zealous Advocate, Double-Agent, or Beleaguered Dealer." *Criminal Law Bulletin* 28 (1992): 419.

Wasserman, David. *A Sword for the Convicted: Representing Indigent Defendants on Appeal.* Westport, CT.: Greenwood, Press, 1990.

Weber, Max. *The Theory of Social and Economic Organization.* Glencoe, Ill.: Free Press, 1947.

Wice, Paul B. *Chaos in the Courtroom.* New York: Praeger Publishers, 1983.

——. *Criminal Lawyers.* Beverly Hills, Calif.: Sage Publications, 1978.

——. *Gideon v. Wainwright and the Right to Counsel.* New York: Franklin Watts, 1995.

——. *Statewide Speedy Trial Reform.* Trenton, N.J.: New Jersey Supreme Court and the Administrative Office of the Courts, 1985.

Wice, Paul B., and Mark Pilgrim. "Meeting the *Gideon* Mandate." *Judicature* 58, 8 (March 1976): 400.

Wice, Paul B., and Peter Suwak. "Current Realities of Public Defender Programs: A National Survey and Analysis." *Criminal Law Bulletin* 10 (1974): 161.

Williams, Jimmy. "Type Counsel and the Outcomes of Criminal Appeals." *American Journal of Criminal Law* 19 (1995): 275–285.

Worden, Alissa. "Counsel for the Poor: An Evaluation of Contracting for Indigent Criminal Defense." *Justice Quarterly* 10 (1993): 613.

——. "Privatizing Due Process." *Justice System Journal* 15 (1991): 390–418.

Worden, Alissa, and Robert Donaldson. "Local Politics and the Provision of Indigent Defense Counsel." *Law and Policy* 11 (1989): 401.

Index

About the Author

PAUL B. WICE is a professor of political science at Drew University in Madison, New Jersey. He received his undergraduate degree from Bucknell University and his doctorate from the University of Illinois. Professor Wice has published nine previous books dealing with the American legal system, as well as over forty monographs and articles. The recipient of several teaching awards, he has held visiting scholar positions at the U.S. Department of Justice, the Center for the Study of Law and Society, and the New Jersey Supreme Court.